quilting and color
MADE EASY

susan mckelvey
and janet wickell

RODALE

This book is a compilation of *Quilting Made Easy* and *Creative Ideas for Color and Fabric*, two volumes in The Classic American Quilt Collection series.

© 2002 by Rodale Inc.

Printed in the United States of America

Rodale Inc. makes every effort to use acid-free ∞, recycled paper ♻.

Cover Designer: *Tara Long*

Interior Designer and Cover Quiltmaker: *Tanja Lipinski Cole*

Cover and Interior Photographer: *Mitch Mandel*

Illustrators: *Mario Ferro and Jackie Walsh*

The photo of Amish Easter Baskets on page 166 appears courtesy of the Collection of the Museum of the American Quilter's Society, Paducah, Kentucky. Photo by DSI Studios, Evansville, Indiana.

Library of Congress Cataloging-in-Publication Data

McKelvey, Susan Richardson.
    Quilting and color made easy / Susan McKelvey and Janet Wickell.
        p.   cm.
    Includes index.
    ISBN 1–57954–554–8   paperback
    1. Quilting.   2. Appliqué.   3. Color in art.
I. Wickell, Janet.   II. Title.
TT835 .M293   2002
746.46—dc21   2002017803

Distributed to the book trade by St. Martin's Press

2 4 6 8 10 9 7 5 3   paperback

RODALE

WE INSPIRE AND ENABLE PEOPLE TO IMPROVE
THEIR LIVES AND THE WORLD AROUND THEM

FOR MORE OF OUR PRODUCTS
WWW.RODALESTORE.COM
(800) 848-4735

Contents

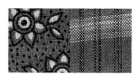

How to Use This Book

. . . the technique of stitchery was passed on by exacting instruction, so also was education in color and design. And the art was controlled and handed down by women, usually mother, grandmother, or aunt. The best elements of teaching were often combined over the construction of a quilt: early and often loving instruction, tradition, discipline, planning and completing a task, moral reinforcement. Quilting was a virtue.

—Patricia Cooper and Norma B. Buferd
The Quilters: Women and Domestic Art—An Oral History

This book was created to provide you with the all the know-how you'll need to re-create classic heirloom quilts, stitch new country-style quilts, or design your own contemporary art quilts. The information goes beyond the basics that come with most pattern directions. Our goal is to help you learn more about quiltmaking, try new techniques, and find ways to build your skills and stretch your creativity, especially when it comes to color and fabric.

Author Janet Wickell is an award-winning quilter, experienced teacher, and technical editor. In the first half of this book, she covers traditional approaches, then goes beyond the time-honored techniques and provides step-by-step directions for newer, speedier methods—methods that can save you time, improve your accuracy, or both. For extra-special time-savers, look for the Blue Ribbon Technique symbol throughout these pages. It's a signal that the technique described is especially quick and easy.

For example, if you've hesitated to try your hand at appliqué because you think it may be too difficult or too time-consuming, take a look at "Quicker and Easier Appliqué." You'll find a variety of ways you can make appliqué work for you. Fusible webs, invisible stitching by machine, or mock hand blanket stitching by machine are all ways you can quickly, easily, and beautifully complete an appliqué project.

Or turn to "Successful Quilting." There are lots of tips on hand quilting—what type of thimble to use, how to choose the right marking tool for your quilt top, and ways to successfully baste the layers of the quilt together. But there are plenty of up-to-the-minute details on machine quilting, too—from how to choose the right thread and batting to practice exercises and full-size quilting designs so you can try our new techniques right away.

You'll find all the basics you need, from step-by-step directions and color diagrams to tools, materials, and insider tips to help you get better results no matter what type of project you're working on.

In the second half of this book, Susan McKelvey, well-known quilter and author, shares her expertise on color. Susan is widely recognized as an authority on color as it relates to quilting. Choosing colors and fabrics for quilts is one of the areas where quilters struggle most. And these days, with so many incredible fabric choices, who doesn't need all the help they can get?

The color section is designed to be a workbook, a tool for you to use as you learn about the different aspects of color. As you read about the color terms, many of which may be new to you, take time out to explore these concepts with fabrics from your collection. There is no better way to learn about a concept and truly understand how it works than to experiment with it. You probably have fabrics in your scrap basket that you've sewn with, but you may not have thought about them in terms of color. You can certainly purchase a few new fabrics in colors that you haven't explored yet, but using the fabrics you already have can be just as rewarding when learning about color. Take time to learn the color concepts in this book by pasting up fabric swatches in the workbooks; you'll have a solid foundation on which to create your future quilts.

We've provided plenty of color exercises and space for you to incorporate your fabrics into this workbook. Use rubber cement or a glue stick so the pages won't warp and pucker. You can also photocopy these pages and paste your fabric samples on the copies. Keep your copied pages in this book or in a notebook that's shelved with this book for easy reference. Wherever you decide to paste your fabrics, just remember that it's important that you do make the fabric samples. When you look back later, your fabrics will be far better reminders than the samples shown in the book because you chose and thought about them. Strive to make your paste-ups different from the ones highlighted here. That way, they'll be of more help to you later.

If you want your swatches to be perfect shapes, make a paper template to guide you in cutting the swatches. Some people want their samples to be perfect; to others that's not so important. Follow your own preferences, and don't worry if you don't have enough examples of a particular concept to fill the space provided. Paste up what you have, or consider working with friends. You will have far more fabrics to choose from if you get a group of quilters together to share, and your friends will enjoy learning about color and fabrics just as much as you will.

"Your Fabric Collection" is a workbook section designed to help you organize your fabrics. You'll be able to see where the gaps are in your stash and what you need to buy on your next trip to the quilt shop. Use the workbook and write directly in your book, or photocopy the pages and put them in your own color notebook and keep adding to it over time.

No matter what your quilting experience is, this book will help you add to your knowledge and skills. You'll learn new techniques and improve the ones you already know. There's something here for anyone who sews or quilts already or just wants to learn. So go through that fabric stash, and get ready to have fun learning about quilting and color!

part one

A QUILTER'S GUIDE TO EASY QUILTING

cutting
MADE EASY

Cutting Made Easy

When our grandmothers made their first quilts, they had to draft their own patterns and make their own templates from newspaper, cardboard, or whatever other suitable materials they could find. Today, there are many cutting innovations available to quiltmakers, from reusable plastic template sets to paper foundation patterns that let us use fabric scraps without having to cut precise, specific-shaped pieces. But to most quilters, the most revolutionary quiltmaking tool on the market is the beloved rotary cutter. Not only has it taken the drudgery out of tracing around templates and cutting individual pieces but it also has taken precision patchwork to a whole new level.

This chapter is full of ideas for making cutting your patchwork pieces quicker and easier, whether you prefer working with templates or with a rotary cutter, mat, and ruler.

IT ALL STARTS WITH FABRIC

PICKING THE RIGHT FABRICS

Whether you plan to rotary cut or use the template marking and cutting method, you need to start at the very same place—by selecting the fabric and making sure it's ready for cutting and sewing.

Today's fabric of choice among quiltmakers is 100 percent cotton. It has a nice *hand* (the term that describes the drape and feel of the fabric), it comes in thousands of prints and solids, and it's easy to work with in both patchwork and appliqué because it frays less than synthetic blends.

Of course, many contemporary or art quilts do contain other types of fabrics, such as silk, lamé, and even nylon netting. But since most traditional quiltmakers prefer 100 percent cotton, this fabric discussion is based on the properties of this versatile fabric.

But before you cut into cotton fabric, it's helpful to know a little more about the fabric and how it should be handled to give you the best results in your quilting projects.

UNDERSTANDING FABRIC GRAIN

Have you ever seen a demonstration of a craftsperson weaving fabric, passing the shuttle back and forth across a loom? Mass-produced cotton fabric is made in the same basic way. Long threads are stretched across a loom and attached firmly to both ends. These threads are referred to as *warp threads*, and they result in what we call the lengthwise grain of the fabric. Next, threads are woven crosswise through the warp threads, moving back and forth from side to side along the entire length. These are referred to as *weft threads*,

and they make up the crosswise grain of the fabric, as shown.

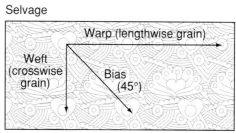

Selvage

Warp (lengthwise grain)

Weft (crosswise grain)

Bias (45°)

Selvage

Lengthwise grain: Warp or lengthwise threads can be thought of as the stabilizers in a piece of fabric, and pieces cut parallel to the lengthwise grain usually won't stretch out of shape. These threads not only gain stability by being firmly attached to the loom during weaving but there are also more of them per square inch than crosswise threads. In addition, their stability is enhanced by the interlaced weft threads that run along their lengths.

Crosswise grain: Weft threads have a bit more give, but pieces cut on the crosswise grain usually won't stretch out of shape unless they are handled roughly. Whenever possible, cut pieces with their edges on either the lengthwise or crosswise straight of grain.

Bias: Although *true bias* is a 45 degree angle from the straight of grain, any cut not parallel to one of the grain lines is called a *bias cut*. Since bias has the greatest amount of stretch or give, pieces cut on the fabric's bias stretch easily and must be handled with care. Triangles are an example of a commonly used shape that has at least one bias edge.

To keep stretch to a minimum, cut pieces so that a bias edge does not end up on the outer edge of your finished quilt block. When possible, bias edges should be sewn to straight of grain for stability.

PREWASHING YOUR FABRIC

Should you or shouldn't you prewash is the million dollar question for quiltmakers. How you intend to use your quilt and what impact shrinkage will have on that use plays a big part in answering the question. Cotton fabrics shrink when washed because the fabric finish is rinsed away. If you'll be using your new fabric for a bed quilt, a lap quilt, or especially a crib quilt, you'll definitely want to prewash it so it won't shrink after you've put all the time and effort into making the quilt. However, if you like the look of the smooth finish *and* you plan to use the fabric in a wallhanging, pillow, or some other project that won't require washing, you can feel perfectly confident in using the fabric without prewashing it.

For projects that aren't prewashed, simply use the fabric attachment on your vacuum cleaner to periodically dust them.

If you decide to prewash, use warm water and mild soap or detergent. Test for colorfastness by first soaking a scrap in warm water. If colors bleed, use a dye-setting solution like Retayne, available at most quilt shops, and follow the instructions on the bottle. Rinse the fabric several times in warm water before using it. If the fabric still bleeds, reserve it for a quilt that won't need laundering, such as a wallhanging that won't get a lot of use.

Dry your fabric in a dryer on medium heat and remove it while it's still slightly damp to keep wrinkles under control. Press the fabric immediately.

If you don't have time to press your fabric right away, be sure to let it dry thoroughly before storing it. Smooth it out flat to dry completely so no set-in wrinkles occur.

WHY DOES COTTON SHRINK?

Everyone accepts shrinkage as a fact of life, but do you know why it happens? Blame it on the need cotton fibers have to relax (something they share in common with all natural fibers).

Storing Prewashed Fabrics

Some quiltmakers like to prewash all of their new fabric as soon as they buy it, so it's ready to use in a project the moment the creative urge strikes. If you prefer to hold off on prewashing, it's helpful to devise a storage system so you can quickly and easily tell if a fabric has been prewashed or not. One easy method is to snip the selvages of fabric that has been prewashed. Or simply store washed and unwashed fabrics on different shelves.

When cotton fabric is produced, both the warp and weft threads are pulled taut in the loom, stretching the fibers into an unnatural, straight position. Coatings used by manufacturers stabilize the newly woven fabric, helping the threads retain their rigid position in the cloth after it is removed from the loom. When you wash and dry the fabrics at home, some of the coatings are rinsed away. And the twisting and spinning movement in the washer and dryer, plus the wicking action of the fibers in water, help the fibers relax and return to a position more like that in which they grew. This relaxation results in what we see as shrinkage.

Don't be surprised if the 45-inch-wide piece of cotton you put in the washer and dryer comes out a mere 42 inches. (That's why when you are making strip sets, the various strips never seem to match up exactly on both ends!)

Synthetic fibers don't possess a wicking action, nor do they have a natural, relaxed position to return to—they tend to remain just as they were manufactured. So, a cotton/polyester blend will shrink less than 100 percent cotton because the synthetic fibers remain rigid, preventing the cotton content from relaxing as much as it would like to.

Most projects take shrinkage into account when determining yardages. In this series, a width of 42 inches is used to figure yardage and cutting requirements to allow for cotton's inclination to shrink.

BEST TECHNIQUES
FOR CUTTING WITH TEMPLATES

A template is an exact copy of a printed pattern that is used to trace the pattern onto the fabric. For this traditional method of marking and cutting quilt fabrics, a template is made for each shape in a block. Templates can be constructed from many materials, including lightweight cardboard, index cards, sandpaper, and freezer paper.

Another popular choice is transparent or translucent plastic made especially for template making, which is available at craft and quilt shops. This flexible plastic can withstand the heat of a moderately hot iron, so it's great for use in the sewing room.

For more information on selecting a template material to suit your needs, see the "Template Materials" chart on page 9.

HOW-TO FOR HAND-PIECING TEMPLATES

A template for hand-pieced patchwork is drawn to exactly match the *finished* size of your piece, normally indicated by the inner, dashed line on printed patterns, as shown.

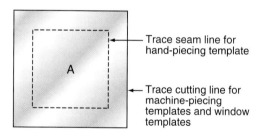

Trace seam line for hand-piecing template

Trace cutting line for machine-piecing templates and window templates

Step 1. To mark the fabric, place the template on the wrong side of the fabric and use a sharp pencil or fine-tip permanent pen to draw around its edges. These lines are the piece's *seam lines.*

You can trace symmetrical templates, such as a square or a heart, faceup or facedown. But templates such as a house roof that angles to one side must be traced facedown on the wrong side of the fabric, so your finished block will look like the one in the project instructions.

Step 2. Draw a seam allowance ¼ inch away from all sides of the piece, and cut it out on the outer lines with scissors or a rotary cutter and ruler. Some hand piecers only draw the seam lines and estimate seam allowances as they cut. The marked seam line is one of the most important elements of a hand-pieced shape, since seams of adjacent pieces are carefully matched before they are sewn together. Hand-pieced seams never extend into the seam allowance, so accurate marking is essential.

If you are a beginner at hand piecing, it's easiest to mark the exact seam allowances onto your fabric pieces so there's no guesswork involved.

View through a Window

A window template makes it easy to mark both the seam line and cutting line with the same template. Trace both lines onto template material. Use scissors to cut out the template on the outer cutting line and a craft knife to cut the template on the inner seam line. The resulting window represents the finished block size and lets you see exactly which part of the fabric design you'll be using, while the outermost edge is used to mark the cutting line.

HOW-TO FOR MACHINE-PIECING TEMPLATES

Templates used for machine-pieced patchwork usually include an exact ¼-inch seam allowance around all sides of the *finished-size* pattern (the size of the piece once it is sewn into the quilt). The *unfinished size* (or finished size plus ¼-inch seam allowances on all sides) is normally indicated by a solid, outer line on a pattern. You only need to trace the outer line when making templates for machine piecing.

Machine-piecing templates can be positioned faceup on the right side of fabric and drawn around as for hand piecing. Pieces are cut out directly on this line, since the seam allowance is already included in the shape of the template. The outer edges of pieces are matched for sewing, and machine-pieced seams *do* extend into the adjacent seam allowance except when a piece will be set in to a seam intersection. (See "Try Set-In Piecing" on page 40.)

Check for Seam Allowances

Throughout *The Classic American Quilt Collection* series, seam allowances are given on all pattern pieces, but be sure to carefully check patterns from other sources, such as magazines, as they often provide only finished-size patterns and you have to add the ¼-inch seam allowances. Use a rotary ruler to measure the ¼-inch seam allowance, or try an Add-a-Quarter template guide, a long acrylic bar that fits over the edge of templates, so you can trace a perfect ¼ inch around them.

PICKING THE BEST TEMPLATE MATERIALS

There's no quick-and-easy answer here, since no single template material is *always* best. Needs vary from project to project, and your choice will

often depend upon the piecing method you're using. The "Template Materials" chart describes the pros and cons of each kind of material, and you should experiment with different ones to learn which will work best for you in different situations.

Using Freezer Paper Templates

Freezer paper is a handy item to keep with your collection of quilting supplies. Patchwork templates are just one use for this versatile paper, which you will see referred to many times in this book. Unlike other template materials, freezer paper templates actually stick to the fabric for tracing and cutting. If you've never used freezer paper templates, follow these simple steps to accurate cutting:

Step 1. To make freezer paper templates for pieced blocks, position a *finished-size* template right side *down* on the nonwaxy, or dull, side of the freezer paper, and trace around it. For simple shapes, you can even use a ruler to help you draw the template's reverse image onto the paper. Repeat for all templates.

You can reuse freezer paper templates several times each so you don't have to cut one for every shape in your quilt. For a large quilt, make duplicates of your freezer paper templates for use when the waxy coating wears off the first batch.

Step 2. Cut out the templates and press them to the wrong side of your fabric, leaving at least ½ inch between templates, as shown. Use a sharp pencil to mark a seam allowance ¼ inch away from all sides of the templates, as shown. Cut out the fabric on the marked lines, leaving the papers in place. As you sew pieces together, use the edges of both the fabric pieces and the freezer paper to help you align and sew accurate seams.

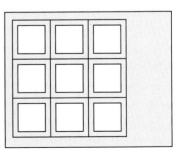

Press freezer paper templates onto wrong side of fabric, leaving ½" between templates. Mark ¼" seam allowance around each piece and cut out.

Template Materials

Type	How It Works	Pros	Cons
Cardboard or posterboard	Lightweight cardboard, such as the type used for cereal boxes, is the traditional choice for templates. Patterns are traced onto tracing or graph paper, then glued to cardboard and cut out. Posterboard adds thickness and stiffness that is easier to trace around than just paper.	If your project calls for a large number of templates that are not used over and over, cardboard or other paper-based materials are a suitable and inexpensive choice.	One disadvantage to cardboard templates is their lack of durability, since edges tend to become worn and distorted with repeated use.
Sandpaper	Glue paper templates onto the smooth side of fine-grit sandpaper (such as 100-grit), then cut them out. Glue the paper templates *right* side down, so when you position the rough side of a sandpaper template on the wrong side of fabric you will be marking the pattern shape correctly. The sandpaper prevents the template from shifting as you mark the fabric.	Your templates won't slip around on the fabric. Also, small pieces of fine-grit sandpaper, such as dots or squares, can be glued to any template to help keep it in place as you mark your fabric.	As with cardboard, sandpaper is not the best choice for templates that are used repeatedly. And cutting a lot of sandpaper templates can create wear and tear on your utility scissors.
Freezer paper	Plain white freezer paper is available at the grocery store, while a gridded version can be purchased at quilt and craft shops. See "Using Freezer Paper Templates" on the opposite page for complete step-by-step directions.	Freezer paper templates are a good choice for blocks with set-in pieces, since individual seam endings are clearly visible. For the same reason, they are also helpful for aligning triangular pieces, where sides must be offset for seams to match correctly, and for hand piecing. They also help to stabilize bias edges, making it easier to stitch a seam without stretching.	You may have to make several freezer paper templates of the same shape, since the paper edges will wear and the waxy coating won't last indefinitely.
Transparent plastic	Patterns can be traced directly onto the plastic, eliminating the need to first trace onto paper. Transparent material also makes it easy to position a template over specific areas of a fabric. Template plastic is available in several thicknesses, in sheets or rolls, plain or gridded, transparent or opaque. Some types are rough on one side to help them stick to fabric during the marking process.	Plastic makes durable templates, since the edges remain intact even after tracing around them many times. Plastic is flexible and easy to see through for tracing.	Plastic costs a bit more, but it's well worth your investment.

Tracing a Fine Line

Use a very sharp pencil or fine-tip permanent pen to trace templates. A consistent, narrow line helps to minimize distortion because it leaves less doubt about exactly where to cut out the shape. Always check all templates for accuracy by piecing one sample block or unit before cutting out all of the fabric for a project.

Marking Templates

Make your life easier by transferring all markings from the original printed pattern onto your own templates (see the diagram below for an example). The following is a list of handy things that you'll need to refer to as you're using your templates.

• **Template name:** This is often a letter of the alphabet or a number, and it is particularly important for avoiding confusion when you have two or more templates that are similar in size and shape.

• **Grain line arrows:** Grain is indicated by a line with an arrow on each end. The template should be positioned with the arrow parallel to the fabric's straight of grain. (For more information about fabric grain, see "Understanding Fabric Grain" on page 5.)

• **Reverse:** The reverse side of a template needs to be traced for some pieces and is sometimes indicated by "R" or "rev." after a template name, such as DR, D rev., or D Reverse.

• **Number to cut:** This information tells you how many pieces to cut from each template.

• **Pattern name:** It doesn't hurt to add the quilt name to your templates, too, to avoid confusion with other templates.

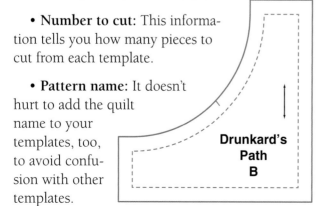

Drunkard's
Path
B

Quick Cutting with Templates

Here's a way to speed up marking and cutting with templates—without sacrificing accuracy!

Step 1. Trace multiple copies of templates onto the wrong side of your fabric. When possible, align the tracings side by side, butting their edges. (Remember that seam allowances must be added when hand piecing.) Continue marking until you have drawn the total number of pieces required for that particular fabric.

Step 2. Instead of cutting out the pieces with scissors, gather other fabrics that will be used for the same template. Stack two to four layers of fabric right side down on your cutting mat. Place the fabric with the template tracings on top. Align the edge of your rotary ruler exactly with the drawn lines, and cut out the shapes with your rotary cutter. Since you are cutting through several layers at one time, you'll be slicing your cutting time dramatically, yet all your pieces will be precise. See "Terrific Techniques for Rotary Cutting" on the opposite page for more information about rotary-cutting techniques.

Before cutting layers of fabric, press them together. Pressing helps the fabrics stick to each other, so your layers won't shift as you cut.

Speedy Reverse Patches

You can cut reverse pieces at the same time you cut standard pieces. For the standard image, draw around the template as you normally would, with it facedown on the wrong side of the fabric. Position the fabric required for the reverse image of the template right side up below the marked fabric, and use your rotary-cutting equipment to cut out both pieces at once.

TERRIFIC TECHNIQUES FOR ROTARY CUTTING

There's no doubt about it. The rotary cutter has sparked a revolution in quiltmaking, giving today's quilters a way to speed up the tedious task of cutting pieces. This section covers the basics and then goes on to give you some clever ways to make your rotary cutting even quicker and more accurate.

THE BASIC TOOLS

Rotary Cutter

This handy tool resembles a pizza cutter, with one exception—its blade is razor sharp. For general cutting, use a cutter with a large blade to easily slice through several layers of fabric at once. Nearly all equipment is suitable for both right-handed and left-handed quilters; however, handles vary, so try out a few different types of cutters before purchasing one to see which feels most comfortable in your hand. Blades should be replaced when cutting requires more pressure than normal or when the blade begins to skip over areas of the fabric as you're cutting. Be sure to retract the blade after each use and to keep your cutters away from young children.

Keep That Wheel Rolling

When you notice your rotary-cutter blade is beginning to skip over a few threads without cutting them, it may be time for a replacement blade. But maybe not. First, unscrew the blade from the handle, and carefully wipe the flat sides of the blade with a soft cloth and a drop of sewing machine oil to remove lint buildup. Replace the blade, and try cutting again. If it still skips over sections of fabric, then replace the blade with a new one.

Getting It Back Together

When you take your rotary cutter apart to clean it or change the blade, it may be a bit tricky to get the pieces back together in the correct order, since the screw and the nut can fit on either side of the handle. To remember where all the pieces go, lay the blade, screw, washer, and nut all in a row on the table from left to right in the same order in which you removed them.

Large: This all-purpose size is great for most cutting. You can cut through four to six layers at a time when the blade is nice and sharp.

Small: The smaller blade is great for cutting curved shapes, such as Drunkard's Path pieces. This size is also handy to keep near your sewing table for trimming triangle corners and cutting strip sets into smaller units.

Jumbo: The jumbo, heavy-duty model is a nice addition to your sewing room if you plan on doing a lot of layered cutting. The larger cutting wheel handles more layers at a faster pace.

Cutting Mat

A special, self-healing cutting mat is a *must* for rotary cutting. The mat protects your table from the rotary blade and protects the blade from dulling too quickly. The slightly

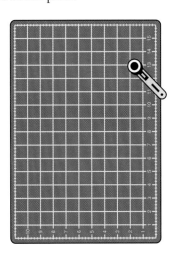

textured surface grips fabric and helps to keep it from sliding around. Choose a mat with a *self-healing* surface (which means that cuts reseal themselves) and your mat will last a long time. Mats are available in several colors and with or without marked grid lines. Some mats are reversible, with a dark color on one side and a light color on the other, giving you the option to use a contrasting background when cutting both light and dark fabrics. An all-purpose size is 18 × 24 inches, but if your work surface will accommodate a larger mat, buy it.

Never leave your mat in a very hot space, such as in a closed automobile or anywhere that the sun will shine on it, because it will warp. Always store the mat flat so it won't curl, making it impossible to use.

Rotary Rulers

Walk into any quilt shop or browse through any quilter's catalog, and you'll be astounded by the variety of rotary rulers on the market. These thick, acrylic, see-through rulers are made so that a rotary cutter can glide easily along their sides. But if you're new to quiltmaking, it's hard to know which one to start with.

And if you've already begun a collection of basic and specialty rulers, it's sometimes hard to keep up with all the varied uses to which they can be put.

Try Before Buying

Before buying a rotary ruler, lay different brands over several different colors of fabric. You'll quickly see which types of markings are easiest for you to see and use. For example, a ruler with only black markings is great for light and medium fabrics, but it may be hard to read when cutting dark fabrics. You may find everything you're looking for in one basic ruler or decide to buy a variety of rulers to suit your cutting needs.

To help end this confusion, here are the basic rulers you'll want to start with.

The basic models: A 6 × 24-inch ruler is a good all-purpose size to start with. This size ruler is the best for squaring up the end of fabric, as described in "The First Step—Cutting Strips" below. For the most versatility, be sure it's marked in ⅛-inch increments and has 30, 45, and 60 degree markings.

A 15-inch-square ruler is another wise investment. It's great for making sure blocks are square, and it can also be used to cut large squares for setting blocks or appliqué backgrounds, to cut setting triangles, and to square the edges of your quilts. See the "Rotary Rulers" chart for more details on other basic rulers.

Choose your basic set of rulers from the same manufacturer. Each company uses a different type of line markings, some thick and some very narrow. It's easier to make accurate cuts when you are accustomed to working with one type of marking.

THE FIRST STEP—CUTTING STRIPS

Cutting long strips of fabric across the fabric's crosswise grain is the first step in making most quick-pieced quilts. Accurately cut strips are essential to the success of any project that starts with rotary-cutting techniques.

Before cutting strips from your fabric, you need to properly fold the fabric and square off one end.

Step 1. Fold the fabric lengthwise with the selvages together. Press the fabric to help the layers adhere to each other. If your mat is small, fold the fabric again, bringing the first fold up to meet the selvages, as shown, doubling the number of layers to cut. You can actually cut up to eight layers at a time; however, the more layers you cut, the less accurate your cuts will be.

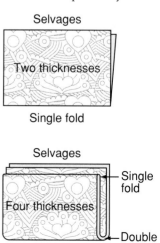

Rotary Rulers

Ruler Types		Uses	Important Markings
Rectangular rulers	6" × 24"	All-purpose ruler for everyday cutting tasks; allows you to cut practically any straight-edged shape	30°, 45°, and 60° lines; horizontal and vertical lines marked in ⅛" increments
	6" × 12"	Handy to take along to quilt class; works well for cutting segments from precut strips or from smaller pieces of fabric such as scraps or fat eighths	30°, 45°, and 60° lines; horizontal and vertical lines marked in ⅛" increments
	3" × 18"	Good for miniature quilts and other small-scale piecework, especially if you are cutting from fat quarters rather than full-width fabric	30°, 45°, and 60° lines; horizontal and vertical lines marked in ⅛" increments. Some have 1/16" grid around perimeter to help in drafting
	1" × 6"	Verifying measurements as you sew	⅛" increments
Square rulers	4", 6"	Helpful for checking the accuracy of miniature and small quilt blocks and for second cuts from larger pieces	Continuous grid of ⅛" increments
	12½", 15"	Cutting background blocks for appliqué, setting squares and triangles, and squaring blocks and quilt corners; the 15" size is most versatile	Continuous grid of ⅛" increments
Specialty rulers	Bias Square— 4", 6", 8"	Designed especially for making fast and accurate triangle squares	
	BiRangle	Designed to accurately cut pre-assembled bias rectangle blocks	
	Scrap Saver	A handy tool for quick cutting squares and triangles from stacks of scrap fabrics	
	45° Kaleidoscope	Designed for cutting 45° shapes from plain or strip-pieced fabrics	
	60° Triangle— 6", 8", 12"	Used for cutting equilateral triangles; allows you to easily cut shapes with 30°, 60°, and 120° angles	
	9° Circle Wedge— several sizes	Used to make speed-pieced circular or fan quilts in 9° increments; many other creative uses also	
	Right triangles	Used to help speed cut half-square and quarter-square triangles	Some include seam allowances in the size of the ruler
	Rolling rulers	Used for measuring and cutting borders, sashing, and other long pieces	

NOTE: This is a sample of common size rulers. Other sizes and shapes are available from several manufacturers.

Step 2. Place a ruled square on the fold, as shown, aligning the bottom edge of the ruler with the bottom fold of your fabric. Slide a 6 × 24-inch ruler flush against the left side of the square, making sure it is positioned far enough onto the fabric that a cut down its right edge will slice through all layers. Hold the long ruler firmly in place, remove the square, and use your rotary cutter to cut from bottom to top along the right edge of the ruler. *Always cut away from yourself.* (If you are left-handed, work from the other end of the fabric.)

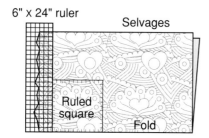

6" x 24" ruler
Selvages
Ruled square
Fold

Step 3. Cut strips as required for your project, beginning with the squared-up edge. Align the prepared edge of the fabric with the lengthwise rule that corresponds to the required width of the strip, and cut through all layers. To make sure you always have a 90 degree angle of the edge, never cut a strip until one of the horizontal rules is aligned with the fold. Think of the ruler's lines as a two-way check system. If the horizontal and vertical lines are both parallel to the edges of your fabric, as shown, your strips will be accurate.

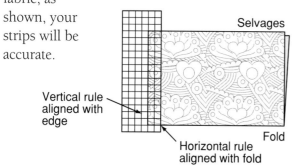

Selvages
Vertical rule aligned with edge
Fold
Horizontal rule aligned with fold

Step 4. Check the strips periodically to make sure they're straight. If your strips are angled in the middle, as shown, the cut edge isn't at a 90 degree angle to the fold. Refold the fabric and square up the edge again. Don't be discouraged; cutting accurate strips takes practice. And it's not un-

common to have to refold and realign periodically, especially if you are cutting many strips from a big chunk of fabric. To fine-tune your skills, practice on pieces of scrap fabric, or divide your fabric and cut shorter strips from an unfolded piece until you are more comfortable with the technique.

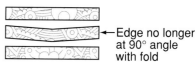

← Edge no longer at 90° angle with fold

Step 5. To cut lengthwise grain strips, fold your fabric in the opposite direction, with the selvages along the ends. If you need to cut extremely long lengthwise strips for borders, you may find that all the folding required can get a bit tricky. In fact, you may be more successful by tearing long strips for borders. These strips will be on the straight of grain and won't have any angles or bends that can occur from cutting through multiple folds.

Tearing Long Borders

To tear long, lengthwise border strips, first make a snip in the fabric just inside the selvage. Tear the selvage away and discard it. Then measure across the end of the fabric the width you want your border to be, plus ½ inch for the seam allowances. Make another snip with your scissors and tear the strip. You'll have a perfect border strip. Repeat for all four borders, and you're in business!

CUTTING OTHER SHAPES

Once you've mastered cutting straight-of-grain strips, you can cut many commonly used shapes from them, including squares, rectangles, triangles, and diamonds. Before cutting shapes with a 90 degree side, such as squares and rectangles, you need to square up one end of a strip by removing the uneven selvage edge, as shown. Remember to align a hori-

Cutting Shapes

Shape	Yield	Strip Width	Segment Length
Squares	1 per cut	Finished height + ½"	Finished length + ½"
Rectangles	1 per cut	Finished height + ½"	Finished length + ½"
Right triangles	2 per square	Finished length of short edge + ⅞"	Finished length of short edge + ⅞"
Right triangles	4 per square	Finished length of long edge + 1¼"	Finished length of long edge + 1¼"
Equilateral triangles	1 per cut	Finished height + ¾"	Finished leg length + ⅞"
Diamonds: *30°*	1 per cut	Finished height + ½"	Finished leg length + 1"
45°	1 per cut	Finished height + ½"	Finished leg length + ¾"
60°	1 per cut	Finished height + ½"	Finished leg length + ⅝"

zontal rule along the bottom edge of the strip so that you create an edge that is at a 90 degree angle to the length of the strip.

The following instructions explain how to cut common shapes with a basic 6 × 24-inch ruler. Keep in mind that there are many specialty rulers available that can make certain cutting tasks even easier. In addition, the "Cutting Shapes" chart shows what strip widths you need to start with to yield different shapes.

SQUARES AND RECTANGLES

Squares and rectangles can easily be cut from strips. If rotary-cutting directions are not provided for a project you are making, you can easily determine how wide to cut your strips. You simply need to know the finished size of the square or rectangle, then add ½ inch to that measurement. By adding ½ inch, you are allowing for the standard ¼-inch seam allowance on both sides of the strip, as shown.

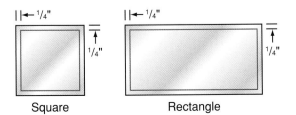

Square   Rectangle

Cut a straight grain strip as wide as your calculated width and square up one end. With the squared-up end to the left, as shown, align the ruler with your calculated measurement marking lined up with the left edge of the strip and cut. For example, for 2-inch finished squares, you will need to cut 2½-inch-wide strips. Then align the 2½-inch marking on the ruler with the edge of the strip to cut a 2½-inch square. Be sure to align a horizontal rule with the strip's bottom edge.

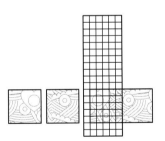

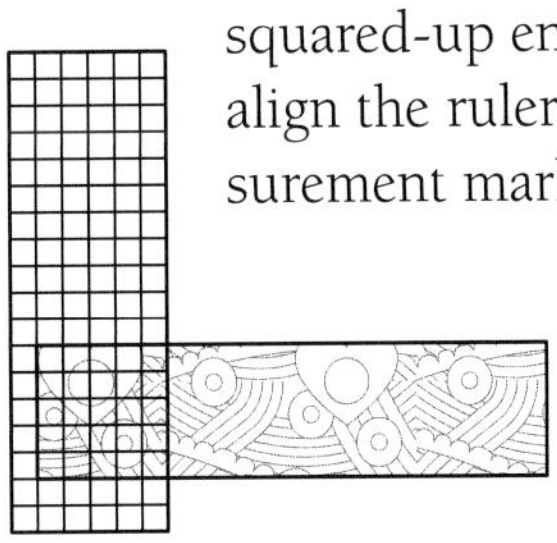

Layered Cutting

To speed the cutting of any shape, stack two or three strips together and cut out several layers at once. Press the layers together before cutting to help them stick together and prevent them from slipping underneath your ruler.

DIAMONDS

If you have a rotary ruler with 30, 45, and 60 degree markings, you can cut diamonds with these angles from precut strips—without templates. To calculate the strip width required for a rotary-cut diamond, add $\frac{1}{2}$ inch to the finished height of the diamond, as illustrated by the arrow in the diagram.

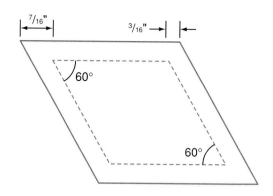

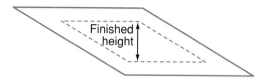

Each side of a simple diamond is the same length. Because the angles at the narrow tips of the diamonds differ, the seam allowance you must add to the finished length of each type also differs. The following three diagrams illustrate the seam allowances for each of the three common diamond variations.

• **30 degree diamond:** Add 1 inch to the *finished* length of the diamond's edge to determine the *unfinished* leg length ($\frac{7}{8} + \frac{1}{8} = 1$ inch).

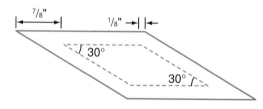

• **45 degree diamond:** Add $\frac{3}{4}$ inch to the *finished* length of the diamond's edge to determine the *unfinished* leg length ($\frac{5}{8} + \frac{1}{8} = \frac{6}{8} = \frac{3}{4}$ inch).

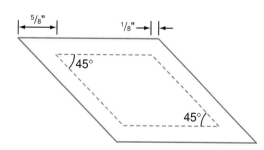

• **60 degree diamond:** Add $\frac{5}{8}$ inch to the *finished* length of the diamond's edge to determine the *unfinished* leg length ($\frac{7}{16} + \frac{3}{16} = \frac{10}{16} = \frac{5}{8}$ inch).

Double-Check Dimensions

To cross-check your strip width and segment length calculations, measure the length of the prepared, angled edge of your fabric strip. If the strip width is correct, the length of the angled edge will equal the finished height of the diamond plus $\frac{1}{2}$ inch.

Rotary Cutting Diamonds

Step 1. Align the ruler on the fabric strip so that the 30, 45, or 60 degree marking is flush with the long edge of the strip. Slide the ruler toward the left end of the strip until one side of the ruler is about $\frac{1}{4}$ inch from the edge of the fabric where the 45 degree line is placed along the long edge of the strip, as shown. Cut along the ruler to remove the corner of the strip.

Step 2. Use the ruler to measure the length of the diamond along the lower edge of the fabric strip. Align the appropriate angle line along the lower edge of the strip as before, and align the diagonal edge of the strip with the marking for the width of the diamond. For example, if you are cutting $3\frac{1}{2}$-inch-wide diamonds, align the $3\frac{1}{2}$-inch line with the diagonal edge. Cut the diamond, then continue realigning the ruler and cutting diamonds in the same manner, as shown.

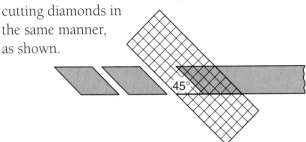

Template-Rotary Ruler Combo

If the size of a piece you need to cut doesn't measure up to a ruler marking (for example, 2⁷⁄₁₆ inches), make a template of the pattern that includes seam allowances and tape it to the underside of the ruler with one edge flush with the edge of the ruler and the adjacent edge flush with the angle line. Match the template with the strip edge to find your cutting line. This method is helpful even if the cutting line you need is marked, since it gives you an instant visual guide that keeps you from having to look at all of the other lines on the ruler each time you move it across the fabric. Masking tape is also handy to frame marked lines on the ruler.

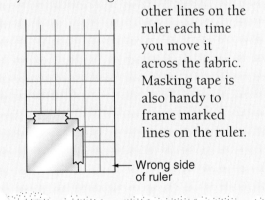

← Wrong side of ruler

RIGHT TRIANGLES

You can quickly cut right triangles from squares using one of two different methods. Choose the method based on which side of the triangle you want to be cut on the straight of grain. Remember that you always want the outside edges of a block or the quilt to be straight of grain, not bias.

Half-Square Triangles

Cutting a square in half once diagonally, as shown, makes two right triangles with the straight of grain on the short sides. Right triangles cut this way are used in blocks where their shortest sides will be on the outside edge, such as in the Shoofly block.

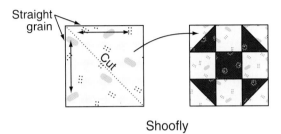

Shoofly

To determine what size square you need to start with to yield the size triangles you need, add ⁷⁄₈ inch (⁵⁄₈ inch + ¼ inch) to the *finished* length of the triangle's short side, as shown. For example, if you need a triangle that finishes 1½ inches long on each short side, you need to cut a 2³⁄₈-inch square (1½ + ⁷⁄₈ = 2³⁄₈ inches).

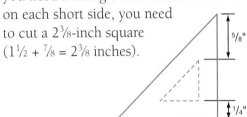

Quarter-Square Triangles

If you cut a square in half diagonally in both directions, you'll make four right triangles, each with the straight of grain on the longest side only, as shown. Right triangles cut this way are needed for blocks where the longest side will be on the outer perimeter, such as the outer triangles in the Windblown Squares block.

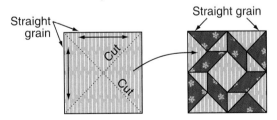

Windblown Squares

To determine the size square you need to start with to yield the appropriate size triangles, add 1¼ inches (⁵⁄₈ + ⁵⁄₈ = 1¼ inches) to the *finished* length of the triangle's longest side, as illustrated. For example, to make an 8-inch Windblown Squares block, the *finished* long sides of the outer triangles need to measure 4 inches each. That means the square you start with needs to measure 5¼ inches (4 + 1¼ = 5¼ inches).

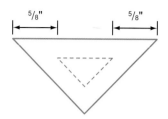

Handy Triangle Formulas

Keep these quick-and-easy formulas handy for times when you need to calculate your own triangle dimensions:

Finished length of short side × 1.41 = finished length of longest side

Longest side + 1¼ inches = size of initial square

If your result is a number that can't easily be measured and cut with a rotary cutter and ruler (such as 2⁵⁄₁₆ inches), round the calculation up to the nearest ⅛ inch. Then, after sewing the triangle to its surrounding pieces, trim it slightly to square up the outer edges.

Grid-Method Triangles

If you need to make dozens or even hundreds of identical triangle squares from two right triangles, there is yet another rotary-cutting method for you to try. This method requires marking and sewing first, then cutting. For more information on this method, see "Making Triangle Squares on a Grid" on page 30. The advantage to this technique is that all of your bias-edge sewing is done before you even cut the fabric, so you'll have less chance of stretching it as you sew.

EQUILATERAL TRIANGLES

Equilateral triangles measure the same length on all three sides (or legs) and have a 60 degree angle at each corner. Follow these steps for cutting equilateral triangles:

Step 1. First, start with a fabric strip that is ¾ inch wider than the *finished* height of the triangle to allow for the ½- and ¼-inch seam allowances, as indicated in the diagram. To determine how long to cut each segment for an equilateral triangle, add ⅞ inch (⁷⁄₁₆ + ⁷⁄₁₆ = ⅞ inch) to the *finished* length of a leg of the triangle, as shown.

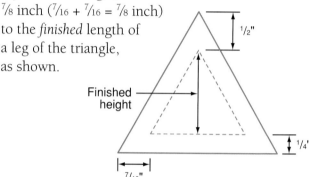

Step 2. Align the 60 degree line on your rotary ruler with the bottom left edge of the strip, and make the cut illustrated.

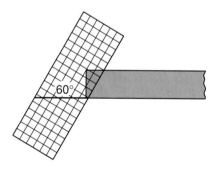

Step 3. Mark the bottom of the strip in increments equal to the *unfinished* length of one side of the size triangle you need, as shown.

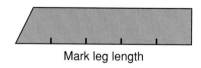

Mark leg length

Step 4. Realign the 60 degree line on the ruler with the bottom edge of the strip so that the ruler is also in line with the very edge of the top of the strip, as shown in **A.** Cut along the ruler to make the first triangle. Continue aligning the 60 degree line of the ruler with the edge of the strip, alternating from the top to the bottom edge, as shown in **B,** to cut additional triangles.

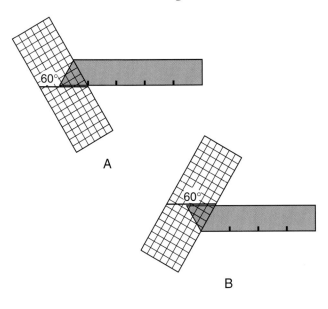

A

B

CUTTING CURVED SHAPES

While most patchwork blocks are built from pieces with straight lines and angled corners, there are a number of wonderful blocks that include curves in their design. Drunkard's Path, Double Wedding Ring, and New York Beauty are a few popular curved patchwork designs. Some of the traditional One Patch or charm quilt shapes include curves, too, such as Apple Core, or Spools, and the Clamshell.

Rotary Cutter and Scissors for Curves

For some curved pieces, the curve is only one side of the block, such as a New York Beauty or Drunkard's Path block. You can rotary cut the basic square shapes first, then use the template to trace the curve and cut out that section with scissors.

Tracing and Cutting Accurate Patterns

Although this sounds like common sense, tracing a long curve with a smooth line by hand isn't as easy as it sounds. Try this quick-and-easy trick for tracing and cutting smooth curved templates for accurate curved piecing.

Step 1. Trace any straight lines first, such as the square edge of a Drunkard's Path block. Then, instead of tracing a solid line over the curve, make a series of dots along the curve, as shown.

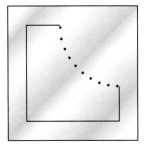

Use dots along curved line

A

Step 2. Now you're ready to cut out the template. Cut the straight lines first, followed by the curve. Simply hold your scissors pointing straight up, and rotate the template material in your other hand so you can cut smoothly from dot to dot, as shown. It's a lot easier to cut a smooth curved line than to draw one.

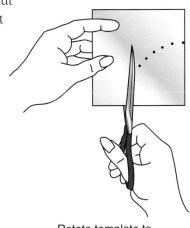

Rotate template to cut along curve

B

Step 3. Trace your template onto the fabric and cut out as for other noncurved pieces.

If you are careful, you can use a small-size rotary cutter to cut around the curved edge of your template. Go slowly so you don't cut through the template material. And use an old cutting mat since curved cuts don't heal.

Acrylic Templates for Rotary Cutting

Some of the more commonly shaped curved pieces can easily be cut with a rotary cutter and purchased acrylic templates. These template sets are available for a variety of blocks, including Double Wedding Ring, Drunkard's Path, and Spools. Some come in a variety of sizes, so be sure to check out the options before purchasing.

Precut Paper Templates

Yet another way to handle cutting curved shapes is to use die-cut paper templates and the English paper piecing method. For more on this hand-piecing method, see "English Paper Piecing" on page 26. To cut the fabric for this method, simply trace around the precut template and then eyeball the seam allowance, which will get basted to the paper.

Small Blade Works Best

If you plan to rotary cut curved pieces with acrylic templates, invest in a small-blade rotary cutter. You'll find the smaller blade handles much better around the curves, which is a must for accuracy. Also note that curved cuts may not heal themselves on your cutting mat, so you may need to reserve a cutting mat specifically for curved cutting and save your best mat for all other rotary cutting.

ANALYZING AND DRAFTING BLOCKS FOR ROTARY CUTTING

The previous information provides you with a variety of ways to speed up the cutting aspect of the quiltmaking process. In this section, you'll learn more about when to apply these cutting techniques to your projects and how to analyze blocks for rotary-cutting possibilities. Then the next time you start a project that provides only templates for tracing and cutting with scissors, you'll be armed with the information you need to transform that project into one that you can rotary cut.

Follow the ⅛-inch rule: When quilt designers print patterns intended for rotary cutting, they usually do so with the standard rotary-cutting tools in mind. Since rotary-cutting rulers are usually marked at ⅛-inch intervals, most designers try to make that the smallest possible increment you would need to measure and cut.

When you're ready to draft your blocks (whether they are your own design or just a size variation of a classic quilt block), remember that it's easier to rotary cut pieces that can be measured with a standard ruler with ⅛-inch increments. An easy way to make sure you'll end up with easy-to-measure pieces is to think of blocks in terms of their grid size and choose a finished block size accordingly.

Keep grids in mind: Most common patchwork blocks are drafted in one of the following grid units: Four Patch, Five Patch, Seven Patch, or Nine Patch, as shown at the top of the opposite page. Within each type of grid, all or part of the original squares in the grid can be divided into smaller units to create an endless variety of patterns. For example, in the Nine Patch variation block, five of the original nine units have been subdivided into small four patch units.

All of the blocks in the illustration are drafted the same size for uniformity. If you actually wanted to make these blocks in the same size, however, you would quickly realize that rotary cutting your pieces would be a problem.

For example, a block based on a nine patch grid is easy to draft to be a 6-inch, 9-inch, or 12-inch block—any number that is divisible by three. A block based on the four patch, however, is more easily drafted—and rotary cut—when the block

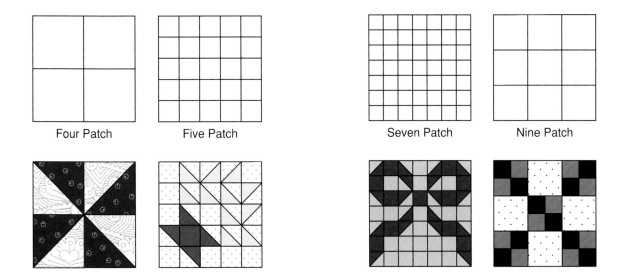

Four Patch   Five Patch   Seven Patch   Nine Patch

size is divisible by two. So for four patch blocks, try drafting 8-, 10-, or 12-inch blocks. This way, even when you divide some of the squares in the grid into two or four triangles, the cut sizes of the triangles can still be readily cut with a rotary-cutting ruler with $\frac{1}{8}$-inch increments.

If you absolutely need to draft a finished Nine Patch block that measures 8 inches, you may find that you will need to use templates for some of the pieces because it is difficult to cut triangles that measure $3\frac{9}{16}$ inches or other odd increments with a rotary ruler.

easy
PIECING

Easy Piecing

Imagine the joy that accompanied the advent of the domestic sewing machine in the 1850s, when the element of speed was introduced to home sewing. Daunting tasks, such as making garments for a large family, became much more manageable. The benefits carried over to quiltmaking as well. Today, sewing machines are quite different from their humble treadle counterparts, and quiltmakers of the twentieth century have the luxury of many new, improved features offered by modern machines.

Hand piecing, too, remains a viable technique for today's quilters because it offers greater flexibility in manipulating set-in pieces and curved seams. Some quilters merely enjoy the relaxation that hand piecing affords, while others see its portability as the only way to work on projects when the demands of a busy schedule take them places where there is no sewing machine.

Whether you prefer hand or machine piecing, this chapter provides the details and expert tips you need to perfect your patchwork.

HAND PIECING WITH PRECISION

Hand piecing offers wonderful benefits like the utmost in control and accuracy, as well as portability. Three popular methods—traditional template, freezer paper template, and English paper piecing—each have particular attributes, so it's a good idea to experiment with each to see which works best for you. Generally, any type of hand piecing requires templates for marking or indicating seam lines or stitching lines on the fabric pieces. Refer to pages 7 to 10 for general information about constructing templates and using them to cut fabric for hand-pieced patchwork and for tips on combining templates with rotary cutting.

TRADITIONAL HAND PIECING

Step 1. Place the first two pieces to be joined with right sides together. Insert a pin through the 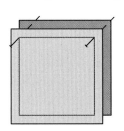 top piece, directly through the end of the marked seam line, and continue through both layers, piercing the second piece at the end of its corresponding seam. Repeat at the opposite end of the seam, again exactly matching the end points. Insert additional pins through the pieces if necessary to hold them firmly in place, taking care to match the marked seam lines each time a pin is used, as shown.

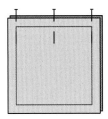

Step 2. Make a single stitch through the pin hole at one end of the marked seam line, pulling the thread through and leaving a tail approximately 1 inch long; do not knot the tail. Backstitch.

Start with thread that's approximately 20 to 24 inches long so you can avoid tangles, yet not run out in a hurry.

Step 3. Use a running stitch of approximately 8 to 10 stitches per inch along the marked line, as shown in the diagram. Backstitch every four or five stitches, and remove the pins as you near them. Secure the tail of thread by stitching over it as you work. When you reach the seam end, make two back-stitches, pulling the needle through the final loop to secure the thread. Clip the thread, leaving a tail about ¼ inch long. Add other pieces to the row as required, and assemble additional rows in the same manner.

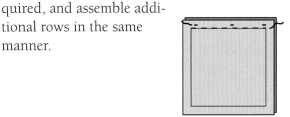

On the Right Track

When hand piecing, turn your work over often to make sure the stitches are exactly on the marked seam lines of both pieces. And try stitching with a "sharp" or "straw" needle. These long, thin needles slip easily through the fabric.

Step 4. To complete the block, align all seams from row to row, as described in Step 3. Sew the rows together. When you cross seam allowances of previously joined units, leave the seam allowances free, as shown at the top of page 26. Backstitch just before you cross the seam allowance, slip the needle through the seam allowance, backstitch just after you cross, then resume stitching the

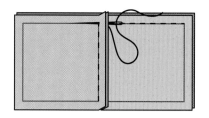

seam. The seam allowances can be pressed later in the direction that best suits the rest of your quilt top assembly.

FREEZER PAPER METHOD

If you find pinning, flipping, and checking for matching seam lines is a bit tedious, try freezer paper. Instead of having to mark the seam line on each fabric piece, you can use *finished-size* freezer paper templates pressed onto the wrong side of the fabric pieces. Use the papers as the guide for aligning seams. The papers provide a visual guide that's further enhanced by your sense of touch, as shown. The stiffness and slight lump you feel through the fabric tells you exactly where your seam line is, as well as where the seam begins and ends. Sew the pieces together in the same manner as you would with traditional hand piecing. Refer to page 8 for information about making templates from freezer paper.

Freezer paper templates can be reused several times each before the waxy coating no longer adheres to the fabric, meaning you don't have to cut quite as many paper pieces as fabric pieces.

The Color Gray

Medium gray thread is a good choice for hand piecing multicolor blocks. The medium tone blends well with a variety of colors and shades, and you won't have to keep changing your thread color.

Stabilize Stretchy Edges

Freezer paper templates make great stabilizers for stretchy bias edges, such as on triangles and hexagons. The paper holds the edges in place while you sew. Carefully peel away the papers after sewing to avoid any unintentional stretching.

ENGLISH PAPER PIECING

This technique became popular in England toward the end of the nineteenth century, when mosaic quilts pieced from silk hexagons were in vogue. Although it began with hexagons, English paper piecing can be used to stitch together pieces of any shape. The basic technique is easy: Fabric is basted to paper templates, which have been cut to the *finished* size of each piece, then edges of adjoining pieces are whipstitched together. Paper piecing does require more time than other piecing methods because you need to baste a paper template to each patch, but, if you like to hand sew, the precision it adds to a project makes the extra time worthwhile.

Choosing the Right Paper

Many types of paper can be used for this method. Card stock–weight paper works well, but since it is thicker than other papers, it is harder to cut through. Some quilters prefer ordinary typing paper, which can be less expensive than other choices. Another option is freezer paper, which also eliminates seam basting.

Precut paper pieces are also available in a variety of sizes and shapes from quilt shops and mail-order quilting catalogs. As long as you can find the shape in the size you want, these precut pieces are a great time-saver. When planning the number of papers you'll need, remember that each paper template is left in place until all neighboring pieces have been sewn to the piece it is basted to.

Try English Paper Piecing

The following example illustrates the basics of English paper piecing using a hexagon, but the steps are the same for all patchwork shapes. A hexagon pattern is given on page 47. Trace it to make a template and try your hand at English paper piecing.

If you are careful in your stitching, papers can be reused in another section of the quilt once they are removed.

Step 1. Make paper templates to match the exact *finished* size of the pieces.

Step 2. Cut corresponding fabric pieces that are about ¼ inch larger on all sides than the paper templates. The seam allowances don't need to be exact because the paper template will control the finished size of the piece.

Step 3. Center a paper template on the wrong side of a fabric piece, and pin it in place. Fold the seam allowance over the paper piece one side at a time and press. Baste the seam allowance to the paper, as shown, making sure you secure areas where the seam allowance overlaps. Repeat for all of the remaining pieces.

Step 4. Place two prepared pieces right sides together, matching edges carefully. Use a whipstitch to sew the edges together from corner to corner along one side, backstitching at the beginning and end of the seam. If your seams are long, take additional backstitches occasionally along the seams. Take small stitches, and avoid sewing into the edges of the paper, as shown. Your stitches should barely show when the pieces are opened.

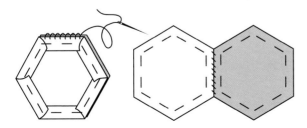

Step 5. Sew the remaining pieces together. (Your project directions will tell you specifically which pieces go together.) Sew each side from end to end in the same manner as before, matching edges carefully. Remember to backstitch at the beginning and end of each seam. Whenever possible, do not cut your thread at the end of one piece; instead, backstitch and continue sewing the next piece along the adjacent edge, as shown in the diagram. Papers should be left in place until all adjacent pieces are sewn to a hexagon. When the hexagon is complete, remove your basting stitches and the remaining papers, then press.

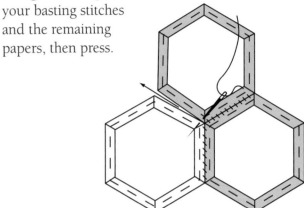

Backstitch where three hexagons meet; continue stitching in direction of arrow.

To Baste or Not to Baste

If you cut your paper pieces from freezer paper, you can skip the basting seam allowances step. Instead, position a paper hexagon with the waxy side up on the wrong side of a fabric hexagon. Use a medium to hot dry iron to press the seam allowances onto the paper. The waxy coating will soften and hold the fabric in place.

Better yet, avoid burning your fingers by replacing your iron with a clean hot glue gun. Make sure no glue is remaining in the gun, then use the hot tip to press the seam allowances to the freezer paper.

PERFECT MACHINE PIECING

There are many quick-and-easy machine-piecing techniques—from chain piecing to strip piecing to foundation piecing—that make quilt-making fun and yield wonderful results. Regardless of the techniques you use, however, it always pays to start with the basics.

SEAM LINES AND ALLOWANCES

Seam lines are usually not marked on pieces that will be pieced by machine. Instead, pieces are positioned with right sides together and their outer edges aligned. A seam is then sewn from raw edge to raw edge through both pieces, using a stitch length of 10 to 12 stitches per inch and a $\frac{1}{4}$-inch seam allowance, as shown. With shapes that have matching angles along their connecting sides, such as the rectangle and square shown,

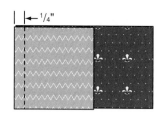

alignment is simple because the seam allowances at those angles are exactly the same.

MATCHING ANGLES

Matching edges can be a bit trickier when you need to align two shapes with different angles, because the tips of one piece may extend beyond the seam allowance of the adjoining piece. For example, when you need to sew a triangle to a square, as shown in the diagram, the tips of the triangle extend beyond the ends of the square.

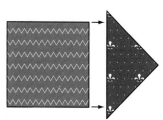

The Right Way: When the pieces are accurately centered and sewn together (see **A**), the finished

unit will look like the one shown in **B**. Notice how the tips of the triangle extend beyond the edges of the square.

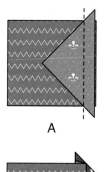

A

If you continue sewing triangles to each side of the square, your completed block should look like the one shown in **C**. Notice that the corners of the squares do not touch the outer edges of the block. That's because a $\frac{1}{4}$-inch seam allowance is included all the way around the block and will be used when this block is sewn to other blocks in the quilt.

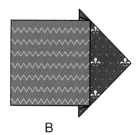

B

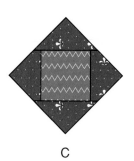

C

When sewing triangles to all four sides of a square as shown, always sew the second triangle to the side opposite the first one to avoid distortion.

The Wrong Way: If the triangles aren't centered when you sew them to the center square, a minor misadjustment on each side turns into a major problem by the time all four triangles are added to the square!

A quick-and-easy way to make sure triangles are centered is to fold each triangle in half and crease to find the midpoint. Fold the square in half in each direction, too. Match the centers, pin, and stitch.

TRIMMING SEAMS FOR ACCURACY

Marking seam lines and measuring alignment is a surefire way to avoid misaligned pieces; but if you're into speed, and especially if you're using a rotary cutter, it doesn't make much sense to re-trace your steps and mark every piece you've cut. Here are a few easier ways to deal with the problem of hard-to-match pieces.

Trim the excess from the tips of triangles, diamonds, and the like, so that all pieces will fit flush with one another when correctly aligned. Or simply start the cutting process with templates that have the tips trimmed off, so your fabric pieces won't have unneeded tips to start with. You can even buy a triangular ruler that has squared-off edges for quick-and-easy rotary cutting of pieces due to built-in alignment guides.

Nubbing Makes Matching Easy

Here's a method for *nubbing* (trimming off the tips that extend beyond the seam) that doesn't require a specialty ruler. This method can be used to make nubbing guides for any shape.

Step 1. Draft a *finished-size* paper template of both the triangle and the square on graph paper. Draw ¼-inch seam allowances around both templates, and cut them out on the outer lines.

Step 2. Align the templates just as you would fabric pieces, carefully matching seam lines. To be certain the pieces are aligned correctly, stack them as shown, and stab a pin through both layers, making sure it pierces each template at the end of a seam line.

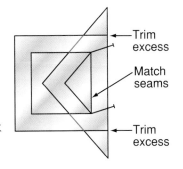

Step 3. Repeat on the opposite end. Trim away the excess nubs from the triangle template to make a nubbing guide, as shown.

Step 4. Tape the nubbing guide to the bottom of a rotary-cutting ruler, as shown in **A,** then align the shape to a stack of your rotary-cut triangles and use it as a guide to trim away the nubs. (Don't stack more than about four pieces at a time, or your cuts won't be accurate because your ruler will wobble.)

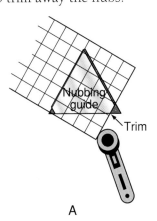

A

Or use the nubbing guide to mark the nubbing lines on the fabric pieces, then align the rotary ruler with the drawn lines and trim the tips, as shown in **B.** Again, you can stack up to about four pieces at a time for trimming, which means you don't have to mark the nubbing lines on all of your pieces. Only the ones at the tops of the stacks need guidelines.

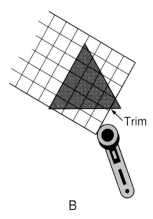

B

CHAIN PIECING

Chain piecing (which is sometimes called assembly line or laundry line piecing) is a time-efficient method for sewing together more than one pair of the same combination of pieces.

Place the fabric pieces with their right sides together and, without lifting the presser foot or cutting the thread, run the pairs of quilt patches through the sewing machine one after another, referring to the diagram. Once all of the units you need have been sewn together, snip them apart and press them open.

Chain Piecing Triangles and Diamonds

Triangles and diamonds can be stitched together using the same chain piecing method, but here's a tip for saving thread. Alternate the direction of the triangles or diamonds as you feed them into your machine. The angles will fit together nicely when alternated, as shown, reducing the distance between pieces. Just make sure you have an accurate ¼-inch seam allowance on both sides of your presser foot or throat plate.

When you chain piece shapes with long pointed angles, the tips can stray a bit. Since it's hard to fit your fingers under the presser foot to keep everything in line (and that's a dangerous place to have your fingers, anyway), try this trick: Pin the narrow tips together so that they will stay in place as they are fed through the machine, as shown in the diagram.

Add a Scrap to the Chain

When chain piecing triangles, all too often the narrow tips on the first set of pieces will be sucked down into the feed dogs, nearly eliminating the timesaving element of this trick! To avoid this annoyance, start your chain sewing with a single scrap of fabric. Start sewing in the middle of the scrap, rather than right at the edge, to prevent this, too, from being pulled into the feed dogs.

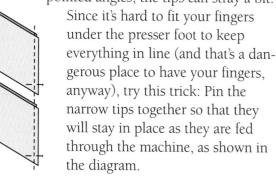

MAKING TRIANGLE SQUARES ON A GRID

Many quilt blocks require a number of identical triangle squares—square units made from two right triangles joined along the long sides. The grid construction method lets you assemble very accurate blocks much more quickly than you could using a more traditional method of sewing together individual triangles.

With this method, two pieces of fabric are cut oversize, placed right sides together, then marked, sewn, and cut apart into individual triangle squares. Careful marking and sewing are musts, but your attention to detail will produce multiples of identical triangle squares. As an added bonus, you won't have to work with bias edges!

This method is especially helpful when you need lots of very small triangle squares (such as 1-inch squares), since you never have to handle individual tiny triangles.

Step 1. To determine the size to cut your two pieces of fabric that will make up the triangle squares, you need to know two important things: how many triangle squares you need to make and what size square you will be making. These two numbers are normally provided in any project directions. The number of squares to draw on the grid will be the total number required divided by two, since each square you draw will yield two triangle squares. The size of the squares you will draw on your grid will be the finished size of the triangle squares plus ⅞ inch.

For example, if you need to make 60 red and blue triangle squares with a finished size of 2½ inches, calculate your fabric size like this:

- 2½ inches + ⅞ inch = 3⅜ inches (the size you'll draw your squares)
- 60 squares ÷ 2 = 30 (the number of squares you'll need to draw)
- A grid of five squares across by six squares lengthwise will give you 30 squares
- Five × 3⅜ inches = 16⅞ inches
- Six × 3⅜ inches = 20¼ inches

It's wise to allow a little extra room on all sides of the grid, so cut your two pieces 22 × 25 inches.

It is easier to work with fabric pieces that aren't too big, so if you need hundreds of identical triangle squares, make two or three separate grids rather than one large, hard-to-manage grid.

Step 2. Working on the wrong side of the lighter fabric, draw a grid of squares with a pencil or fine-tip permanent pen, as shown in **A.** Draw the grid at least ¹/₂ inch from the raw edges of the fabric. Referring to **B,** carefully draw a diagonal line through each square in the grid.

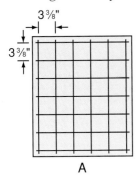
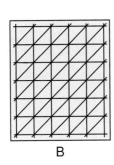

A   B

Step 3. Position the marked fabric right sides together with the second piece of fabric. Pin the fabrics together, using one pin in about every other square. Using a ¹/₄-inch seam allowance, stitch along both sides of the diagonal lines, as shown. Use the edge of your presser foot as a ¹/₄-inch guide. If your presser foot isn't exactly ¹/₄ inch, draw a line ¹/₄ inch from each side of the diagonal lines.

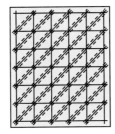

Instead of breaking the stitching at the end of each diagonal line, as shown, simply lift the presser foot, rotate the fabric grid, and start stitching in the next direction without clipping the thread each time.

Step 4. Use a rotary cutter and ruler to cut the grid apart. Cut on all of the marked lines, as indicated in **A.** Carefully press the triangle squares open, pressing each seam toward the darker fabric. Trim off the triangle points at the seam ends with your rotary cutter and ruler, as shown

in **B.** Continue marking and cutting triangle squares until you have made the number required for your quilt.

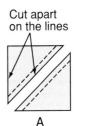 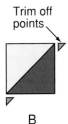

Cut apart on the lines   Trim off points

A   B

TRIANGLE SQUARES FROM BIAS STRIPS

Bias strips can also be used to construct triangle squares. In this method, developed by Nancy Martin, long bias strips are sewn together, pressed, and cut apart into ready-made triangle squares, eliminating the need to handle bias edges on individual triangles.

As with other methods, there are pros and cons to this technique. In this case, you will need extra fabric, and there will be some waste, but the accuracy, especially for small triangle squares, can outweigh wasted bits of fabric. Although other rulers can be used, the Bias Square ruler, available in three sizes, was developed specifically for this method.

Step 1. Lay the two fabrics for the triangle squares with one on top of the other and right sides up, and press. Make an initial cut on the bias, as shown, by aligning the 45 degree line of a 6 × 24-inch rotary ruler (or a Bias Square ruler) with the lower, straight edge of the fabric. Continue cutting bias strips through both layers in a width equal to the *unfinished* size of the triangle square. For instance, 2-inch-wide strips will result in blocks that are 2 inches square before sewing. If you need 2-inch *finished* blocks, you need to cut the strips 2⁷/₈ inches wide.

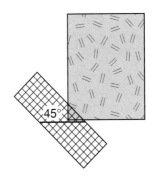
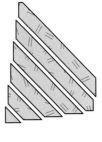

45°

Step 2. Place two contrasting strips right sides together and sew along the longest sides, using a ¼-inch seam allowance. See the diagram. Press the seam allowance toward the darkest fabric, taking care not to stretch the fabrics, since the long edges are cut on the bias.

Step 3. Align the 45 degree line on the Bias Square (or rotary) ruler with the seam line, and cut the first two sides of the block, as shown in **A**. Turn the strip around, align the 45 degree line with the seam, and align the appropriate ruler markings with the two cut edges of the square, as shown in **B**. For instance, if you are cutting 2½-inch squares, align the 2½-inch markings on each side of the ruler with the cut sides of the square. Cut along both edges of the ruler to yield one triangle square, as shown in **C**.

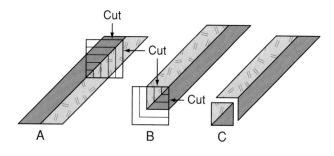

Step 4. Continue cutting squares in the same manner, cutting away the excess triangles, as shown in the diagram, and then cutting the remaining two sides of each square.

TRIANGLE SQUARES FROM SQUARES

Another way to eliminate handling bias edges when making triangle squares is to cut squares, sew them together diagonally, then cut them apart to yield two triangle squares. This method is useful for larger squares or for when you need squares stitched from an assortment of fabrics.

Step 1. Determine the size square required by adding ⅞ inch to the desired finished size of the triangle square. Cut two squares to this size; or, if you prefer, you can cut the squares slightly larger, and the resulting triangle squares can be trimmed to the finished size after sewing. This extra trimming step adds a bit more work, but it improves the accuracy of the finished block.

Step 2. Draw a diagonal line from corner to corner on the reverse of the lightest square, as shown below.

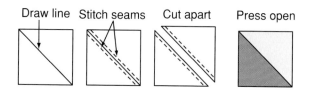

Draw line   Stitch seams   Cut apart   Press open

Step 3. Match the edges of squares carefully, then stitch the squares together, sewing ¼ inch from each side of the drawn line, as shown. After sewing on both sides of the line, cut the squares in half on the drawn line with a rotary cutter and ruler. Press the seam allowance in each triangle square toward the darkest fabric. Trim off tips from the triangle points, as shown on page 31.

TIMESAVING STRIP PIECING

In traditional patchwork, each piece in a block is cut and sewn individually. Multiply the time spent cutting, sewing, and pressing just one multipatch block by the number of blocks required for your quilt, and traditional piecing can seem more like a task than fun.

Unless you are making a charm quilt, where no fabric is repeated in the design, or a scrap quilt, where you want to randomly mix up all of the fabrics, strip piecing can often be used to shorten the assembly time.

In this timesaving technique, long fabric strips are sewn together into a large strip set. The seams are pressed, then the strip set is cut apart into shorter segments that will be used as rows or sections of the quilt block. This system eliminates the individual cutting, sewing, and pressing steps, and it can even improve the consistency among your quilt blocks.

rics used in the four patch. In this example, you would cut the strips 2 inches wide (1½ inches + ½ inch = 2 inches).

Try Strip Piecing

Take a look at the Milky Way block shown and the step-by-step directions that follow for a clearer understanding of how strip piecing is used and how it can be combined with other piecing methods to complete a wide variety of popular quilt blocks.

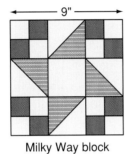

Milky Way block

Step 1. Since the finished Milky Way block shown is 9 inches square, then each of the three units that make up the block, as shown, has a finished size of 3 inches square. For other types of blocks, you can determine the finished size of the components in the same manner.

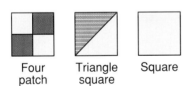

Four patch   Triangle square   Square

Step 2. The four patch unit above is made by sewing together two long strips of contrasting fabric to make a strip set, which will be cut into segments, as shown. Two segments are joined to make each four patch. To determine how wide to cut your strips, start with the finished size of the four patch. Since the block is 9 inches square, and the four patch has a finished size of 3 inches, then each small square in the four patch must measure 1½ inches square. Add ¼ inch to each side of the small square's finished width (a total of ½ inch) to determine the strip width for each of the two fab-

Step 3. Sew the two strips together lengthwise to make the strip set. Press the seams toward the darker fabric. Use your rotary ruler and cutter to square up one end of the strip, then cut 2-inch segments (the same width as the width of the original strips) from the strip set, as shown.

Step 4. Place two segments together with right sides facing. Because the seams are all pressed toward the darker fabric, they will be facing in opposite directions in your two pieces. This will allow you to butt, or nest, the seams together, as shown, for perfect seam alignment. You will be able to feel the seams aligning. Once you have the seams where you want them, pin the pieces together. Pin on each side of the stitching line rather than directly over it. Stitch the seam, using a ¼-inch seam allowance. Make four such pieces for the Milky Way block.

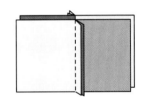

Step 5. To complete the block, you'll need four triangle squares and one square, as shown earlier. Refer to pages 29 to 32 for several quick-piecing methods for triangle squares. Both the square and the triangle squares need to measure 3½ inches (including seam allowances) like the four patch unit.

Step 6. Now that you have all of the individual components ready for the Milky Way block, you are ready to sew them together. The block is assembled in three rows, as shown. Press seams in

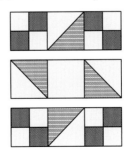

adjoining rows in opposite directions, then match the seam intersections carefully and sew the rows together. For more information on row assembly, see page 44.

Many Uses for Strip Piecing

As you become more familiar with strip piecing, you'll be able to quickly analyze blocks for strip-piecing potential. A few examples of blocks that can be strip pieced are shown.

Rail Fence

Puss in the Corner

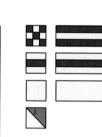

Goose in the Pond

Cutting Double

Slash your cutting time in half with multiple strip sets using this simple trick. Layer two strip sets together with right sides facing, but with the contrasting fabrics on top of one another. Carefully nestle or butt the seams together as you would with the individual segments. Then cut your segments. Each segment will be paired with another, aligned, and ready to sew!

FOUNDATION PIECING: CONSISTENT, PRECISE, AND FUN!

In the nineteenth century, quilters used foundation piecing to construct many of their quilts, sewing fabric pieces to either the front or back side of a foundation onto which a copy of the block had been drafted. Foundation piecing is now enjoying a strong revival, with more and more quilters designing blocks specifically for foundation piecing. Today, most of the foundations are paper rather than muslin fabric, since the paper can be removed. Fabric foundations remain in the quilt, making it a bit heavier and harder to quilt through.

Recycle used dryer sheets (the white fabric type, not the colored sponge kind) for a great foundation material that can either be left in or removed.

When to Use Foundation Piecing

Foundation piecing is especially helpful for the following types of blocks or those with similar characteristics:

• **Log Cabin and Pineapple:** These strip, or log-style, blocks, particularly versions with narrow logs, are an excellent choice for foundation piecing. The foundation ensures that your blocks will be perfectly square with no puckers in the middle.

• **Miniature quilt blocks:** Miniatures are often foundation pieced, since larger pieces of fabrics can be attached to the foundation, and trimmed, thus avoiding the need to start with very tiny pieces, which can be difficult to work with.

• **Pickle Dish, New York Beauty, and Wedding Ring:** Any variations of these designs that have long or narrow points set into curved pieces are easier to piece accurately on a foundation.

• **Flying Geese and Sawtooth borders:** Lots of piecing is required to complete a long stretch of border, and all the seams can lead to distortion. Foundation piecing eliminates the distortion, and the result is a perfect-fitting border.

Making the Foundations

One disadvantage of the foundation piecing method is that separate foundations must be prepared for individual blocks. This requires additional preparation time and added materials. But there are benefits that help offset this extra preparation. Cutting time is decreased because you don't have to cut individual pieces to exact sizes. In many cases, you'll work with scraps or long strips that are trimmed as you go, which means the actual sewing moves along quickly.

First, you need to draw the block to scale on the foundation material. It can be a permanent foundation, such as muslin, which remains in the quilt forever, or a removable foundation, such as paper, which is pulled away from the block after the quilt top is assembled. Various types of paper are commonly used for foundation piecing. "Paper Choices for Foundation Piecing" on page 36 outlines the pros and cons of each.

Hot-Iron Transfers

An alternative to repeatedly tracing your pattern onto foundations is to use a hot-iron transfer pen to draw the full-size block onto tracing paper. The image can usually be ironed onto a foundation material five or six times. Retrace the original transfer for additional ironing, being careful to mark over the existing lines exactly. A transfer pen can be used on both fabric and paper foundations, but do a test first to be sure it will work on your chosen material.

Foundation Piecing Basics

There are a few basic rules and pointers to keep in mind when using foundation piecing. But once you've got these down pat, you're sure to enjoy the instant expertise foundation piecing brings to your patchwork.

• **Flip and sew:** The most common method of foundation piecing involves positioning the fabric on the reverse side of the foundation (the side without the sewing guide lines), and sewing on the opposite, or marked, side. Seams are stitched directly onto one of the marked lines of the foundation. If you are unfamiliar with this technique, it may at first seem awkward. But if you position the fabric correctly and are careful to sew on the lines, every piece in every block will be perfect, no matter how small or narrow its finished size.

• **Drafting foundations:** Since the fabric will be sewn to the back of the foundation, the finished block will always be a *mirror image* of the template. For example, if you want a Schoolhouse block with the door on the right side of the block, the foundation template needs to be drafted with the door on the left side. For symmetrical blocks, such as a Log Cabin or Pineapple, drafting is not as confusing as where your colors or fabrics are to be placed. Jot the colors or another code for your fabrics onto the foundation before sewing to help you keep track of their position in the block.

• **Cutting fabric:** For maximum strength and stability and minimum distortion, fabric should be cut along its lengthwise or crosswise grain. Ideally, the straight of grain should be parallel with the outer perimeter of your block. Grain placement is most important if you are using removable foundations that won't remain in the quilt as permanent stabilizers. You can use long strips of fabric and trim them off after stitching your seams. Just remember to cut them wide enough to cover the section of your foundation plus ½ inch for a seam allowance on each side.

Try Foundation Piecing

The only seam allowance included on the foundation template is the one around the outer perimeter of the design. The foundation for an arc in an Indian Wedding Ring variation is illustrated here. The piecing on this type of quilt design would ordinarily be quite complicated, but the foundation method makes stitching these curves and points just about fail-proof. Simply

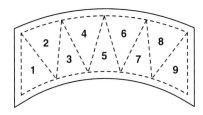

Paper Choices for Foundation Piecing

Types of Paper	Benefits	Disadvantages
Copy machine paper	Readily available; can be used to make multiple copies of block pattern	Can be difficult to remove; photocopying pattern can lead to distortion on some copiers; copier ink can come off with the heat of an iron
Freezer paper	Fairly easy to remove; available in most grocery stores; many quilters have on hand	Waxy coating can make it slippery to sew on; need to take care when pressing due to waxy coating
Newsprint (blank)	Inexpensive; easy to remove	Pencil and ballpoint ink can smear; use permanent ink only
Tissue paper	Transparency makes it easy to see how fabrics are aligned; readily available; easy to remove	Can't be used in copy machine, but suitable for other means of transferring pattern
Tracing paper	Very easy to trace onto with pencil or fine-tip permanent pen; easy to sew through and remove	Can't be used in copy machine, but suitable for other means of transferring pattern
Typing paper	Readily available; relatively inexpensive	"Erasable" types can smear; use permanent pen or nonerasable paper for patterns

follow the numbers on the pattern for the order in which to sew the pieces to the foundation. To try this method yourself, make a paper foundation of the Wedding Ring Arc pattern on page 46.

Right Side Up Rule

The first piece of fabric sewn to the foundation is always positioned right side up (the wrong side of the fabric faces the wrong side, or unprinted side, of the foundation). All remaining pieces are positioned right side down (facing the the wrong side of the foundation) for sewing.

Step 1. Make an exact copy of the foundation pattern. In this example, paper is used. Photocopies are fine, but make sure they are accurate

reproductions before using them. Cut out the paper pattern, leaving about ¼ inch of paper beyond the outermost lines.

Step 2. Determine how wide you need to cut your strips, and be sure to allow enough for seam allowances. In fact, when you first try foundation piecing, it's usually best to add an additional ⅛ to ¼ inch to the calculated strip width. The extra bit of fabric will give you more flexibility as you position your strips onto the back of the foundation, and the excess will be trimmed away after sewing. Cut two contrasting fabric strips to your calculated width. Place the strips right sides together, with the lightest strip on top. Lay your paper pattern piece on top of the strips (with the marked lines

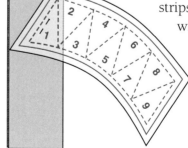

Pin fabric strips
underneath section 1

facing you) so that when you look through the paper arc, the strips completely cover the triangle marked 1. They should also extend at least ¼ inch beyond the seam lines, as shown in the diagram on the bottom of the previous page. You may find it helpful to pin the fabrics in place.

Step 3. Set your stitch length to 14 to 18 stitches per inch. This shorter-than-usual stitch length will perforate the paper more closely, making it easier for you to tear away the paper when the block is completed. Stitch directly on the paper along the dotted line that separates triangles 1 and 2, as shown. Start and stop your stitching slightly beyond the curved seam lines.

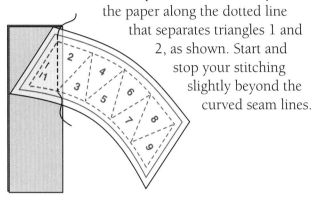

Stitch on line between
sections 1 and 2

There's no need to backstitch when sewing on a paper foundation since the short stitches won't pull out.

Step 4. Remove the foundation from your sewing machine and turn the paper over to trim the seam allowance to a scant ¼ inch, as shown. Then flip the dark fabric strip so it's right side up. Finger press in place or press with a warm iron. Trim away the excess fabric strips, making sure you leave enough of the dark fabric so that at least ¼ inch overlaps all points of the line between triangles 2 and 3.

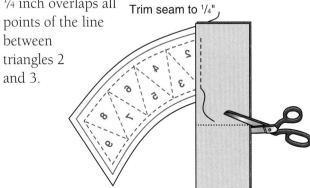

Trim seam to ¼"

Trim off bottom of strips

Also be sure that the light fabric extends beyond the ¼-inch seam allowance at the end of the arc. See the diagram.

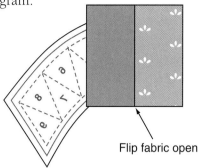

Flip fabric open

Step 5. Place a light strip against the dark fabric that was just sewn to the paper with right sides together. Position the light strip so it extends at least ¼ inch beyond the sewing line between triangles 2 and 3. Holding or pinning the fabric in place, sew along the dotted line separating triangles 2 and 3, as shown in the diagram. Remove the foundation from the machine, flip it over, trim the seam allowance, and finger press as you did before. Continue alternating fabrics and adding the remaining pieces in exactly the same manner until the paper arc is completely covered.

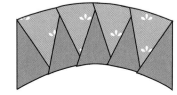

Place light fabric strip underneath foundation. Stitch on line between sections 2 and 3.

Step 6. When all pieces have been sewn to the foundation, press with a warm iron. Use a rotary cutter or scissors to cut on the outermost line of the foundation to remove the excess fabric and paper. The diagram shows a completed arc. To remove the paper arc, fold it along the seam lines and gently tear it away from the stitching.

Completed arc with seam allowances

Raid your cosmetic bag for a pair of tweezers—a great tool for removing those last little bits of foundation paper without damaging your stitching.

String Piecing on Foundations

String piecing is another technique that uses foundations. But instead of sewing fabric to pre-drawn or preprinted lines, you sew fabric strips to the base in a freestyle manner. Strips can also be sewn together without a foundation base. The method you choose depends on how you intend to use the resulting patchwork and on the lengths of your strips.

Short strips are handy to cover single templates. Long strips of fabric can be sewn together to create an entire panel of fabric that can be cut in any way you choose.

Try String Piecing

Step 1. Draft and cut a foundation out of paper or muslin. If you want to make a triangle as in the example here, start with a large square (about 9 × 9 inches) and cut it in half diagonally. Be sure to include a ¼-inch seam allowance around the shape's outer edges. For easier and more accurate trimming, leave a bit of excess foundation paper or muslin beyond the edges of the desired template shape.

This example illustrates string piecing a triangle, but the technique can be used for any shape you choose. As with the previous foundation method, muslin will remain in the quilt, while paper will be removed.

Step 2. Select a strip of fabric and position it right side up on the marked side of the foundation, as shown, making sure the fabric extends past the marked lines. (If you prefer to mark the seam line on the front and sew on the back side, keep in mind that the resulting piece will be a mirror image of the template's front.)

Step 3. Select a second strip of fabric and position it right side down on top of the first fabric. Align the lower edges of the two strips and stitch ¼ inch from the edge of the strips, as shown.

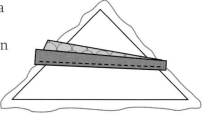

Step 4. Flip the second strip open so it is right side up, as shown, and finger press.

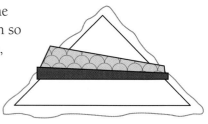

Step 5. Align a third strip of fabric right side down along the edge of the first strip and stitch, as shown.

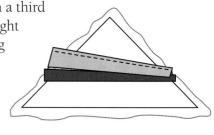

Step 6. Flip the third strip right side up and finger press. The front of your foundation should now resemble the diagram.

Step 7. Continue adding strips in the same manner until the entire template is covered, as shown. Strips can be any width you choose and can be sewn to the foundation in an angled manner.

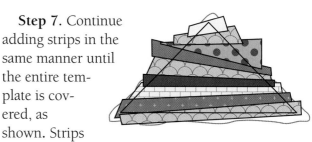

Step 8. Press the finished patchwork lightly, then turn it over, align your rotary-cutting ruler to

the marked edge, and trim away the excess fabric and foundation. Be sure to leave ¼-inch seam allowances intact. The finished strip-pieced triangle should look like the one illustrated.

STRING PIECING FABRIC

String piecing your own fabric is a fast, fun, and creative way to make a project uniquely yours. Cut a variety of fabric strips, varying the colors, patterns, strip widths, and even the angles. Sew the strips together lengthwise, press the seam allowances, and you have a custom-made piece of fabric. Don't be afraid to mix colors that don't seem to go together. The variety will add visual interest. If you've decided to angle a seam more than the original cut of the strips, trim the excess seam allowances to reduce bulk.

Use the string fabric in the same way you would any other piece of fabric. You can cut templates from it, as shown.

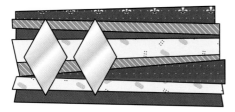

Or rotary cut it into squares, triangles, or other shapes or strips as shown, or use it for appliqué. The choice is yours!

FUSED CRAZY QUILTING

Pieces cut from random-width strip-pieced fabric can be made to look like Victorian crazy quilting when decorative stitches are added. To

keep the stitching intact, be sure to tie off beginning and ending threads on the back of your work. Establish a design on paper first, then transfer the lines to your background fabric and use fusible web to fuse the pieces, such as the Wedding Ring melon shape shown, to it.

STITCHING SMOOTH CURVED SEAMS

Many popular quilt patterns involve curved seams, including Drunkard's Path, Double Wedding Ring, and New York Beauty. Although the degree of the curves varies from block to block, the objective is to align a convex edge with a concave edge and sew the two together so the seam lies smooth and flat, with no puckering. When you look at the two shapes needed to make a Drunkard's Path block, shown here, the task may seem daunting.

However, achieving a smoothly curved seam on your sewing machine really is possible.

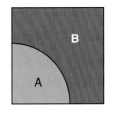

Try Curved Piecing

Using the Drunkard's Path A and B patterns on page 47, make templates and cut out fabric shapes and try your hand at precision curved piecing on the sewing machine.

Step 1. Make a ⅛-inch mark or notch in the center of both curves, as shown. You can mark these with pencils or by making a snip in the seam allowance with the tip of your scissors.

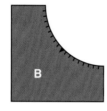

Center notches are often printed on curved patterns, but if they aren't, you can determine match points by folding each piece in half along the diagonal and creasing.

Step 2. To make the edge easier to manipulate, make tiny (1/16-inch) clips in the seam allowance on the concave piece, as shown. Use just the tip of the scissors so you don't cut into the seam allowance.

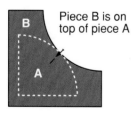

Step 3. Place the curved pieces with right sides together. Match and pin at the center notches, as shown in the diagram. Add additional pins along the length of the curve and at each corner, manipulating the curves to fit, as shown. If necessary, make more tiny clips in the concave curve.

Piece B is on top of piece A

Step 4. Sew the pieces together, using a ¼-inch seam allowance. Move slowly, removing pins just before you get to them. Open up the patchwork and press with the seams toward the convex curve.

SETTING IN PIECES

Some quilt blocks have pieces that need to be set into angles created by other pieces, such as in a LeMoyne Star or Eight-Pointed Star or in the Tumbling Blocks shown. In the Tumbling Blocks example, three 60 degree diamond pieces (the pattern is on page 45) are stitched together to make a cube. When the third piece is attached, it needs to be set in where the other two diamonds are joined. When setting in by machine, it is helpful to remember the basic hand-piecing rule— sewing takes place only on marked seam lines and never extends into the seam allowance. For precise set-in seams, it is helpful to mark the seam lines on the wrong side of all pieces that are involved in a setting-in procedure.

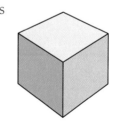

If you are experienced at set-in piecing, you may find that simply marking the seam intersections with an X or a dot is sufficient for indicating where to start and stop stitching.

Try Set-In Piecing

Step 1. Stitch together two diamond shapes, beginning and ending the seam ¼ inch from the edge of the fabric and backstitching at each end, as shown. Remove from the machine. By stitching only to the dot, which indicates the seam line intersections, you will be sure to keep the seam allowances open where the next diamond is to be set in.

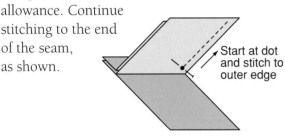
Stitch direction →

Step 2. Open up the pieces and place the third diamond right sides together with one of the other two diamonds. Pin the pieces together, placing a pin directly through the dot, or seam line intersection. Begin stitching at the dot and backstitch, being careful not to stitch into the seam allowance. Continue stitching to the end of the seam, as shown.

Start at dot and stitch to outer edge

Step 3. Rotate the pieces so that you are ready to sew the other half of the set-in seam. Pin the seam, again pinning directly through the dot where the seam allowances intersect. Keeping the seam allowances free, sew from the dot to the end of the pieces. Refer to the diagram.

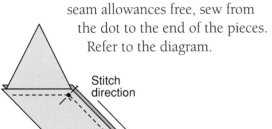
Stitch direction

Step 4. Press the seams so that as many of them as possible lie flat. The Tumbling Blocks unit should now look like the one shown on the previous page.

PRESSING FOR PERFECT PATCHWORK

Proper pressing can make a big difference in the appearance of a finished block or quilt top. It allows the patchwork to open up to its full size, permits more precise matching of seams, and results in smooth, flat work. Just as a ¼-inch seam allowance is the accepted standard width for patchwork seams, pressing the seams to one side, rather than open, is the rule.

Steam or Dry?

Quilters are divided on the issue of whether a steam or dry iron is best; experiment to see which works best for you. But whether you prefer steam or dry, remember that there is a difference between pressing and ironing. While assembling blocks, you press, lift up the iron, and set it down on the next area without sliding it around. This prevents the seams from becoming distorted by the drag and pull of the iron. When a quilt top is finished and all of the seams are pressed, you can iron the quilt carefully from the top, which means you move the iron across the entire surface of the pieced quilt.

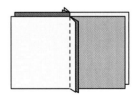
For the most accurate results while piecing, keep an iron close by your sewing machine and press all seams before adding additional pieces.

When a seam allowance is pressed to one side on the back of a patchwork unit, the two layers of seam allowances push the fabric in front of it up slightly, creating a loft. You can take advantage of this loft by pressing seams in adjoining segments in opposite directions. When segments are positioned with right sides together for sewing, the lofts butt up to each other, as shown, distributing the bulk and helping to align seams.

Pressing Directions

When possible, seams should be pressed toward the darker of the two fabrics being joined, but analyze the block you are working on before pressing to be sure doing so will result in units that will be easy to sew together. In part **A** of the diagram, strips in the two segments have been pressed toward the dark fabric. This keeps the dark seam allowance from showing through the light fabric and provides opposite lofts to help match the center seam when segments are joined.

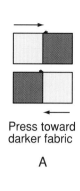

Press toward darker fabric

A

After sewing the two sections together to form the four patch block, as shown in **B**, you need to determine the direction to press the joining seam. That is usually determined by what type of unit it will be attached to next. For example, if you are simply sewing the four patch to a plain square, you can press the seam in either direction. If you will be attaching it to another four patch, you will want the seams in the two four patches to be pressed in opposite directions for a smooth fit.

Completed four patch

B

Once assembled, the back of the four patch with pressed seams will look like **C**.

Wrong side of four patch with seams pressed correctly

C

Set Seams First

To get the best results from your pressing, first "set" the seam. Place the *unopened* unit on the ironing board with the darkest fabric on top and the sewn edge away from you. Press with the iron to set the stitches. (The threads are flattened, making your seam lie flatter once it is opened.)

Once the seam has been set, lift the top piece to open the unit. Set the iron on the portion nearest you, and press gently toward the dark fabric to direct the seam allowance in that direction, unless you determined that you need to press your seams to the lighter fabric for adjoining seams to match properly. In that case, simply start with the lighter fabric on top, set the seam, and continue in the same manner.

EIGHT-SEAM JUNCTIONS

Templates for Eight-Seam Joins

You can machine piece an Eight-Pointed Star with a center seam that lies as flat as if you had sewn it by hand. For pinpoint accuracy, first make a nubbing guide for trimming the tips of the eight diamonds in each star. By trimming or nubbing the tips, the diamonds will align perfectly with each other for sewing.

Step 1. Make two templates of the 45 degree diamond on page 46, both including seam allowances. Position the templates with one on top of the other and seam lines matched, as shown. Trim the points, as shown.

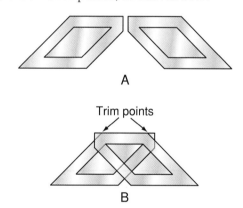

Trim points

A A

Step 2. Rotate templates so the trimmed tip edges are facing, as shown in **A**. Overlap the templates again, matching seams exactly, and trim away the smaller points, as shown in **B**.

A

Trim points

B

Step 3. Overlap the templates shown in **A** one more time, matching seams carefully and using the nubbed tip of each template to trim the pointed tip of the other template. Referring to **B**, use one of the completed templates as a guide to trim the tips from your fabric diamonds. The edges will now match perfectly for sewing an Eight-Pointed Star.

A **B**

Try Piecing an Eight-Pointed Star

Step 1. Before sewing, arrange all of the pieces as they will appear in the finished block. After you stitch the pieces together, replace them into the layout so you can keep track of their positions in the block and the orientation of outer and inner tips. When the diamonds are sewn together, the seam allowances that will be on the outer perimeter of the star must be left open to allow for setting in the squares and triangles that make up the star's background. These openings are illustrated by the small dots in the diagram. For more details on set-in seams, see "Setting In Pieces" on page 40.

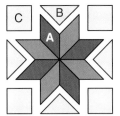

Step 2. Pin two diamond pieces together, placing a pin exactly ¼ inch from one tip. This end will become the outer edge of the star. Using a ¼-inch seam allowance, begin sewing directly at this point. Backstitch, taking care not to stitch back into the ¼-inch seam allowance. Stitch to the end of the seam, as shown in **A**.

When the diamonds are open, the back of your patchwork will look like **B**. Sew the remaining three pairs of diamonds together in the same manner, and press all seams in the same direction.

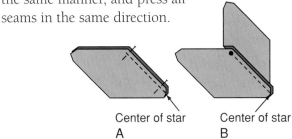

Center of star
A

Center of star
B

Step 3. Sew together two pairs of diamonds to make half of the star. Begin and end this seam ¼ inch from *both* ends, as shown.

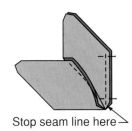

Stop seam line here →

Step 4. Press all seams in either a clockwise or counterclockwise direction, as shown. Repeat to assemble the other star half.

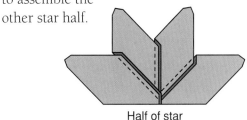

Half of star

Step 5. Pin the two star halves together with right sides facing. Rather than sew completely across the star from one side to the other, start stitching at one edge of the star and sew toward the center, stopping exactly at the point where all of the eight seams meet. Finger press the seam allowances out of the way. Refer to part **A** of the diagram. Sew the remaining seam, starting at the opposite side and stitching to the star center. End the stitching exactly at the center point. By leaving all of your seam allowances free in this manner, you will be able to press this final seam in your star by fanning out all of the seam allowances in the same direction, as shown in **B**.

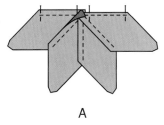

A

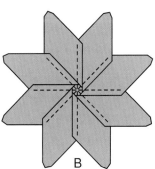

B

Step 6. To complete the Eight-Pointed Star block, refer to "Setting In Pieces" on page 40 to attach the B triangles and C squares to the star diamonds. (Cut a 5¼-inch square diagonally in quarters for B triangles; cut four 2⅞-inch C squares.)

When setting in seams, start at the inner corners and stitch toward the outer edge of the block.

When assembling an Eight-Pointed Star or other similar block with set-in triangles and squares, it is always best to set in the triangles first, followed by the squares. Sewing bias diamond edges to bias triangle edges can be a bit tricky if they are stretched out of shape. By sewing the triangles in first, you won't risk having to work with an overhandled star. Then setting in the straight-of-grain squares will be easy.

ASSEMBLING BLOCKS, ROWS, AND QUILT TOPS

Once you've pieced the components, such as triangle squares and four patches, for your quilt blocks, you're ready to combine the elements into the actual quilt blocks. Often these can be chain pieced together, just as you did for smaller units within the blocks. Completed blocks are then sewn into rows, and the rows are sewn into a quilt top. For more information on setting your blocks together, see "Sets and Sashing," beginning on page 73.

Chain Piecing Blocks

A Four-in-Nine Patch block is used for this example, yet just about any basic quilt block can be chain pieced together. The finished block is shown in the diagram. The vertical rows are labeled Rows 1, 2, and 3. The horizontal rows are labeled Rows A, B, and C.

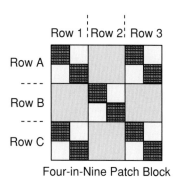

Four-in-Nine Patch Block

Step 1. Lay out all components of your quilt block as they are to appear in the finished block. For the Four-in-Nine Patch block, we will have nine components, laid out in three rows of three units each, as shown.

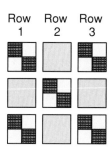

Step 2. Flip the Row 2 units onto the Row 1 units so their right sides are together. Sew the Row 2 units to the Row 1 units, using the chain piecing technique. Feed each pair of units through your sewing machine until all units in Rows 1 and 2 are attached, as shown in **A**. Open up the pieces, as in **B**. Don't press yet.

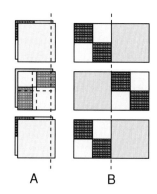

A   B

Step 3. Flip the Row 3 units onto the Row 2 units so their right sides are together. Pin in place. Chain sew these rows together as you did in Step 2. Open up Row 3, as shown.

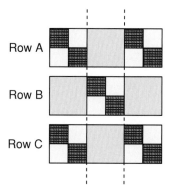

For perfect seam matching, it is more important to press seams in opposite directions than toward the darker fabric.

Step 4. Press the seam allowances so that adjoining seams are pressed in opposite directions. Whenever possible, press toward the darkest fabrics or to the side with the fewest seam intersections. In this example, you will press toward the large, unpieced squares rather than toward the Four Patch squares. Refer to the diagram.

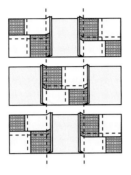

Wrong side.
Press seams toward
large squares.

Step 5. To sew the first horizontal row, fold Row A down so its right side is facing Row B. Align the seam intersections by feeling the hump where the seams are pressed in opposite directions. The two seam allowances should nestle together for a smooth, flat fit. Refer to the diagram. Pin each seam allowance in place and stitch. Repeat for the horizontal seam of Rows B and C.

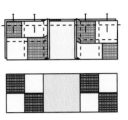

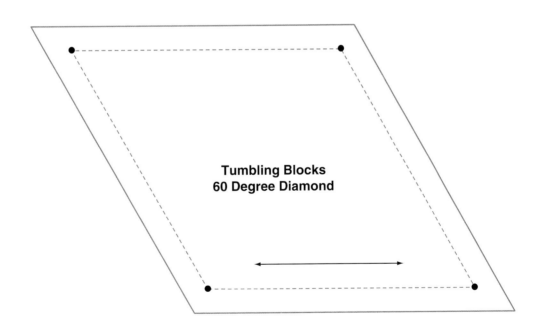

**Tumbling Blocks
60 Degree Diamond**

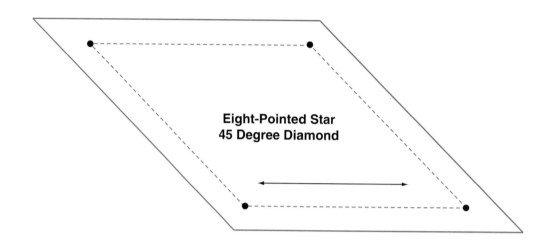

**Eight-Pointed Star
45 Degree Diamond**

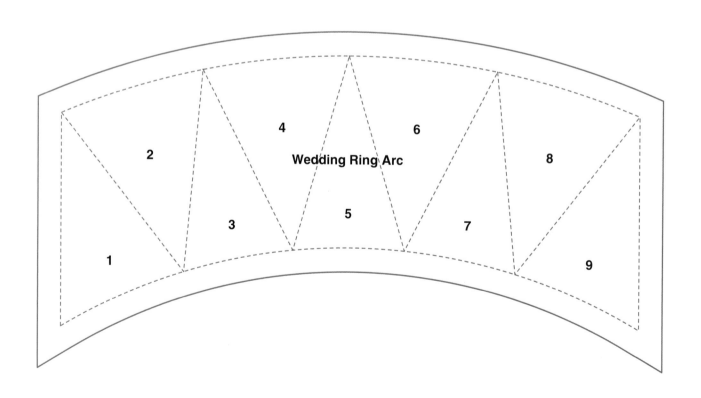

Wedding Ring Arc

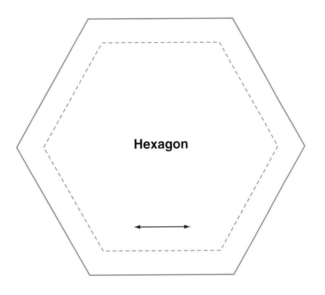

Hexagon

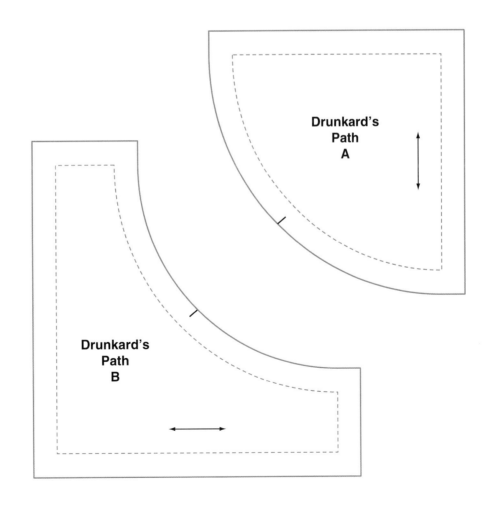

Drunkard's Path A

Drunkard's Path B

One-half of Basket

quicker and easier APPLIQUÉ

Quicker and Easier Appliqué

Appliqué, the art of applying shapes cut from one fabric onto a background fabric, has long been an artful way for quiltmakers to express themselves. Realistic shapes, layers of color, swirling vines, and embroidery embellishments all contribute to the art of quiltmaking in a way that patchwork alone cannot. From the refinement of a Baltimore-style album quilt to the whimsical fun of a modern folk art quilt, the designs created with appliqué are limitless. In this chapter, you'll learn today's quickest and easiest ways of incorporating the look of appliqué into your next project, whether you prefer hand or machine stitching.

GETTING READY TO APPLIQUÉ

START WITH THE BEST SUPPLIES

Whether you prefer traditional hand appliqué methods or want to try your hand at a quicker machine technique, you'll save time and enjoy better results if you have the right tools and supplies. In addition to normal sewing supplies, there are a variety of other products that can help make appliqué work fun and beautiful.

• **Scissors:** Sharp scissors are important for cutting both fabric and templates. In addition to your normal shears, a small pair of scissors that cuts all the way to its points is useful for appliqué. Some people like to use curved scissors for cutting curved areas.

• **Template materials:** Plastic, cardboard, freezer paper, and fusible web can all be used as template material, depending on the appliqué method you will be using. The different techniques described in this chapter specify the best template material for each individual method.

• **Freezer paper:** Found in your local grocery store or quilt shop, this plastic-coated paper is great for hand appliqué templates.

• **Tracing paper:** See-through yet durable, this office-supply-store find is helpful for combining individual pattern pieces into one overall block layout. It can also be used for tracing patterns from books to transfer to template material.

• **Spray starch:** Borrow this item from your laundry room. It's a quick-and-easy helper for keeping edges turned under.

• **Thread:** *For hand appliqué,* choose 100 percent cotton or silk thread to match the color of the piece being appliquéd. The

lighter the thread weight, the easier it is to make invisible stitches.

For machine appliqué, most quilters choose a 60 weight cotton machine embroidery thread for the top needle and a 60 or 80 weight thread for the bobbin. Since most machine embroidery stitches are visible, color depends on the look you are trying to achieve. For some decorative machine stitches, such as the blanket stitch, use a heavier weight cotton thread.

• **Clear nylon thread:** This thread is used for invisible machine appliqué, but it can also be used for hand sewing. Use the hair-fine 0.004 size in clear for light appliqués or smoke for dark appliqués.

• **Needles:** For *hand appliqué,* choose a thin needle, such as a sharps or milliners. For invisible *machine appliqué,* use a fine needle, such as a size 60 or 70. For *satin stitch appliqué,* try a size 70/10 machine needle.

• **Marking pens and pencils:** In addition to regular pens and pencils used for other quilting methods, hot-iron transfer pens are handy for appliqué projects. They are available in many colors. If possible, choose one with a sharp point. Ultra fine-point permanent pens work well for tracing patterns onto fabric for needle-turn appliqué.

• **Straight pins:** Short sequin pins are handy to tack shapes to the background. If you prefer longer pins, use very narrow ones, such as silk pins.

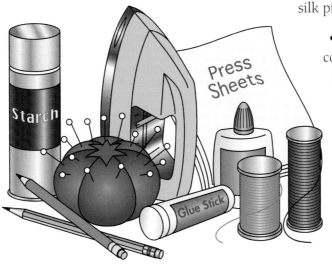

• **Glue stick:** A glue stick comes in handy for unruly edges and for helping pieces adhere without pins or basting. Be sure to purchase the type made especially for use with fabric.

• **Press sheets:** These are translucent sheets used when fusing fabrics to a fusible web. The fusible web doesn't stick to the press sheet as it would to your iron.

- **Fusible web:** Used to fuse pattern pieces to the background for machine appliqué. See page 64 for characteristics of different types of fusible web.

- **Stabilizers:** These nonwoven products are used behind the background fabric during machine appliqué to give added support to the fabric and to help prevent puckering.

- **Fray Check:** This is the brand name for a clear liquid that can be used at any spot where you are afraid the fabric may ravel, such as at a cut made to the fold line at an inside point of an appliqué piece.

- **Presser feet:** For satin stitch and other decorative machine stitches, use a special appliqué foot if possible. If a specialty foot is not available to fit your sewing machine, refer to your owner's manual for the type of foot recommended by your machine's manufacturer.

Many of the recommended supplies are available at quilt shops. If you can't find a particular item, see the "Buyer's Guide" on page 243.

GETTING THE BACKGROUND FABRIC READY

Folded Guidelines

If you are planning a rather simple appliqué block (one with a limited number of pieces that overlap), finger pressing guidelines into the background fabric may be all you need to help you lay out the pieces, especially when identical blocks are not required. Fold the square in half vertically, then horizontally, finger pressing after each fold. Fold and finger press the square on both diagonals, too. The resulting creases shown in the diagram form instant positioning guidelines that "erase" when the block is pressed.

Light Sources

If your background fabric is light enough to see through, use a marker to trace the appliqué pattern onto tracing paper. Then center your background fabric over the paper pattern and trace the lines directly onto it using a pencil. If the pattern lines are difficult to see, a light positioned underneath a glass coffee or dining table provides a quick, temporary light box. If you don't have one of those, try a window on a sunny day.

Traced Guidelines

For complex designs on blocks or larger background pieces, or for designs that must be positioned identically from block to block, you can transfer patterns easily using hot-iron transfer pens. These pens are available in many colors. Using more than one color may help you to differentiate between the guidelines for individual pieces. It is also helpful to record the color of each piece on the master layout and its order in the design.

Step 1. Use a transfer pen to trace the entire pattern onto a sheet of tracing paper that is exactly the same size as the unfinished block. Make sure the lines are thin, especially any that will be embroidered rather than covered with fabric.

Step 2. Align and iron the tracing onto the background, as shown. Before transferring the image, double-check the position of the pattern to make sure it's centered correctly. One tracing can often be used several times. When the transfer fades, reink the lines, being careful to follow the original image.

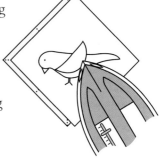

Press transfer onto appliqué background

To be sure lines don't show after pieces are positioned, try tracing on the inner edge of the pattern lines.

MAKING APPLIQUÉ TEMPLATES

Appliqué templates are made much like templates for patchwork, so refer to page 7 for general information about constructing templates.

However, appliqué templates generally do not include a seam allowance. The most important line to trace around is the actual finished outline of each shape. And that line is traced directly onto the right side of the fabric. It is used as the fold-under line unless you are using paper-backed fusible web for template material. The appliqué techniques beginning on page 54 provide specific information about the templates, if necessary, such as how to use freezer paper or fusible web.

There are many different types of appliqué. Often, a combination of techniques is used within the same project, since some methods work better with different shapes than others. Experiment with as many methods as you can—both hand and machine—to help you evaluate which works best in different situations.

Visit the Office-Supply Store

Large sheets of heavy-duty tracing paper are available at office-supply stores. These sheets eliminate the need to tape pages together to draw medallion-style quilts, large appliqué blocks, or sections of appliqué borders.

The large paper is especially useful when you must build the appliqué block layout from individual template pieces, since you can trace around the templates directly onto your paper. This is necessary when the complete layout is not printed to scale in a book or pattern.

Test Thread for Colorfastness, Too

Most often, thread won't bleed. However, you'll occasionally come across a thread that isn't colorfast, so it's best to test before you use any new thread for appliqué. Simply place a sheet of white paper on your ironing board, wet a strand of the thread, and press it dry on top of the white paper. If no color runs onto the paper, the thread is safe to use.

TESTING FOR COLORFASTNESS

As you know, prewashing fabrics is important since you don't want your finished quilt to shrink or your color to run when you wash it.

While checking for colorfastness is an important step for patchwork quilts, colorfastness is especially critical to appliqué projects, since so often vivid colors are surrounded by a white background. Just imagine how it would look if a beautiful red flower was to bleed onto a white background.

Of course, you can prewash fabrics just as you would for patchwork. Here's another way to preshrink fabric and test its colorfastness at the same time. This method is especially useful for smaller fabric pieces often used for appliqué.

Step 1. Using a dime-store variety misting bottle, spray your appliqué fabric until it is completely wet.

Step 2. Place a piece of muslin on your ironing board and lay the appliqué fabric on top. Set your iron on steam and press the fabric until it is completely dry. The heat from the iron will shrink the fabric, and you'll be able to see if the fabric is colorfast by checking for bleeding on the muslin.

Step 3. If the fabric bleeds, don't use it.

PRECISION HAND APPLIQUÉ

MASTERING NEEDLE-TURN APPLIQUÉ

With this classic method, appliqué shapes are cut out and pinned to the background fabric. The edges are then turned under as you sew.

Step 1. Make a finished-size template for each different piece in the design. Position a template right side up on the fabric, and lightly draw around it using a fine point pencil or fine-tip permanent pen. (The edge will get turned under, so the mark will not show in the end.) Cut out the shape, leaving approximately $^3/_{16}$ to $^1/_4$ inch for a seam allowance around all sides of the traced fold line, as shown. Refer to the diagram. Repeat for the remaining pieces.

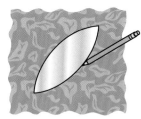

Trace around finished-size template

Cut out shape, leaving $^1/_4$" seam allowance

Step 2. Pin or baste the pieces to the background fabric, always working in order from the background to the foreground. See page 52 for information on preparing the background fabric.

Step 3. Again, working from the background forward, choose a piece to appliqué. Thread your appliqué needle with matching thread, and bring it up from under the appliqué piece, exactly on the drawn line, as shown. Fold under the seam allowance on the line to neatly encase the knot.

Step 4. With the point of your needle, turn under about $^1/_4$ inch along the

fold of the appliqué piece, as shown in **A**. Finger press the fold and hold it in place with your thumb while you stitch. Insert the tip of the needle into the background fabric right next to where the thread comes out of the appliqué piece. Bring the needle back up through the background fabric approximately $^1/_{16}$ inch away from where it went in, and pierce the very edge of the fold, catching just a few threads of the piece. Reinsert the needle into the background and repeat, as shown in **B**.

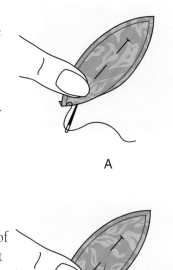

A

B

Step 5. Continue sewing in the same manner, using the tip of your needle to fold under only a small portion of fabric at a time. Make sure you tug on the thread slightly at the end of each stitch. Stitches that are too loose are more likely to be visible in the finished piece. But don't pull too tight, or you'll pucker your background fabric.

Step 6. When you've appliquéd the entire piece to the background, end your stitching by bringing the needle to the back of the fabric. Take one small stitch in the background fabric only, leaving a loop on the surface of the fabric, as shown in **A**. Run the thread through the loop and pull it tightly into a knot on the fabric

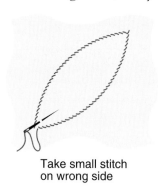

Take small stitch on wrong side

A

Pull needle through thread loop

B

surface, as shown in **B**. Slide the needle through the background fabric, being careful not to poke through the appliqué piece. Tug the thread to pop the knot between the layers, referring to **C**, then cut the thread.

Tug knot between background and appliqué layers

C

STITCHING SMOOTH CURVES

For easier turning and a neater finished edge on a concave, or inside, curve, make clips perpendicular to the fold line before sewing. Make tiny clips, as shown at the top of the next column, using the tips of sharp scissors. Be careful not to

clip all the way to the fold. There is no need to make clips into convex, or outside, curves.

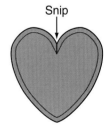

Clip to fold line on concave curves

No need to clip convex curves

Fold line

Step 1. Begin sewing the piece along one side. When you near the area of an inner point, such as the two joints where the tulip petals meet or the deep inner point on the heart, make a perpendicular cut, as shown. Be sure to stop at the beginning of the turn line.

Snip   Snip   Snip

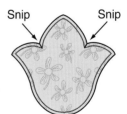

To prevent fraying, it's best not to clip the inner points, or even the curved areas for that matter, until you are ready to turn that section under.

Step 2. Fold under the seam allowance as you work. Take a few extra stitches at the clip to help reinforce the fabric. You can apply a drop of Fray Check to the cut so the fabric doesn't unravel.

Toothpick-Turn Appliqué

Needle-turn appliqué can also be referred to as toothpick-turn appliqué if you try this tip. Instead of using the slippery needle to make your appliqué edges turn under, use the rougher edge of a wooden toothpick. The wood grasps the fabric, making it turn under neatly on the first try. And the toothpick is particularly helpful for managing inner points, such as on a tulip. If you still have a bit of trouble with a loose thread or two where you snipped the inner point, try a dab of glue stick on your toothpick. It works wonders on stray threads.

PERFECTING POINTS AND ANGLES

Perfect points are the sure sign of an expert appliqué artist. Your appliqué points and angles can be perfect every time when you follow these steps.

Step 1. When you get to a point, trim the tip slightly, as shown, to reduce the bulk. It's very hard to fit the seam allowance from both sides, plus the tip, under a narrow appliqué point.

Trim

Step 2. Fold under the seam allowance as usual, and stitch the shape to the background right up to the point. Refer to **A.** Use your needle or a toothpick to fold the extended seam allowance under on the other side of the point, as shown in **B.** If the seam allowance is too bulky, pull it out and

A

trim a bit more. You can trim it as close as $\frac{1}{16}$ inch from the fold line. Continue stitching along the other side of the point.

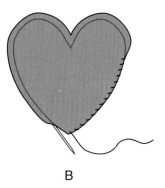

B

To fit the seam allowance under a narrow point, simply use your needle to fold the top or squared-off end of the tip under first, followed by the side seam allowance. Work a little at a time for a perfect fit.

PERFECT CHERRIES, GRAPES, AND OTHER CIRCLES

Grapes, cherries, berries, and other round or oval motifs are favorites of appliquers. Here's a way to make sure all fruits, nuts, and flower buds have nicely curved edges with no puckers.

Step 1. Cut the finished-size circle or oval pattern from template material. Cut a fabric circle or oval that is $\frac{3}{8}$ inch larger than the template.

Index cards make great circle templates. They're sturdier than freezer paper, yet they bend easily enough to remove them from your finished appliqué.

Step 2. Hand baste around the outer edge of the circle, just slightly inside the seam allowance, as shown.

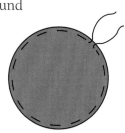

Hand baste in seam allowance

Template

Gather and press

Step 3. Center the template on the wrong side of the fabric circle, then gather the basting stitches. Pull the seam allowance around the template, as shown. Smooth and press the fabric, then remove the template. If any tucks remain, smooth them with your needle as you appliqué the piece to the background.

A Break with Tradition

Traditionally, the grain of appliqué pieces runs in the same direction as the grain of the background fabric. However, you may find it easier to fold under the seams of some shapes, particularly those with deep inside curves, if they are cut on the bias. Another reason for breaking with tradition is that you may want to target a specific design in the fabric to use for a particular shape. If this means you need to cut on the bias, go ahead and do so.

FOOLPROOF FREEZER PAPER APPLIQUÉ

Quiltmakers who have taken freezer paper out of the kitchen and into the sewing room know it can make many appliqué projects much easier. Templates are cut from the paper, then pressed onto the fabric, making a firm edge for turning under the raw edge of the fabric. Some people who hand appliqué prefer the freezer paper pressed onto the top of the fabric; others like it on the wrong side. You'll find both techniques described below. If you've never used freezer paper, you can find the plain white variety at the grocery store (be careful not to purchase wax paper). Gridded freezer paper is available at quilt shops.

Freezer Paper on the Bottom

This method actually starts with the freezer paper pressed on the right side of your fabric for cutting out the appliqué shapes, but the paper is then peeled off and pressed on the wrong side of the fabric for stitching.

Step 1. Use a template to draw your patterns onto the dull (nonplastic) side of the freezer paper.

Step 2. Cut out the shapes exactly on the line. Do not add a seam allowance.

Step 3. Use a medium to hot, dry iron to press the shiny (plastic) side of the shapes onto the right side of your fabric, as shown. The iron will soften the paper's coating, adhering it to your fabric.

Step 4. Cut out the shapes from fabric, leaving a $1/4$- to $3/8$-inch seam allowance around all edges of each template, as shown.

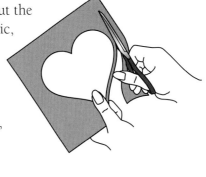

Step 5. Peel away the freezer paper, and center it with the shiny plastic side up on the reverse of your fabric piece. Use the iron again, but this time press your seam allowance over the template, as shown. The plastic coating will again soften and hold your seam in place, just as a basting stitch would, in a short amount of time.

Even though the freezer paper holds the seam allowance in place, it is still a good idea to clip the curves and points for a smooth look.

Step 6. Appliqué the pieces to the block, then make a small slit in the background fabric and use a pair of tweezers to gently pull out the freezer paper. Be careful to cut only the background fabric!

Freezer Paper on the Top

Follow Steps 1 through 4 in "Freezer Paper on the Bottom" on page 57. Then, instead of peeling off the paper and pressing it to the wrong side, leave it stuck to the right side of your fabric. Pin the appliqué piece to the background and turn under the seam allowance as you stitch the appliqué to the background.

This method works similarly to needle-turn appliqué, but it allows you to use the edge of the freezer paper as your guide for the fold of the fabric. After the appliqué is stitched in place, gently peel off the freezer paper.

SEW-AND-TURN APPLIQUÉ

Lightweight, nonwoven, *nonfusible* interfacing can be used to achieve perfect edges on appliqué shapes. You can also use clothes dryer fabric softener sheets that have been run through a dryer cycle in place of the interfacing. It's a clever way to recycle, but be sure to use only the stiff white sheets, not the colored foam types.

Step 1. Trace around the template onto the interfacing or used dryer sheet. Cut out the shape, leaving roughly a ¼-inch seam allowance around all edges.

Step 2. Place the wrong side of the cutout shape against the *right* side of the appliqué fabric, then machine sew the two together directly on the traced line, as shown.

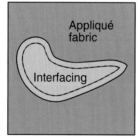

Appliqué fabric

Interfacing

Step 3. Sew completely around the piece, using a slightly shorter than normal straight stitch. Trim the seam allowances slightly and clip into the curves where necessary. Trim excess fabric away from points, too, as indicated in the diagram.

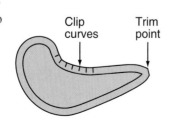

Clip curves

Trim point

Step 4. Make a small slit in the center of the interfacing or dryer sheet. Do not cut too close to the stitching. Insert tweezers into the opening, grab the fabric, and pull it through the opening, turning the piece right side out. Run a blunt-edge tool, such as one used for stuffing dolls, very gently along the seam inside the shape to eliminate puckers. Press the piece, and it's ready for appliqué.

It may be tempting, but don't use the points of your scissors for smoothing out the edges of a sew-and-turn appliqué, or you may end up with a hole in your fabric.

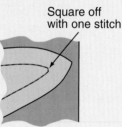

Square Off Inner Points

When using the sew-and-turn appliqué method, take an extra stitch across any inner points to square them off, as shown. While the stitching doesn't quite look like a point, you'll be surprised how nice and neat your inner points look when you turn the appliqué piece right side out and press.

Square off with one stitch

MAKING BIAS HANDLES AND VINES

Many appliqué quilts have curvy vines and flower stems. Even patchwork quilts sometimes require curved appliqué strips, such as pieced baskets that have appliquéd handles. Bias strips work best for these situations, since fabric cut on the bias is easy to curve and shape. Follow these steps for making bias for your next project.

Step 1. Use a rotary-cutting ruler to mark a 45 degree line on the fabric, as shown at the top of the opposite page.

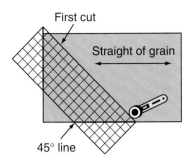

First cut

Straight of grain

45° line

Step 2. Cut bias strips parallel to the marked line, as shown. Each strip will be folded in thirds before it's appliquéd, so multiply your desired finished handle or vine width by 3, add approximately ¼ inch to that figure, and cut your strips that wide. For example, if you want a vine that is ¾ inch wide, cut your bias strips 2½ inches wide.

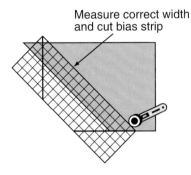

Measure correct width and cut bias strip

Step 3. Fold each strip into thirds, as shown. Make sure the raw edges will be concealed by the folded edges when stitched to the background. Press carefully.

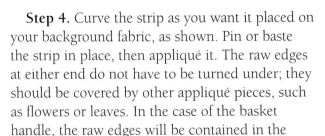

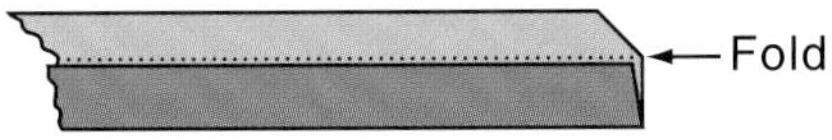

← Fold

Step 4. Curve the strip as you want it placed on your background fabric, as shown. Pin or baste the strip in place, then appliqué it. The raw edges at either end do not have to be turned under; they should be covered by other appliqué pieces, such as flowers or leaves. In the case of the basket handle, the raw edges will be contained in the seam where the handle portion of the block is sewn to the basket bottom.

Vine

Basket handle

To appliqué smooth curves, sew the inner, or concave, curves first, followed by the outer, or convex, curves.

USING BIAS BARS

Using a bias bar is particularly helpful when you need long, narrow stems or vines. Bias bars are sold in sets of varying widths and are made to withstand an iron's heat.

Step 1. Cut a bias strip, as shown in Step 1 of "Making Bias Handles and Vines." The chart lists cut widths for three sizes of bias strips. (These widths apply only to strips cut for bias bars, not for strips that you fold into thirds, as described previously.)

Finished Width	Cut Width
⅛ inch	⅞ inch
¼ inch	1⅛ inches
⅜ inch	1⅜ inches

Step 2. Fold the strip in half lengthwise, with *wrong* sides together. Press lightly to hold the edges of the fabric together as you stitch. To avoid stretching, do not move the iron back and forth—press with an up-and-down motion. Sew the raw edges together using a standard ¼-inch seam allowance. Trim the seam to approximately ⅛ inch. Refer to **A**.

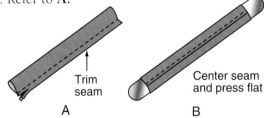

Trim seam

A

Center seam and press flat

B

Step 3. Insert the appropriate-size bias bar into the tube. Turn the tube slightly to center the seam along the flat edge of the bar. See **B**. Dampen the fabric with water or spray starch, and press the seam allowance to one side.

Step 4. Flip the tube over, and check to make sure the seam will be hidden when the bias tube is appliquéd to the quilt. Press the top of the tube and remove the bias bar. You're ready to appliqué.

APPLIQUÉ MAGIC WITH YOUR MACHINE

DECORATIVE AND INVISIBLE STITCH APPLIQUÉ

For years, seamstresses have been appliquéing one fabric to another with their sewing machines. Straight stitch appliqué was used very early on, although most antique appliqué quilts exhibit hand stitches rather than machine stitches.

Many of today's quilt designers include appliqué projects in their pattern lines because the designs can range from elegant to whimsical. And with products like stabilizers, fusible interfacings and fusible webs, decorative threads, invisible threads, and the like, the creative possibilities that machine appliqué offers are just about limitless.

Decorative machine stitches, hand embroidery, embellishments, and more can be added to make your own creations. Invisible machine appliqué, which also starts with fusible fabric, can give the impression of fine hand appliqué. Four appliqué methods are explained step by step in the pages that follow. Each one is illustrated with the same appliqué block, so you can see how the different stitch types will vary the appearance.

If you've ever admired a beautiful, classic appliqué quilt but felt you didn't have the time to recreate it yourself, take a look at the variety of fast, fun, and fabulous ways you can make appliqué part of your quiltmaking repertoire.

SIMPLE STRAIGHT STITCH APPLIQUÉ

This quick-and-easy technique was used early on to appliqué shapes when the only stitch on home-sewing machines was the straight stitch. The shapes, from curved handles appliquéd to patchwork baskets to entire flower blocks, are simply pinned to the background, then stitched very close to the edge with matching thread, as shown in the diagram at the top of the next column.

Take it slow around the curves so that your stitching line is evenly spaced from the edge of the appliqué shape.

Straight stitch

Step 1. Prepare your appliqué shape as described in "Sew-and-Turn Appliqué" on page 58. Or, if you prefer, you can simply turn under the seam allowances and hand baste or press them in place.

Step 2. If your machine has an edge stitch foot, such as that shown here, attach it so you can maintain a consistent stitching distance from the edge of the appliqué shape. Otherwise, use a regular open-toe presser foot.

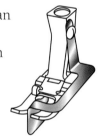

Edge stitch foot

Step 3. Stitch about ¹⁄₁₆ to ⅛ inch from the edge of your appliqué shapes, working with the pieces in the background first, using the 12-stitches-per-inch setting on your machine. (For a European-made machine, set your stitch length at 2.5.)

Start and stop your stitching where the appliqué shape will be covered by another shape, if possible, to hide your starting and stopping points. Pull your threads to the back of the work and tie them off.

For a professional look, match your thread color to the fabric as closely as possible; darker threads tend to blend better than lighter ones.

SATIN STITCH APPLIQUÉ

The same flower motif can be appliquéd with a satin stitch, as shown.

Satin stitch

Satin stitches are simply closely spaced zigzag stitches, as shown. Unlike invisible appliqué, where the goal is to attach a piece with stitches that cannot be seen, satin stitch is very visible on the finished project. The stitches can blend with the patches or contrast with them, depending on your desired look.

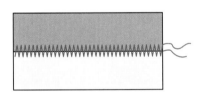

Here are a few guidelines to keep in mind as you design and sew your project:

Use stabilizer: A stabilizer under the background fabric, such as Tear-Away fabric stabilizer, grocery-store variety freezer paper, and lightweight, nonwoven, nonfusible interfacings, are great for satin stitching. They help you avoid puckers, hold your work smooth and firm while you stitch, and can be removed easily when you're finished stitching.

Use heavier-weight background: The weight of your background fabric should be a bit heavier, or at least the same, as the pieces that will be appliquéd to it. Stitches around heavy pieces placed on a lightweight fabric tend to pucker.

Adjust zigzag width: The lighter the weight of your fabrics, the narrower your zigzag stitches

should be, since lightweight fabrics tend to pucker when a wide satin stitch is used, and a bulky line of thread looks cumbersome on delicate fabrics.

Adjust stitch length: The length of the zigzag stitch should be set so that the stitches are close enough together that no background fabric shows through, but not so close that the stitches overlap one another.

Tighten bobbin tension: To avoid tension in you, the quiltmaker, the tension in the bobbin should be tighter than the tension in the top thread. For most normal sewing, the bobbin and top thread tensions are balanced, which means the threads come together midway through the depth of the fabrics being sewn. When the bobbin tension is tighter, the top thread is pulled toward the bottom of the layers.

The smoothest line of satin stitching is produced when only the top thread is visible. So an increased bobbin tension allows the top thread to be pulled toward the underside and keeps the bobbin thread at a lower level, preventing it from popping through the front side of your work.

Relieving Tension

The easiest way to change the balance of tension on your machine is by lowering, or decreasing, the tension in the top thread. Refer to your sewing machine's manual for instructions on that procedure. Before beginning your project, experiment with your machine's settings, and practice the satin stitch using the instructions that follow. Remember that settings will change from project to project, depending on many factors, including the thickness and weight of your fabrics, the type of bonding and stabilizing materials used, and the threads used.

Wind lightweight thread on bobbin: The thread in the bobbin should be a lighter weight than the top thread. A finer bobbin thread helps reduce bulkiness. Try an 80 weight 100 percent cotton machine embroidery thread in the bobbin and a 60 weight 100 percent cotton machine embroidery thread through the needle.

Try Satin Stitch Appliqué

If you have an appliqué foot, attach it to your machine. Otherwise, refer to your owner's manual to see which standard foot is recommended for satin stitching—most often, it's your regular zigzag foot. Use a size 70 needle and, if possible, a slightly lighter weight thread in the bobbin than in the needle.

Most owner's manuals also include instructions for satin stitching, so you may want to refer to it for tips specific to your sewing machine.

Step 1. Cut a sample 10-inch square of background fabric, and make a sample appliqué shape (patterns are on page 69) using the techniques on page 54. Then pin, baste, or fuse the shape to the front of the square, as shown. (For more information on fusing fabrics, see "What Is Fusible Web?" on page 64.)

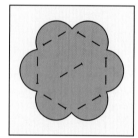

Pin, baste, or fuse
appliqué to background

Step 2. Cut a 10-inch square of freezer paper. Place your sample block facedown on the ironing board, and press the shiny side of the freezer paper to the back of the fabric square, as shown. The freezer paper acts as a stabilizer and will not become part of the finished piece. Stabilizers give the fabric extra support and help elimi-

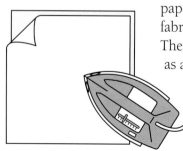

Press freezer paper to
wrong side of block

nate puckering. If you prefer, you can replace the freezer paper with a piece of tear-away paper or nonfusible interfacing. Make sure the stabilizer is larger than the area of your appliqué shape. Pin the stabilizer in place.

If you are pinning the appliqué shape to the background, press the freezer paper on the background fabric first, then pin the shape through both the fabric and the paper.

Step 3. Set your machine for a zigzag stitch that is approximately ⅛ inch wide. Begin to sew, and adjust the stitch length until the stitches are very close together, but not overlapping. The fabric should feed freely through the machine with no coaxing from you. If stitches are too close, the machine will jam, and the fabric won't move. Adjust your machine's settings until you achieve a solid, smooth line of stitching. Remove the square from the machine.

Before sewing around the appliqué shape, practice the satin stitch in an open area of the square.

Step 4. Examine your stitches. If the bobbin thread is visible along the outer edges of the line of stitching, decrease the upper thread tension slightly and try again. Continue to adjust the upper tension until you have achieved a smooth satin stitch where only the upper thread is visible. The diagram shows examples of common satin stitch problems and their causes.

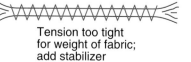

Correct satin stitching

Top tension too tight;
bobbin thread shows

Tension too tight
for weight of fabric;
add stabilizer

Step 5. Once your thread tension is set, you're ready to appliqué your shape. Leave about 3 inches of thread free at the beginning. Turn the flywheel until your needle moves to the right. Position your fabric beneath the needle, and turn the flywheel again so that the needle enters the fabric just slightly to the right of the appliqué shape, as shown. Lower the presser foot, and sew along the edge of the appliqué, making sure the stitching covers all raw edges. Stop sewing when you reach a corner, leaving your needle in the down position, as shown. Make sure the needle is to the right of your appliqué or on the outside edge of your appliqué when you stop.

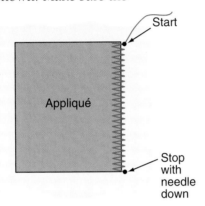

If your machine has an automatic needle-down option, use this function for satin stitch and other decorative stitch appliqué. If not, simply turn the flywheel manually to keep it in the fabric when you stop.

Step 6. Raise the presser foot and pivot. Continue satin stitching to the next corner or point where you will need to turn. Stop again with the needle down, as shown. Repeat the same procedures on each side until you have stitched around the entire piece.

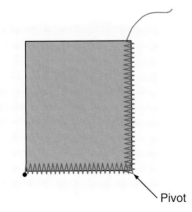

Step 7. Remove the appliqué work from your machine, leaving another tail of thread. Pull it to the back of your work, tie off all threads, and clip tails.

Stitch over Tails

Another way to start your satin stitching is to pull up the bobbin thread to the top layer and stitch over the tails of thread. After you have taken a few stitches, trim the tails, so you will only have to sew over about 1/2 inch or so rather than 3 inches. Your threads will be secure, and you won't have to tie off as many tails.

Perfect Satin Stitch for Any Shape

Other appliqué shapes are satin stitched in much the same way. Here are some helpful pointers for common design elements.

Curves: It is usually necessary to stop and pivot the needle slightly on a regular basis to achieve a smooth stitch around the object. It's time to stop and pivot if the outer edge of the needle begins to enter the background fabric too far away from the edge of your fabric shape. Try to keep the stitching line consistent. For very deep curves, this may mean pivoting as often as every other stitch.

For *outer* curves, pivoting is done when the needle is to the outside of the appliqué shape (in the background fabric), as shown.

For *inside* curves, you will need to pivot when the needle is in the appliqué shape, as shown. Remember to make frequent pivots for deep curves, such as at the inner corner of the bow shown below, rather than a few wider pivots.

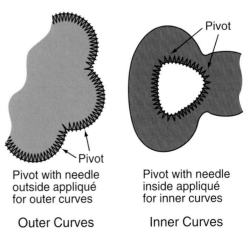

Pivot with needle outside appliqué for outer curves

Outer Curves

Pivot with needle inside appliqué for inner curves

Inner Curves

Inside corners: Stitch past the end of the shape a distance equal to the width of the satin stitch. Pivot the fabric and resume stitching, as shown.

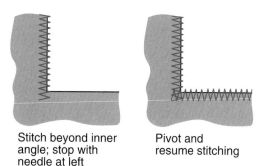

Stitch beyond inner angle; stop with needle at left

Pivot and resume stitching

Outside points: Stop sewing at the tip of the point, ending with the needle in the background fabric. Pivot the fabric and resume sewing on the adjacent side, as shown.

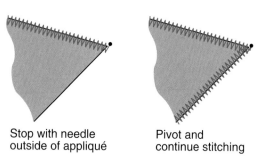

Stop with needle outside of appliqué

Pivot and continue stitching

If the outer point is very narrow, try this. After you pivot, start sewing with a narrower zigzag stitch for a few stitches, and your stitches won't extend way beyond the narrow point.

Practice Makes Perfect

As the adage says, practice does make perfect. Prepare a variety of circles, squares, flowers, hearts, or any other shape you may want to appliqué from your scrap fabrics. Fuse them to a background and use them to practice stitching, whether satin stitch, a decorative stitch, or invisible stitch.

WHAT IS FUSIBLE WEB?

One of the biggest revelations in appliqué has been the advent of fusible web. This amazing, lightweight webbing lets you apply layers of shapes and colors onto a background almost instantly, with just the help of a household iron. Quiltmakers and seamstresses alike are taking advantage of this wonder material to make all sorts of appliqué projects, from re-creating vintage-Victorian looks to creating rustic folk art and whimsical kids motifs. (For more on fusible web, see page 67.)

Fusible web is a nonwoven material that contains a fabric glue that is heat activated. Similar to fusible interfacing, which is sticky on only one side, fusible web will adhere to fabric on both sides. This means you can adhere it to a red heart on one side that can then be fused to a white background fabric.

Fusible web comes either with or without a paper backing. Paper-backed fusible web is the most versatile option for quick-and-easy appliqué, since you can trace templates or draw shapes freehand right onto the paper. It is also available in lightweight (which you can stitch through after fusing) or heavy duty (which will gum up your sewing machine needle if you sew through it).

Fusible web can be used as the starting point for many of the machine appliqué methods described in this section, while invisible machine appliqué requires fusible interfacing. When shopping for these materials (which are available in most quilt shops and fabric centers), be sure to let the sales clerk know exactly what you want so you are sure to bring home the right type of fusible. If you're not certain about the type of web or interfacing you need, explain your project, and the sales staff can point you in the right direction.

FUSING APPLIQUÉS TO THE BACKGROUND

Appliqué pieces that will ultimately be attached to the background by satin stitch or other decorative stitches can be fused to the background first. There are many advantages: no fraying edges, no need to turn under the edges, no slipping appliqués, and the stability provided by the fusible web.

Of course, along with the advantages come one or two disadvantages. By knowing about them before you begin, however, you can make sure you get the results you're looking for. With fusible web, the main thing to consider is the stiffness it adds to the project. Fusible web is usually fine for wallhangings, place mats, craft projects, and the like, but it is not always suitable for a bed quilt that you want to snuggle under.

Keep Your Iron Clean

Since fusible web is a heat-activated product, you need your iron. Using a press cloth is the best way to avoid getting glue stuck onto your iron. However, you may, on occasion, find yourself faced with a gummy iron.

To remove fused web from your iron, try rubbing the sole plate lightly with fine-grade steel wool. You can do this while your iron is still warm. Wipe the sole plate with a clean, dry paper towel, and you're back in business.

Note: Don't use steel wool if your iron has a Teflon sole plate.

Or try a commercial product available in sewing centers called Clean & Glide. This goop comes in a tube and instantly takes off unwanted residue from your iron.

Try Fusing

This technique uses paper-backed lightweight fusible web, such as Wonder-Under or Heat n Bond, which can be purchased either in packages or by the yard. The appliqué shapes are bonded to fusible web, cut out, and then fused to the background before any decorative stitching is added.

If using fusible web is new to you, make some practice appliqué shapes from the patterns on page 69 before you begin to fuse shapes to your actual project.

Don't Press Too Long

If you're tempted to press your fusible appliqués for just a bit longer than the directions state, thinking they will stay on that much better, remember that more is not always better with fusible web. It really is best to follow the manufacturer's directions regarding pressing time, or you'll run the risk of having appliqués that lift off. Too much heat breaks down the bonding and will result in peeling edges—the very thing you're trying to prevent.

Step 1. Position a template *right side down* on the paper side of the fusible web, and trace around its outer edges. The paper side of the web is going to become the back of your appliqué shape, so if you trace right side up, your final appliqué shape will be backwards. Repeat for all shapes required for your design. Add a small seam allowance to shapes that will be overlapped by other pieces.

Step 2. Cut out the shapes just outside of the drawn lines, as shown. Position the pieces, fusible side down, on the *back* of the appropriate appliqué fabrics and press for several seconds. (Do not iron back and forth.) Refer to the package instructions for recommended pressing time and heat setting for your fabric type.

Step 3. Cut out the fabric pieces exactly on the traced lines, as shown.

Cut out shape
on drawn line

Step 4. To determine correct appliqué placement, refer to "Getting the Background Fabric Ready" on page 52. Either draw an outline of the design onto your background fabric, or simply use the folded guidelines technique. If you draw a pattern outline, make sure all drawn lines will be covered by the fabric pieces when they are fused.

Step 5. Position the fabric pieces on the background, beginning with those in the back and working forward. The edges of front pieces should overlap the extra fabric left on back pieces, as indicated by the dotted lines in the diagram. When you are satisfied with the layout, cover the design with a press cloth and fuse. The project is now ready to embellish with stitches, if desired.

BLANKET AND BUTTONHOLE STITCH APPLIQUÉ

The blanket stitch and buttonhole stitch are made using the same technique, but buttonhole stitches are simply stitched closer together than blanket stitches. Both stitches can be used to embellish fusible appliqué, either by hand or by many newer sewing machines. However, the blanket stitch is the more commonly used method, especially if a folk art look is what you're after. The flower block shown illustrates a machine blanket stitch.

Blanket stitch

These two stitch names are often used interchangeably, yet they are two visibly different stitches, as you can see in the diagram. When deciding upon a stitch to cover the raw edges of your fabric, keep in mind that blanket stitches will not completely encase the edges, so the pieces can ravel if washed, unless they are firmly fused to the background. However, many decorative machine stitches, including buttonhole and blanket stitches, hold raw edges more securely than their hand-stitched counterparts.

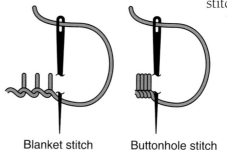

Blanket stitch   Buttonhole stitch

Fuse Everything at Once

If your pieces overlap, you can fuse all elements of a design together, then fuse them to the background as one unit. To do this, place an appliqué pressing sheet over the background before positioning pieces. Be sure to purchase a pressing sheet made specifically for fusible appliqué, since only this type of sheet is nonstick and won't remove the bonding.

Since these sheets are transparent, you can easily place your appliqués accurately over the drawn or folded guidelines. When all pieces are in place, lay another press sheet over the design and fuse. The entire unit can be lifted away and positioned on the background. Although this technique can be used any time, it is particularly helpful when working on a large background with appliqués in many areas. If a placement error is made in one section, it only affects that section. It's much easier to redo one section rather than your entire project.

INVISIBLE MACHINE APPLIQUÉ

With practice, this type of machine appliqué can look very much like fine hand appliqué. Although the invisible stitch example illustrated below doesn't really look invisible, when you do this stitch using clear thread the stitches will be nearly impossible to see.

Invisible stitch

A blind hem stitch, as shown below, and clear nylon thread are used around each shape, with the jump stitches catching the fold of the appliqué piece at short intervals. For best results, use a sewing machine that allows you to control both the stitch length and width.

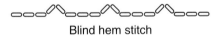

Blind hem stitch

Fusible Interfacing vs. Fusible Web

Invisible machine appliqué can be used on appliqués that are fused to a background; however, the look of the appliqué will be flatter than that of hand appliqué, where the turned-under seam allowances will give some loft to the design.

If you want to duplicate the look of hand appliqué, it's best to use fusible interfacing (sticky only on one side) and the sew-and-turn technique described on page 58. This method still lets you fuse your appliqué shapes to the background, but it also involves turned-under seam allowances, so it will be hard to tell that your appliqués weren't finished by hand.

Try Invisible Machine Appliqué

Step 1. Sample appliqué patterns are on page 69. Prepare your appliqué templates, fabric pieces, and background using the sew-and-turn method on page 58, with one exception. You can use lightweight, nonwoven *fusible* interfacing so you won't have to baste or pin your appliqués in place. Sew your appliqué fabric to the interfacing with the right side of the fabric facing the glued side of the interfacing. Stitch around the shape completely. Make a small slit in the interfacing and pull the fabric through with tweezers.

Step 2. Use a fine needle (size 12/80) in the machine so that the hole made when it enters the fabric is nearly invisible. Use size 0.004 invisible quilting thread in the needle and a lightweight machine embroidery thread in the bobbin.

Invisible thread comes in two colors: clear and smoke. Use clear for light-color fabrics and smoke for stitching darker fabrics.

Step 3. Set your machine for a blind hem stitch, which was shown. Adjust the stitch width so that the jump stitches will catch just a few threads on the fold of the fabric, as shown. Adjust the length so that the distance between the jump stitches is 1/8 to 3/16 inch, or even shorter if you prefer. Make sure the bobbin thread isn't visible on the top of your work. Reduce the tension in the top thread until only the invisible thread remains on the top.

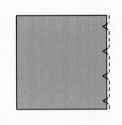

Make adjustments to your machine, and practice stitching on a scrap appliqué until you are happy with the results. Record your stitch settings for future reference.

Step 4. Stitch the appliqué to the background, pivoting at corners and stitching slowly around curves. See "Satin Stitch Appliqué" on page 61 for pointers on handling curves and angles with machine appliqué. To begin your stitching, pull the bobbin thread to the top surface, as shown. Take two or three stitches in the same place to lock your threads.

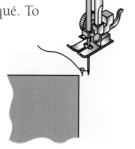

Pull loop of bobbin thread to top surface

Step 5. Stitch around the shape completely, then end the threads in a similar manner. Stitch in place to lock the threads before cutting them.

Weave the thread tails between the layers of your appliqué, as shown, and clip the ends.

Thread tails on needle and weave under appliqué. Pull through and clip tails close to fabric.

BLUE RIBBON TECHNIQUE

FASTER AND EASIER BIAS VINES

Details for making bias strips for hand appliquéd vines, stems, and basket handles are given on page 58. There are a few shortcuts, however, for machine appliqué that will speed up the process but still produce excellent results.

Step 1. Measure, cut, and prepare your bias strips following the directions in Steps 1 and 2 of "Using Bias Bars" on page 59. Trimming the seam allowance is optional if your stem is really wide. You may want to grade the seam allowances to reduce bulkiness if the bias stem is narrow.

Step 2. Pin or baste your bias strip to the background fabric to suit your quilt design. The stitching line on the strip should be exactly aligned with the left edge of where you want your vine or stem to be. Refer to the diagram.

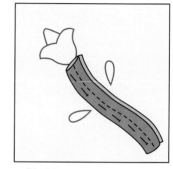

Pin bias over traced lines

Step 3. Stitch the bias strip to the background, sewing directly on your previous stitching line. This will attach one side of the bias strip so that only one, rather than both, sides have to be appliquéd. See the diagram.

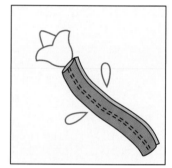

Sew over the previous stitching

Step 4. Fold the bias strip over so that the stitching and raw edges are covered. Trim the seam allowance if necessary. Appliqué the other edge in place, as shown, using either a hand or machine blind stitch.

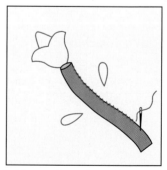

Fold over the strip and appliqué the edge in place

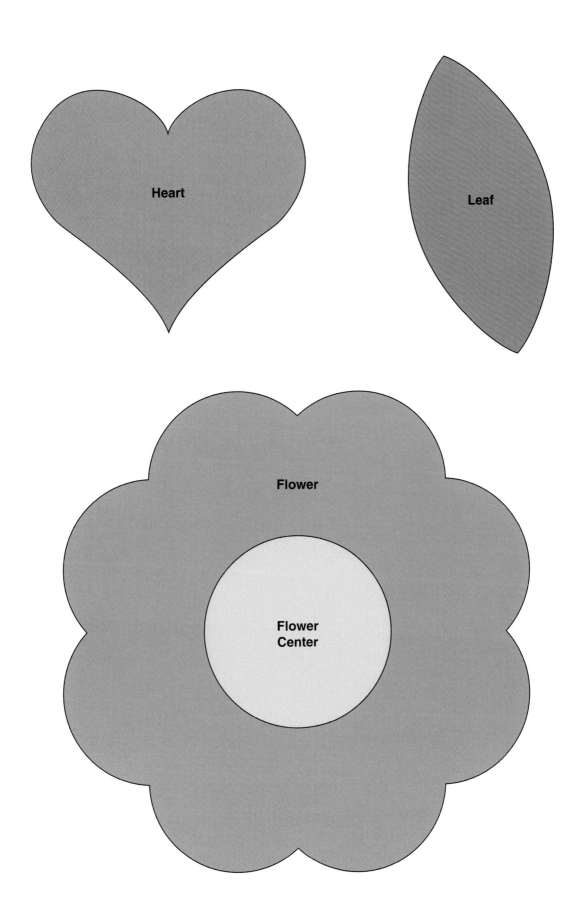

Heart

Leaf

Flower

Flower
Center

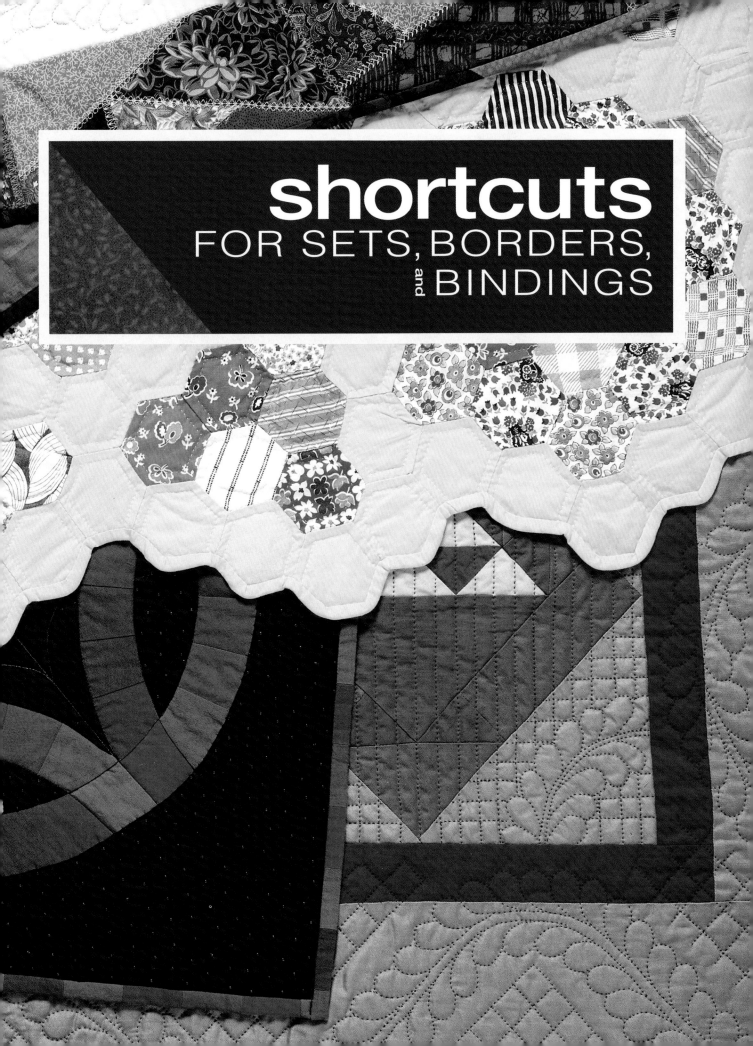

shortcuts
FOR SETS, BORDERS, and BINDINGS

Shortcuts for Sets, Borders, and Bindings

Quite often we hurry through the final stages of making the quilt top, perhaps because we can't wait to have a finished project or maybe because this area of quiltmaking is simply perplexing because it is rarely explained in detail.

Whatever the reasons have been, you'll see in this chapter that there are still many design possibilities for your quilt after your blocks are completed but before they are stitched together. From adding a bold red sashing to accent your blocks, to adding a whimsical pieced border that makes your quilt more playful, to choosing a binding fabric and method that gives your quilt the perfect finishing touch, this chapter will provide you with dozens of ideas—and quick-and-easy techniques—to liven up your quilts.

SETS AND SASHING—
FROM SUBTLE TO SNAZZY

The way in which quilt blocks are arranged together to form the quilt top is called the *set* or *setting*. When strips of fabric are used to separate the blocks in a quilt setting, the strips are called *sashing* or *lattice*.

There are many options regarding the set of your quilt that can dramatically change its final appearance. From straight sets to diagonal ones, from plain sashing to pieced sashing to no sashing, from alternate blocks to all pieced or appliquéd blocks, the combinations seem endless.

To take the pressure off, you should realize that there is no best way for your quilt to be set together. The decision should be based on your personal taste, whether or not you like to do a lot of quilting (such as is usually found in large alternate blocks), how much fabric you have available (you don't want to run out), how big you want your quilt to be, and how bold or subtle a look you want.

Since a variety of sets could possibly work well for your selected type of quilt block, this section of the chapter focuses on the different options available for sets, tips for the easiest ways to handle different sets, and ways to calculate sizes and efficiently cut alternate blocks and setting triangles.

Graph It!

The best way to make your decisions about sets is to draw your options on graph paper (or on your computer!) and color them in to see how you like those royal blue setting squares you were thinking about. Or see how different your quilt blocks look set together as compared to when they are set with 2-inch-wide red sashing.

Once you've decided on a particular setting, you'll be armed with all the information you need to set the blocks together for a spectacular quilt.

SIMPLE STRAIGHT SET

In a straight-set quilt, the sides of the blocks are parallel to the outside edges of the quilt. For a simple straight set, blocks are sewn into horizontal or vertical rows, then rows are sewn together, as shown here with Ohio Star blocks.

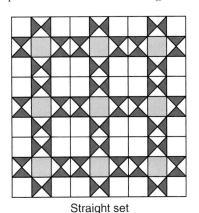

Straight set

STRAIGHT SET WITH SETTING SQUARES

The Ohio Stars look very different when they are alternated with plain setting squares, as shown in this straight-set variation. The setting squares provide lots of blank space where you can show off your hand- or machine-quilting skills or a large-scale print fabric.

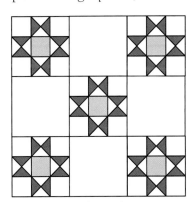

Straight set with setting squares

Adding setting squares is an easy way to enlarge your quilt without increasing the time you spend cutting and piecing additional blocks.

The look changes again when the plain squares are replaced with pieced Snowball blocks, which link the stars together and visually give the design a diagonal look, as shown. The Snowball pattern is just one example of a simple block that is commonly used as a filler to add a new dimension to the quilt top. Other popular pieced blocks used for alternate setting or filler squares include Broken Dishes, Pinwheels, and Puss in the Corner.

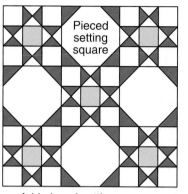

Add pieced setting squares

Option 2

Option 3

STRAIGHT SETS WITH SASHING

Another way to change the look of a straight set is to add sashing between the blocks. Sashing separates the blocks, can make a bold or subtle statement depending on the fabrics and style used, and increases the size of the quilt without having to piece additional blocks. Sashing can be pieced or solid strips, as shown. Option 1 shows plain sashing with contrasting plain sashing squares. Option 2 has strip-pieced sashing to give the quilt a striped look. Option 3 also contains pieced sashing, but in this case, the sashing strips have half-square triangles added to the ends to form a secondary design element in the quilt—a smaller star.

Continuous Sashing

For this type of quilt setting, short strips are sewn to the sides of the quilt blocks to divide them. Then longer strips are added between rows and around the perimeter of the quilt, as shown, without the interruption of sashing squares.

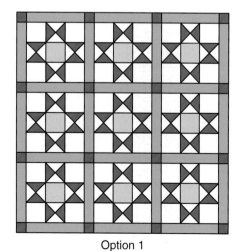

Option 1

Continuous sashing

Step 1. Determine how wide you want your finished sashing to be and add ½ inch to that width. This is the cut width for all sashing strips. For example, if you want 3-inch-wide sashing, you will need to cut your sashing strips 3½ inches wide.

Step 2. After cutting strips for sashing, determine how long to cut the individual shorter strips that go between the blocks. They should be the same length as your unfinished block, or the finished-size block measurement plus ½ inch. So, if your blocks are 12½ inches square and will finish to 12 inches square, cut the strips into 12½-inch lengths.

Step 3. Cut and sew a short sashing strip to the right of each block, except for the last block in each row, as shown in **A.** Sew the block/sashing units together in horizontal rows, as shown in **B.** Press the seams toward the sashing strips.

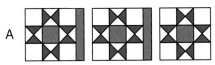

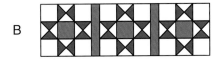

Step 4. For the long horizontal sashing strips, cut the number of strips required for your quilt. You will need one more strip than the number of block rows in your quilt. To determine how long to cut the horizontal strips, refer to your quilt diagram and use the following calculations:

- The *finished* block size × the number of blocks across, *plus*
- The *finished* sashing width × the number of sashes across, *plus*
- ½ inch for a seam allowance on each end of the sashing strip

Step 5. Mark matching points on each long strip to help you align the strips with the horizontal rows of blocks. (Taking the time to match ensures that the blocks in the assembled quilt will all line up vertically.) The first mark should be ¼ inch from the end of the strip for the seam allowance. From the first mark, measure the width of the quilt block and make a second mark, as

shown. Then measure the width of the sashing strip and mark again. Continue measuring and marking, alternating between the width of the blocks and the width of the sashing, as shown.

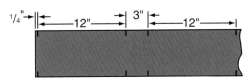

Mark matching points

You can mark matching points with a pencil or by simply making a tiny snip (no deeper than ⅛ inch) at each matching point with the tip of your scissors.

Step 6. Sew a horizontal sashing strip to the top and bottom of the top row and to the bottom of all remaining rows, as shown. Be sure to match and pin marked points accurately. Press the seams toward the sashing, then stitch the rows together.

Cut on the Same Grain

For consistency, it's best to cut all of your sashing strips along the same grain, either crosswise or lengthwise. Cut the longer strips first. When cutting on the crosswise grain, it may be necessary to piece longer sashing strips.

Step 7. Cut two vertical sashing strips for the sides of the quilt, and match marked points on each to help you align the strips with the side of the quilt as you did for the horizontal strips. Use the following method to determine the cut length for the two outer vertical sashes:

- The *finished* block size × the number of vertical blocks, *plus*
- The *finished* sashing width × the number of vertical sashes, *plus*
- ½ inch for a seam allowance on each end of the sashing strip

Step 8. Sew a vertical sashing strip to the quilt sides, as shown. Press seams toward the sashing.

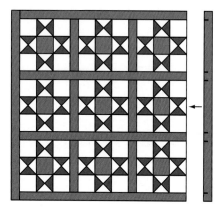

Sashing Squares in a Straight Set

Sashing squares break up the continuous line of the sashing by adding a splash of another color where the horizontal and vertical sashing strips intersect. Sashing squares can be simple squares cut from one fabric or pieced squares, such as Diamond in a Square, Variable Stars, Nine Patch, or other designs. The following directions explain how to calculate and cut sashing when sashing squares will be used.

Step 1. Refer to your quilt layout to determine how many sashing squares are needed. Determine their size by the cut width of your sashing strips. For instance, if you cut 3½-inch-wide sashing strips, you will cut your sashing squares 3½ × 3½ inches. Or, if you want to use pieced sashing squares, make them 3-inch finished-size squares with ¼-inch seam allowances on all sides.

Step 2. Cut the sashing strips to the same length as your *unfinished* blocks.

Use Your Fabric Wisely

Continuous sashing can be sewn to the quilt with the short strips on the top and bottom of blocks and long strips running vertically through the quilt top. Base your placement decisions on the amount of fabric you have and how long your strips need to be.

For example, if you are making a quilt that is longer than it is wide (a typical bed-size quilt) and you have 2 yards of fabric, you may want to cut vertical continuous sashing strips from the length of the fabric. You'll need to cut fewer long strips than if you cut strips for all of the horizontal rows. Plus, the fabric width probably won't be enough for a full horizontal sashing strip, but cutting the horizontal strips from the length of your fabric will give you strips that are too long, and therefore you'll waste fabric.

Step 3. Sew together a horizontal row of blocks and sashing strips, beginning and ending with a sashing strip, as shown below. Press the seams toward the sashing strips. Repeat for all block rows.

Step 4. Sew together a horizontal row of sashing strips and setting squares, beginning and ending with a sashing square, as shown. Press the seams toward the sashing strips. Repeat, making one more sashing row than block row.

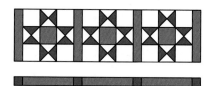

Step 5. Sew a sashing row to the bottom of each block row, matching seam intersections. Press the seams toward the sashing rows.

Step 6. Sew the rows together, again matching seam intersections. To complete the quilt top, sew the remaining sashing row to the top of the first row of blocks.

Sashing width is up to you, but in general, a narrower sashing will produce a more delicate-looking quilt.

DIAGONAL SETS

In a diagonal set, blocks are positioned *on-point,* which means their straight sides are at a 45 degree angle to the outer edges of the quilt. The diagram illustrates a quilt layout for blocks set on point.

On-point layout

The blocks are sewn together in diagonal rows, then the rows are sewn together to complete the top. To fill in the jagged edges along the outside of the

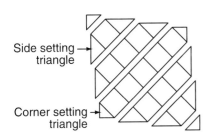

Side setting triangle →

Corner setting → triangle

quilt top, setting triangles are added. Smaller triangles are used to complete the quilt's corners, as shown.

Diagonal sets offer the same range of design possibilities as straight sets. On-point blocks can be used alone, with plain or pieced setting blocks and triangles, or with sashing to separate the blocks. Three traditional diagonal settings are shown here.

Option 2

Option 3

More Diagonal-Set Variations

Diagonal sets offer other design options, such as a medallion-style quilt, which uses large corner triangles to encompass a cluster of blocks, as shown.

Option 1

Medallion set

A Zigzag, or Streak of Lightning, set has blocks offset vertically, using triangles rather than setting squares to create the zigzag effect, as shown.

Zigzag set

QUICK CUTTING FOR DIAGONAL SETS

You can quickly and easily double the size of your diagonally set quilt simply by offsetting the pieced or appliquéd blocks with plain setting squares and triangles, as shown in Option 2 on page 77. Step-by-step directions are provided here, or take a look at "Setting Squares and Triangles" on the opposite page for quick-cutting dimensions.

Setting Squares

Step 1. To determine the size square you'll need to cut, add ½ inch to the finished size of your patchwork block.

Step 2. Cut the setting square fabric into strips the width you calculated; cut strips into squares.

Setting Triangles

For setting triangles, it's best to have the longest edge of the triangle on the straight of grain so your finished quilt top will have a stable outer edge. The easiest way to cut these triangles is to start with a square and rotary cut it into triangles, as follows:

- Finished length of block side × 1.41
- Round up answer to nearest ⅛ inch
- Add 1¼ inches to the calculated figure for the size square to cut

Here's an example. If you have a finished block size of 12 inches, multiply 12 × 1.41. The result is 16.92 inches, which rounds up to 17 inches. Add 1¼ inches to allow for triangle seam allowances; 17 inches + 1¼ inches = 18¼ inches. Cut 18¼-inch squares from your setting square fabric, then cut each square diagonally in each direction, as shown. These triangles will have the straight of grain on their longest edges, so your finished quilt will have a stable outer edge.

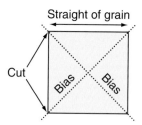

Straight of grain

Cut

Bias   Bias

Corner Triangles

You will need four corner triangles, which can easily be cut from two squares. It's best to cut corner triangles by cutting two squares in half rather than by cutting one larger square in quarters as you did for setting triangles. This way the bias edge of each triangle will be attached to the quilt top, and the straight grain sides will become the outer corner edges. Straight grain corners will give your quilt the stability it needs to stay in shape.

Follow the step-by-step directions for calculating what size squares to start with.

Step 1. Divide the finished diagonal measurement of the block (finished side × 1.41) by 2, then add ⅞ inch. For example, with the 12-inch block, 12 inches × 1.41 = 16.92 inches; 16.92 inches ÷ 2 = 8.46 inches. Round up to 8½ inches. 8½ inches + ⅞ inch = 9⅜ inches.

Step 2. Cut two squares to your calculated size (9⅜ inches in our example). Cut each square in half diagonally, as shown, to yield four triangles—one for each corner.

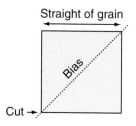

Straight of grain

Bias

Cut →

Setting Squares and Triangles

Finished Block Size	Finished Diagonal	Setting Squares	Setting Triangles*	Corner Triangles†
4"	5¾"	4½"	7"	¾"
5"	7⅛"	5½"	8⅜"	4½"
6"	8½"	6½"	9¾"	5⅛"
7"	9⅞"	7½"	11⅛"	5⅞"
8"	11⅜"	8½"	12⅝"	6⅝"
9"	12¾"	9½"	14"	7¼"
10"	14⅛"	10½"	15⅜"	8"
11"	15½"	11½"	16¾"	8⅝"
12"	17"	12½"	18¼"	9⅜"
13"	18⅜"	13½"	19⅝"	10⅛"
14"	19¾"	14½"	21"	10¾"
15"	21¼"	15½"	22½"	11½"
16"	22⅛"	16½"	23⅞"	12¼"

*Setting triangles are cut from the size square listed; cut the square diagonally into quarters.
†Corner triangles are cut from the size square listed; cut the square diagonally in half.

When Bigger Is Better

For a precise edge around the perimeter of the quilt, cut setting and corner triangles from squares that are slightly larger than your calculated size. Then, after your quilt rows have all been assembled, you can use your rotary-cutting equipment to square up the outer edges of the quilt top to perfection. Be sure to leave a ¼-inch seam allowance around all edges of the quilt when you trim, as shown.

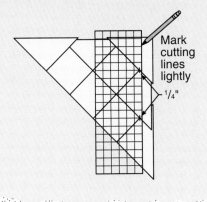

Mark cutting lines lightly

¼"

SASHING FOR DIAGONAL SETS

Sashing for diagonally set quilts is made in much the same way as for straight sets. Short sashing strips are sewn between the blocks in diagonal rows, then longer strips are added to separate the rows.

If sashing squares are used, as shown in the diagram, notice that along the outer perimeter of the quilt you will need to use sashing triangles rather than squares.

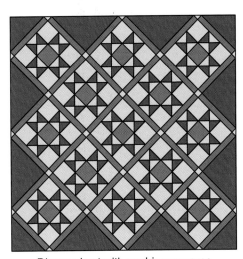

Diagonal set with sashing squares

WORKING WITH ODD-SIZE BLOCKS

Friendship block swaps are as popular now as they've ever been. Often, when you gather all of the blocks made for you by different quilting friends, you'll find that finished sizes vary. The differences are the result of many things, including a slight variation in seam allowances and cutting lines or even a difference in the way blocks were pressed as they were assembled.

If you find yourself faced with a collection of blocks that vary in size by about ½ inch or so, try pressing the too-small blocks first, opening up the seams to their full capacity. If the sizes still vary, the differences can be minimized by using setting squares or sashing between the blocks.

Here's one method to help you sew together a group of odd-size blocks more accurately by first bonding each one to freezer paper. You'll get better results than you would if you simply chopped off the seam allowances from the largest blocks!

Step 1. Cut a piece of freezer paper of the correct unfinished size for each block. Mark the ¼-inch seam allowance around all sides on the dull side of the paper. Draw additional lines to divide the block in half horizontally, vertically, and diagonally, as shown, or draw the actual block layout onto each piece, which may take more time, but often results in more accurate piecing.

Step 2. Place a block right side up on your ironing board, and align the freezer paper with the top side of the block, matching strategic points by stabbing pins through the paper, then through the corresponding portions of the block, as shown. In many cases, seam allowances will be slightly inside outer edges of the paper. If they are very near the marked seam line, there will likely not be enough fabric for a stable seam allowance. Remove the pins and press the block again, working to stretch it a bit toward the insufficient seam allowances. Place the paper on top of the block again and match strategic points.

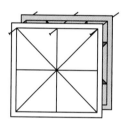

Step 3. When the freezer paper drawing matches the block as closely as possible, press it to the top of the block. Repeat with the remaining blocks and sew the quilt together, using the seam allowances on the freezer paper as guides. Remove the papers from the blocks after all edges have been joined to their neighboring blocks or sashing.

BEAUTIFUL BORDERS— QUICKLY AND EASILY

Borders are yet another way you can dramatically change or enhance the look of your quilt. And as with quilt setting options, the possibilities are numerous. Here are some of your options:

- Appliquéd borders
- Border print fabric
- Corner blocks
- Mitered corners
- Pieced borders (simple or intricate)
- Single, double, or multiple border strips
- Butted corners

TYPES OF BORDERS

No matter how simple or complex a border you plan to add to your quilt top, the corners where the top, side, and bottom borders meet are usually finished in one of three ways: *butted corners,* where the border seams run parallel to either the top or side of the quilt, *mitered corners,* where the borders are joined at a 45 degree angle, or *corner blocks,* where a pieced block is added to the intersection of the side and top and bottom borders. The basic shells for all three basic border types are shown.

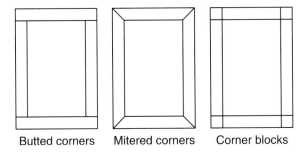

Butted corners   Mitered corners   Corner blocks

These borders can be made up of one or more strips of fabric sewn together lengthwise. They can be pieced, such as a checkerboard border, or appliquéd with beautiful floral motifs. They can even be cut from special *border fabrics* (fabrics that are printed with a repeated striped pattern, designed especially for borders). The same is true for corner squares—they can be as simple or as elaborate as you choose.

How Big a Border?

Not only do you need to decide on a type of border, but you need to determine how wide to make your border. Here's an easy way to help you decide.

Borders look most appealing if their width is proportional to the overall size of the quilt and to the size of the blocks in the quilt, so choose a border width that evenly divides into your block size. For example, if you have 12-inch blocks in the quilt, a border width of 2, 3, 4, or 6 inches would be appropriate. You might want to reserve a 6-inch border for a larger quilt, however, and try a 3- or 4-inch border on a wallhanging. If you plan to use multiple borders, keep those same measurements in mind. Combine a narrow 2-inch border with a wider outer border of 4 or 6 inches.

CUTTING BORDERS

Borders can be cut on either the crosswise or lengthwise grain. For bed-size quilts, crosswise strips must be pieced together end to end to achieve the length required for border strips. Lengthwise strips can be cut in one segment if enough yardage is available. Be sure to cut lengthwise strips first, before using the fabric for other portions of the quilt.

Cut each border a bit longer than the length you've calculated from your quilt design. Sometimes variances in seam allowances can make a quilt with a lot of pieces "grow" to larger than the calculated length or width, and it's easier to trim away excess border than to have to add on to a border that's too short.

MAKING BORDERS WITH BUTTED CORNERS

Step 1. Measure the length of the quilt top, taking the measurement through the vertical center of the quilt rather than along the top or bottom edges, as shown. Cut or piece two border strips this exact length.

Measure vertically through center

If you need to piece border strips, use a diagonal seam, which will be much less noticeable than a horizontal seam.

Step 2. Fold one border strip in half crosswise and crease to mark the center. Unfold it and position it right side down along one side of the quilt, with the crease at the horizontal midpoint of the quilt top. Pin at the midpoint and ends first, then along the length of the entire edge, easing in fullness if necessary. Sew the border to the quilt top using a ¼-inch seam allowance. Press the seam allowance toward the border. Repeat on the other side of the quilt.

If your border is longer than the quilt top and needs to be eased in to fit, it will be easier if you sew the pieces together with the border on the bottom. The feed dogs can help ease in extra fullness.

Step 3. Measure the width of the quilt, taking the measurement through the horizontal center of the quilt and *including* the width of the side borders, as shown. Cut or piece two border strips this exact length.

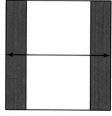

Measure horizontally through center

Step 4. Sew the top and bottom borders to the quilt top in the same manner as for the side borders, pinning at the midpoints and ends first, then easing in fullness if necessary.

All Borders Aren't Alike

Though most traditional quilts have borders on all four sides, there's no hard-and-fast rule regarding the number of borders you add to your quilt. Some quilts are bordered only on three sides, with the edge that tucks under your chin at night left plain. Other quilts may have an inner border on the sides only to extend the width of the quilt and then an outer border on all four sides.

In addition to where the borders are placed, you can change the look of your quilt by changing the size of the borders, too. For more of a folk art look, sew wider borders on the top and bottom than on the sides. Or, if your goal is a more contemporary look, make all borders different widths for an off-center quilt.

ADDING CORNER BLOCKS TO BORDERS

Corner blocks are a nice addition to butted borders, adding interest to both wall and bed-size quilts. Corner blocks can simply be a repeat of blocks in the quilt top or a small-scale version if the borders are not as wide as the central blocks.

Another option is to choose a different block entirely. For example, if you are making a medallion quilt with a large floral or basket motif, consider making a small pieced basket block for each corner of the quilt top to enhance the central motif without taking away from its beauty.

Of course, corner blocks do not have to be pieced. You can simply use plain squares from fabric that complements your quilt and border.

Corner Block Construction

Step 1. Measure the length of the quilt, as detailed in Step 1 of "Making Borders with Butted Corners." Cut or piece two border strips this length.

Step 2. Measure the width of the quilt as explained in Step 3 of "Making Borders with Butted Corners." Cut or piece two border strips this length.

Step 3. If you are using multiple border strips, repeat Steps 1 and 2 to measure and cut all border fabrics. Sew the strips for each border together, and press the seams toward the outer strips.

Step 4. Cut or piece four border squares equal to the finished width of the border, plus ½ inch. (If your finished border will measure 10 inches, cut 10½-inch corner squares, or piece blocks that have a finished size of 10 inches). Sew a border square to each end of a top and bottom border. Press the seams toward the border.

Step 5. Sew the side borders to the quilt top. Press the seams toward the borders. Attach the top

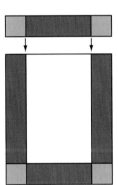

and bottom borders to the quilt in the same manner as in "Making Borders with Butted Corners," making sure you carefully match the seam intersection of the side borders with the corner squares for a nice, neat finish, as shown.

Always press seams toward the border, even if your corner squares are a little darker than the border fabric. That way, your seams will always be ready for a perfect match with the quilt top when you're ready to add the top and bottom borders.

MITERED BORDERS

Mitered borders take a bit more fabric to make than straight borders, but many quiltmakers prefer the finished look of the mitered corners and consider the extra fabric a worthwhile expense. If you choose a print specially designed for borders, such as a paisley or other motif that is printed in a

striped design, mitered borders are the way to go. With mitered corners, the print can form a continuous design around the entire quilt, as shown.

Matched   Unmatched

Mitered corners are also an appropriate choice for multiple borders that don't use corner squares. By mitering the corners, you'll be able to match the various fabric strips in your borders, just as you can match the design in a printed striped fabric. The diagram shows the difference a mitered corner can make.

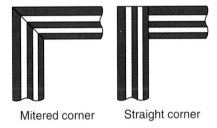

Mitered corner   Straight corner

How to Miter Corners

Step 1. First calculate how long to cut your borders. Measure the length of your quilt top through the center, as described in "Making Borders with Butted Corners" on the opposite page. To that measurement, add two times the width of your border, plus 5 inches. This is the length you need to cut or piece the side borders. For example, if the quilt top is 48 inches long and you are making 4-inch-wide borders, you'll need border strips that are 61 inches long (48 inches + 4 inches + 4 inches + 5 inches = 61 inches).

Cut or piece two border strips this length. If you are using multiple borders, cut or piece additional strips the same length and sew the strips together along their long edges. Press the seams toward the outer border.

Step 2. Calculate the length needed for the top and bottom borders in the same manner, measuring the width of the quilt through the center and adding two times the width of your border, plus 5 inches. Cut or piece two border strips this length. Again, if you are making a multiple-strip border, repeat for all strips.

Step 3. Sew each of the borders to the quilt top, beginning and ending all seams ¼ inch from the ends of the quilt, as shown by the dots in the diagram. You will have excess border fabric extending from each end of your borders, as shown. Press the border seams flat from the right side of the quilt.

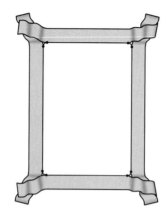

Step 4. Working on one corner of the quilt, place one border on top of the adjacent border. Fold the top border strip under so that it meets the edge of the outer border and forms a 45 degree angle, as shown. If you are working with a plaid or striped border, check to make sure the patterns match along this folded edge. Press the fold in place.

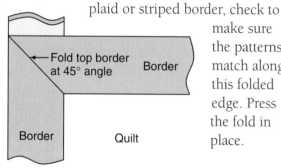

Step 5. Fold the quilt top with right sides together and align the edges of the borders. Use the pressed fold as the corner seam line and sew from the inner corner to the outer corner, as shown in the diagram. Be sure to keep the quilt top out of the way as you stitch.

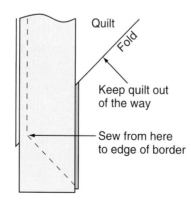

Step 6. Unfold the quilt and check to make sure that all points match and the miter is flat. Trim the border seam allowance to ¼ inch, and press the seam open for a flat corner seam. Repeat from Step 4 for the three remaining corners.

APPLIQUÉING THE QUILT TOP TO A BORDER

Some quilts, such as a Double Wedding Ring or traditional One Patch quilts like Grandmother's Flower Garden, have irregular outer edges. These quilts can be bound around their edges (see "Mock Binding" on page 87), or borders can be attached to them for straight-edge finishing, as shown in the diagram.

To accurately piece straight borders into the curved or angled edges would be time-consuming and, in many cases, difficult to accomplish. If you want to extend such a quilt with borders, you can solve the problem by cutting straight borders, sewing them together to form a frame, and then appliquéing the quilt top to the preassembled border. Either straight or mitered borders can be used for this technique.

How to Attach a Preassembled Border

Step 1. Determine how wide you want your borders to be. You will need to allow extra width for the quilt top to overlap the border. Measure the distance from the widest part of the quilt to the innermost curve or angle on the edge to determine just how much extra width you will need. Then add an extra inch to your border width for insurance.

Step 2. Measure the quilt top to determine the length needed for your borders, following the instructions in "Making Borders with Butted Corners" on page 82 or "How to Miter Corners" on page 83. Sew the strips together at the corners to form a border frame, as shown, and press the seams.

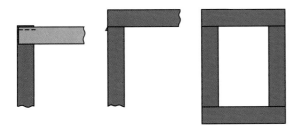

Step 3. Prepare the edges of the quilt for your favorite method of appliqué. A freezer paper template can be used to stabilize the quilt edges for appliqué, as shown. Center the quilt faceup on top of the border unit. Pin or baste in place, with basting stitches about ⅝ inch from the edge of the quilt top. Hand or machine appliqué the quilt edges to the border. Remove the basting stitches and press.

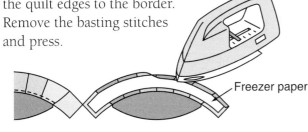

Freezer paper

QUICK-AND-EASY PIECED BORDERS

Pieced borders can be as intricate or as simple as you like to suit the style of your quilt. This section focuses on ideas for quick-and-easy pieced borders to enhance your projects.

BLUE RIBBON TECHNIQUE

Checkerboard Borders

For an easy checkerboard border, determine the size of the checkerboard by the size of the blocks used in the quilt. For example, if your blocks are 12 inches square, your individual checkerboard units should evenly divide into 12, as shown. That means each finished checkerboard square could measure 1, 1½, 2, or 3 inches.

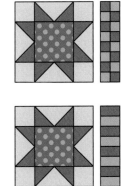

In addition to size, you have options when it comes to color. You can limit your checkerboard border to just two colors, or use a mix-and-match color scheme to incorporate more fabrics from your quilt blocks.

Don't limit yourself to checkerboard squares; rectangles are just as easy to calculate and sew together. (See the purple and blue rectangles shown above.)

Step 1. Cut strips that measure the finished width plus ½ inch for seam allowances. If you want your squares to be 1½ inches when finished, cut your strips 2 inches wide.

Step 2. Sew the strips together into a strip set, alternating colors. You can make two-color strip

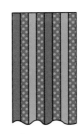

sets as well as multicolored strip sets, as shown. Notice that the first strip and the last strip are *not* the same color. Press all seams in one direction.

Step 3. Cut the strip set into thirds, as shown. Each segment should measure about 14 inches long. Then sew the segments together side by side. If your quilt is longer than your new strip set, continue making strip sets and cutting and resewing them in this manner.

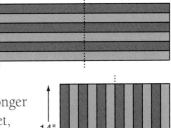

Step 4. Cut the new strip set into segments that measure the width of your original strips. In this case, cut the segments 2 inches wide.

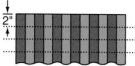

Step 5. Sew two of the long segments together along their long edges. Be sure to flip one of the segments so that you are sewing opposite color squares to one another, as shown. Continue

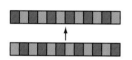

adding strips until you have a checkerboard border in your desired width.

String-Pieced Borders

String-pieced borders are another fast and fun way to add interest to your quilt. Cut long strips of rolled paper (noncoated freezer paper works well) slightly wider and longer than the measurements required for your borders. Use the technique in "String Piecing on Foundations" on page 38 to sew strips of fabric to the paper. Trim the borders to the exact width and length needed, and sew them to the quilt.

Evenly measured strips: For a planned, measured look, measure and mark strip-width increments on your paper border foundation. Stitch your fabric to the paper exactly on the lines.

Random strips: For a more whimsical look in your border, add strips of different widths and at different angles. You can premark the paper strip or simply add strips randomly so they have a free-form look, as shown.

Borders That Really Add Up

Rolls of adding machine paper are handy for string piecing narrow strips of sashing or even borders for wall-hangings or miniature quilts.

FOLK ART PIECED BORDER

For the quickest and easiest of all pieced borders, try this trick to give your pieced or appliquéd quilt top a fun folk art look. Instead of piecing together strips of the same fabric to make border strips long enough to fit your quilt, mix and match fabrics within each border, and your quilt will have a time-honored "she had to make do" feeling.

You don't have to measure each fabric strip to a certain length. Simply piece a bunch of strips together, preferably with horizontal seams, then trim the long strips to the lengths you need. There's no faster way to make a pieced border! You can even use this technique with multiple borders, and no seam matching is required. Each border should be pieced individually and completely at random, as shown.

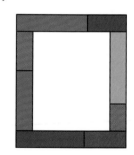

Crazy-Patch Borders

Borders, like the rest of your quilt top, can be crazy pieced and embellished with decorative threads and stitches. If a crazy patchwork border is the look you want, combine the border technique in "Random Strips" with the techniques for "Fused Crazy Quilting" on page 39. The stitching is quick and easy, and the results are stunning!

BINDING ACCENTS AND OPTIONS

If you've ever gotten to the point where your quilt top was finished right down to the last quilting stitch and all you wanted to do was bind it and get it done, you're not alone. Most times, when quilters think of finishing their quilts, the decision is merely whether to use straight-of-grain or bias binding. However, there are a variety of options that can change the look of the quilt or add a final festive touch.

From a country look bias plaid binding to a folk look scrap-pieced binding to the perky feel of prairie points, you still have design options at this final stage of the quiltmaking process that can make your quilt look like a million bucks and not add a significant time investment on your part.

SELF-BINDING

With this finishing technique, the quilt backing is cut larger than the quilt top and batting. After quilting, the backing is folded to the front of the quilt, folded again, and blind stitched in place. It is one of the earliest finishing methods, as evidenced by many antique quilts. A word of caution, however: Self-binding does not wear as well as applied bindings because it causes stress and strain to the backing fabric. This method is quicker than attaching separate binding, but it should be reserved for projects that won't get a lot of wear, such as wallhangings.

How to Make Self-Binding

Step 1. Trim the batting even with the quilt top, taking care not to cut the backing fabric.

Step 2. Multiply your desired finished binding width by 3. For example, if you want your completed binding to be ¼ inch, trim your backing fabric so it extends ¾ inch beyond the quilt edges.

Step 3. Beginning along one side, fold the backing toward the front of the quilt so the raw edge just meets the edge of the quilt, as shown. Then make another fold to bring the folded edge of the backing to meet the ¼-inch seam allowance

line of the quilt. Pin the folded edge in place as you continue to fold the backing over the quilt edge.

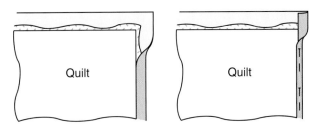

If you want a puffy rather than flat binding, use the scraps of batting trimmed off to stuff in the fold of your binding.

Step 4. When you near a corner, trim the tip of the backing fabric on the diagonal. Then fold the trimmed edge of the corner to meet the corner of the quilt top, as indicated in the diagram. Next, fold in one side of the backing followed by the other, as shown, to make a mitered corner.

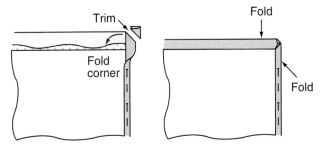

Step 5. Fold the backing and pin it to all sides of the quilt in the same manner. Use thread that matches the backing fabric and blind stitch the self-binding to the front of the quilt. Take a few stitches in each corner to secure the folded edges.

MOCK BINDING

Mock binding is another classic finishing technique. It is easier to finish the outer edges of curved, scalloped, or deeply angled quilts by turning under the seam allowances on the front and backing, then blindstitching them together than it is to apply double-fold binding. This technique can be used on any quilt, but you'll probably want to reserve it for the types of projects mentioned, as the edges will tend to wear more quickly than if they were bound.

How to Make Mock Binding

Step 1. Quilt to within ⅝ inch of the edges of the quilt.

Step 2. Trim the batting so that it lies ¼ inch inside the edges of the quilt top. This will allow the batting to reach completely to the edges of the quilt after you've finished sewing.

Step 3. Carefully trim the backing even with the edges of the quilt top.

Step 4. Turn under the ¼-inch seam allowances of both the quilt top and the backing, encasing the batting inside one of the seam allowances as you work. Blind stitch all around the edges of the quilt.

Step 5. Quilt at the edges of the quilt to secure the batting in place.

APPLIED BINDINGS

Whether you choose straight-of-grain binding or bias binding, the bindings are applied in the same manner once the binding strips are cut. Here you'll find information about the benefits and possible drawbacks of each type of binding, how to calculate the amount of binding you'll need, and directions for applying different types of binding.

Straight-of-Grain Binding

This type of binding can be cut on either the crosswise or lengthwise grain of your fabric.

Pros: Straight binding is easier to measure, cut, handle, and match patterns with than bias binding. It's best used for wallhangings and other projects that won't get a lot of daily use, which can put strain on the fibers.

Cons: When strips are folded and sewn around the perimeter of your quilt, threads that lie along the grain lines at the fold remain in a slight, but continuous stress and may weaken over time with heavy use. Since the threads involved are continuous along the perimeter of the binding, a weakness would probably affect the binding for the entire length of the strip involved.

Because of their rigidity, straight-grain strips are not suitable for binding around curves.

Bias Binding

This type of binding is cut on the true bias, or at a 45 degree angle to the straight of grain.

Pros: Bias binding wears well with age and use because stress in a thread is more likely to affect only a small area since the straight of grain does not follow the length of the strip.

The slight stretchiness of bias strips makes bias binding the best choice for binding around curves and quilts with angular edges, such as Grandmother's Flower Garden.

Cons: Making bias binding requires more fabric than straight-of-grain binding. Plus, when you start cutting on the bias, you'll get some shorter strips from the corners. If you're frugal with your fabric and want to use every bit possible, you'll end up with lots of seams in your binding strips.

When you want to give your project a warm and cozy country feel, try a plaid or striped fabric, rather than a plain or print fabric, for your bias binding.

HOW MUCH BINDING DO YOU NEED?

Estimating the Length

To calculate the length of binding needed, add the lengths of all sides of the quilt, then add another 9 to 12 inches to your total, depending on the overall size of your quilt. Measure carefully around curved edges, and add more insurance inches to compensate for the extra tucks and mitering that are required.

Estimating the Yardage

Now that you know how long you want your binding strip to measure, how do you figure out how much yardage you need to make a strip that long? If your quilt pattern doesn't provide binding yardage requirements, here's what to figure.

Straight-of-grain binding: Divide your total binding length by 42 (the number of inches across your fabric after it's been prewashed). That will tell you how many cross-grain fabric strips you need to cut. Then multiply the number of strips by the width of your binding strips (see "Determining Binding Width" below). The answer is the number of inches of fabric you'll need to make your binding. As an example, say you need 350 inches of binding. 350 inches ÷ 42 inches = 8.33 strips. You'll need to cut a total of nine strips, and if you're cutting them $2\frac{1}{4}$ inches wide, you'll need to buy a minimum of $\frac{5}{8}$ yard of fabric.

Just to be safe and to allow for shrinkage, round your amount up to the next $\frac{1}{8}$-yard increment.

Bias binding: Calculating bias binding yardage is a bit tricker, and a calculator with a square root function key is a big help. For continuous bias binding, start with a square of fabric with dimensions equal to the square root of the number of inches of binding you need. For example, if you need 200 inches of binding, multiply 200 by the strip width, say 2 inches. Your answer is 400. The square root of 400 is 20, so, the size square you need to start with is 20 inches. For other binding amounts or widths that don't leave you with such an even number, remember to round up.

For most bed-size quilts, $\frac{3}{4}$ to 1 yard of fabric is sufficient to make bias binding.

Determining Binding Width

Wallhangings and miniature quilts are often bound with strips that finish to $\frac{1}{8}$ or $\frac{1}{4}$ inch wide, while $\frac{3}{8}$- or $\frac{1}{2}$-inch-wide binding is commonly used for bed quilts. In addition to knowing how wide you want the finished binding to be, you need to decide if you'll be making single- or double-fold binding.

Single-Fold Binding

Single-fold binding refers to binding that is made from a single layer of fabric. For single-fold binding, cut strips that are twice as wide as your desired finished width *plus* $\frac{1}{2}$ inch for seam allowances. For example, if you want $\frac{1}{2}$-inch-wide finished binding, cut your strips $1\frac{1}{2}$ inches wide ([2 × $\frac{1}{2}$ inches] + $\frac{1}{2}$ inch = $1\frac{1}{2}$ inches). If you are using a high-loft batting, add another $\frac{1}{4}$ inch to the strip width.

Single-fold binding works well for quilts with curved or angled edges, such as a Wedding Ring or Grandmother's Flower Garden, since you won't have as much bulk to maneuver around the curves or angles.

Double-Fold Binding

Double-fold binding is, as the name says, made from two layers. In general, double-fold binding is more durable than single fold, so use it for bed quilts and other projects that will have heavy use. Cut strips for double-fold binding four times the finished binding width plus $\frac{1}{2}$ inch for seam allowances. That means for a finished $\frac{1}{2}$-inch-wide binding, cut your strips $2\frac{1}{2}$ inches wide ([4 × $\frac{1}{2}$ inch] + $\frac{1}{2}$ inch = $2\frac{1}{2}$ inches). Again, add an extra $\frac{1}{4}$ inch if you are using a high-loft batting.

Demystifying Binding Jargon

Don't get confused between straight-of-grain and bias binding and single- and double-fold bindings. Straight of grain versus bias has to do with the direction of the grain, while single and double fold have to do with how wide you cut your bindings and whether they will be double thickness or not. Whichever direction of the grain you cut your binding on, you can cut it wide enough to be either single- or double-fold binding.

SEAMING BINDING STRIPS

Whether you are making straight-of-grain or bias binding, you will have to piece the binding strips before attaching them to the quilt, unless your quilt is a miniature one.

Straight of Grain

Place the binding strips right sides together and perpendicular to each other, as shown. Stitch from corner to corner, as indicated, and trim away excess seam allowance. Diagonal seams not only distribute the seam allowance once the binding is folded but they are also less obvious than horizontal ones. Press your binding seams open to reduce bulk in the finished binding.

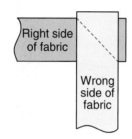

Bias Strips

Bias strips normally have a 45 degree angle at their ends, making it easy to align strips for diagonal seaming. Simply use your rotary-cutting ruler to verify the angle, and correct it if necessary. Then align the strips with right sides together, as shown, offsetting the tips. Stitch the strips together with a ¼-inch seam allowance. Press the seams open.

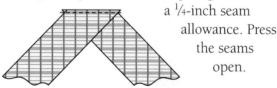

If you prefer this method, you can assemble straight-grain strips in the same way. Simply trim the ends first with your rotary-cutting equipment, then align and stitch.

ATTACHING DOUBLE-FOLD BINDING

Before you attach the binding, trim the excess batting and backing even with the quilt top. Rotary-cutting equipment is very handy for this step. Then attach the binding following either the folded end method or the diagonal seam method.

Folded End Method

Step 1. Fold the long binding strip in half lengthwise, wrong sides together, and press. Beginning in the middle of a side, not in a corner, place the strip right sides together with the quilt top, align the raw edges, and pin. (If you like, pin short sections at a time.)

If you are working with bias strips, be careful not to stretch them as you press. Mist with spray starch to help keep bias edges firm.

Step 2. Fold over about 1 inch at the beginning of the strip and begin stitching ½ inch from the fold, as shown. Sew the binding to the quilt, using a ¼-inch seam and stitching through all layers.

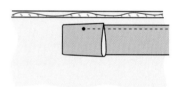

Step 3. As you approach a corner, stop stitching ¼ inch from the raw edge. Backstitch and remove the quilt from the machine. Fold the binding strip up at a 45 degree angle, as shown. Fold the strip back down so there is a fold at the upper edge, as shown. Resume sewing at the top edge of the quilt. Stitch all corners in the same manner.

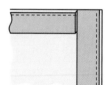

Step 4. To finish the binding seam, overlap the folded-back beginning section with the ending section. Stitch across the fold, allowing the end to extend approximately ½ inch beyond the beginning fold.

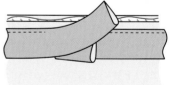

Step 5. Turn the binding to the back of the quilt and blind stitch the folded edge in place, covering the machine stitches with the folded edge. Fold in the adjacent sides on the back and

take several stitches in the miter. Add several stitches to the miters on the front of the quilt, too.

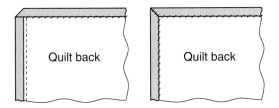

Quilt back   Quilt back

Diagonal Seam Method

The binding is attached in the same manner as for the folded end method except at the starting and stopping points (Steps 2 and 4 on the opposite page).

Step 1. Fold the long binding strip in half lengthwise, wrong sides together, and press. Beginning in the middle of a side, not in a corner, place the strip right sides together with the quilt top, align the raw edges, and pin.

Step 2. Instead of folding over the starting end of the binding, leave about a 2- or 3-inch length of binding unsewn at the start, as shown.

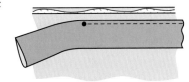

Step 3. Miter the corners, as described in Step 3 of "Folded End Method" on the opposite page.

Step 4. When you near the starting point, stop sewing and backstitch, leaving about an 8-inch space unsewn. Leave enough of a tail on the binding to meet up with the starting end of the binding.

Step 5. Open the folds of both ends of the binding. Fold the tails at 45 degree angles where they meet and crease, as shown. Then, with the right sides of the binding tails facing and the folds aligned, pin the two binding ends together. Make sure you have just enough binding to fit the un-sewn edge of the quilt. If it's too long it will gap; if it's too short, the quilt will buckle.

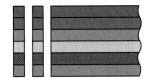

Crease

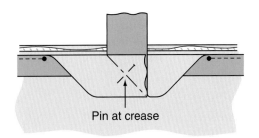

Pin at crease

Step 6. Sew the binding ends together with a diagonal seam, as shown. When you are sure that the binding is the correct length for your quilt, trim the excess binding, leaving a ¼-inch seam allowance. Press the seam open, then refold the binding. Stitch the binding to the quilt.

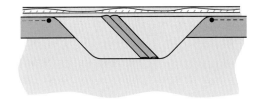

Step 7. Hand sew the binding to the back of the quilt, as described in Step 5 of "Folded End Method" on the opposite page.

BLUE RIBBON TECHNIQUE

Easy Pieced Bindings

Pieced bindings can be made from leftover strip-pieced fabrics or can be pieced specifically to coordinate with your quilt top.

Straight-Pieced Binding

Step 1. Sew strips of fabric together side by side to make a strip set, as shown. Use your rotary-cutting equipment to trim seam allowances slightly, then press the seams open.

Step 2. Square up one end of the strip set, and cut segments from it in the width needed for your binding. Sew the strips together end to end until you have enough binding for the quilt.

For more variety, make multiple strip sets from different fabrics, and sew units together randomly.

Diagonal-Pieced Binding

Step 1. Make a strip set, offsetting the ends of the strips slightly, as shown (below left). Trim the seams slightly and press them open.

Step 2. Make a 45 degree cut at one end of the strip set, as shown, using your rotary-cutting equipment. Continue to cut segments from the strip set, and sew them together end to end to make the total length of binding for your quilt. Your finished binding will look like that shown below (right).

Faux-Pieced Binding

For a fast binding with a pieced look, make your binding from striped or checked fabric cut on the bias.

BINDING AROUND CURVES AND ANGLES

To calculate the amount of binding needed, measure the length of one side of the hexagon, the length of the curve of the spool, or the side of whatever unusual shape you need to bind. Then multiply this measurement by the number of those sides, hexagon angles, or spool curves along the outside edges of your quilt. The total is the number of inches of binding you'll need. Add

about 10 to 15 inches extra as a little insurance. And remember to cut *bias* binding for a smooth finish. For best results, hand sew the binding in place.

Step 1. Make narrow single-fold bias binding (cut strips about 1 inch wide) in the length you just calculated. It's easier to apply a narrow binding around angles and curves.

Step 2. Trim the batting and backing even with the edges of the quilt top and pin about 6 inches of the binding to the quilt at a time. With a single strand of thread, work from the top side and sew a ¼-inch seam allowance through the binding and all three layers of the quilt. Use a running stitch, backstitching occasionally.

Step 3. For hexagons, pivot at each outer and inner corner, as shown.

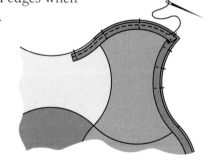

For spools or clamshells, you will also need to pivot at the quilt's corners, as shown. Also, when stitching binding around curves, be careful not to pull the bias binding too tight, or you will have rippled edges when you are finished.

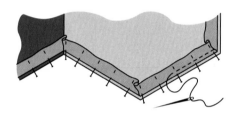

Step 4. Fold the binding to the back of the quilt and blindstitch it in place, forming tucks at each inner corner and slight miters at each outer point, as shown.

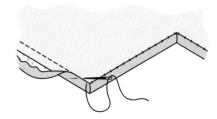

TRADITIONAL PRAIRIE POINTS

Prairie points are a fun way to use up scrap fabrics and add a whimsical touch to your quilt at the same time. Actually, this decorative edge can be made from many different scraps, as described in the two folded square methods. Or continuous strips of prairie points can be made from two contrasting or coordinating fabrics. This is the speedier of the two methods, but you may want to choose your method to suit the style of your quilt.

Folded Squares

Small, folded squares of fabric form triangles that are overlapped and sewn to the quilt edges in place of binding. There are two basic methods for folding the squares, but first you need to determine what size squares to start with.

Decide how big you want your finished prairie points to be, then use this formula: Height of the finished point × 2 + ½ inch = size square to cut.

For example, if you want 2-inch finished prairie points, start with 4½-inch squares (2 inches × 2 + ½ inch = 4½ inch), as shown.

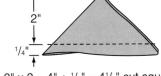

2" x 2 = 4" + ½" = 4½" cut square

Method 1

Step 1. Fold a square of fabric diagonally, wrong sides together, and press. Fold it a second time, as shown, to create a triangle and press again.

Step 2. Nest the prairie points one inside the other, as shown, to form an edging. Pin the prairie points to the edge of the quilt, adjusting the amount of the overlap to fit the length of your quilt. To finish the edge, proceed to "Finishing the Edges."

Method 2

Step 1. Fold a square in half with wrong sides together to form a rectangle and press. Make two diagonal folds from the midpoint, as shown, to create a finished triangle with a vertical fold. Press both new folds.

Step 2. Overlap the prairie points, as shown, to form the edging. Pin them to the quilt, adjusting the amount of overlap to fit your quilt.

Finishing the Edges

Prairie points are usually sewn to the quilt top after it has been quilted. However, you should leave about 1 inch unquilted around the edges of your quilt until after the points have been attached.

Step 1. Trim the batting and quilt backing even with the edge of the quilt top. Then fold the backing away from the batting and pin to keep it out of the way.

Step 2. Beginning at a corner, place the prairie points along the quilt edge, with raw edges even and the triangle points facing in toward the quilt center. Adjust the positioning as needed to fit your quilt top, and pin in place.

Step 3. Sew the prairie points to the quilt top and batting only, using a ¼-inch seam allowance.

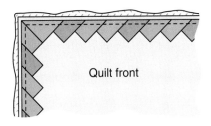

Quilt front

Step 4. Trim the batting and prairie point seam allowance at the quilt corners to reduce bulk. Then remove the pins in the quilt backing and fold under a ¼-inch seam allowance in the quilt backing. Finger press the seam allowance in place.

Pin the backing in place to cover the base of the prairie points, making sure to cover the stitching line. Hand stitch in place, as shown.

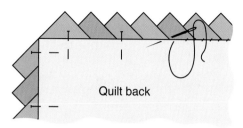

Quilt back

How Many Prairie Points?

Here's a handy formula to help you calculate just how many individual prairie points to make for each side of your quilt: length of quilt ÷ finished base of prairie point × 2.

For example, if your quilt is 90 inches long, you'll need 60 prairie points for each side (90 inches ÷ 3 inches = 30; 30 × 2 inches = 60). Calculate the number for the top and bottom edges in the same manner.

CONTINUOUS PRAIRIE POINTS

This easy technique makes quick work of constructing a whole string of prairie points. While the technique is quick, it does limit your color scheme to just one or two fabrics.

One-Color Prairie Points

Step 1. Cut a strip of fabric using this formula: Desired height of prairie point + $\frac{1}{4}$ inch × 4. For example, if you want your points to finish 2 inches high, cut your strip 9 inches wide (2 inches + $\frac{1}{4}$ inch × 4 = 9 inches).

You can cut your strips any length, but very long strips can get unwieldy. It's easier to cut strips that yield about 10 or 12 prairie points, then nest several strips together to complete your quilt edging.

Step 2. Fold the strip in half lengthwise with *wrong* sides together, and press a crease along the fold. Open the strip and place it right side down on your table.

Step 3. Beginning on the lower right side, mark $4\frac{1}{2}$-inch segments (half the size of the strip width), as shown. Draw lines perpendicular to the crease. Then, on the left side, mark one segment that is $2\frac{1}{4}$ inches, followed by the $4\frac{1}{2}$-inch segments, as shown. Cut along each marked line from the outer edge just to the fold. Cut away the $2\frac{1}{4}$-inch segment and discard.

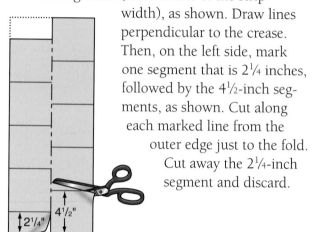

$2\frac{1}{4}$" $4\frac{1}{2}$"

Step 4. Beginning on the lower right side, fold the first segment (A) to form a triangle, as shown. Press. Then fold the upper corner of the triangle down, press, and pin the corners together, as shown.

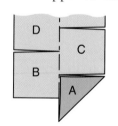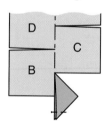

Step 5. On the lower left side, fold the bottom corner of the first segment (B), as shown, and press. Then fold prairie point A over the partially folded point B, as shown. Finally, make the second fold in B, so that A is nested in B.

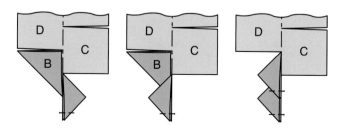

Step 6. Continue folding and nesting points, alternating sides of the strip, until the entire strip has been folded. Stitch the raw edges of the row about ⅛ inch from the edge to hold the prairie point folds in place until you are ready to attach them to your quilt.

Two-Color Prairie Points

Step 1. For two-color prairie points, cut two strips, each the finished height × 2 + ¾ inch. For example, if you want 2-inch finished points, cut your strips 4¾ inches wide (2 × 2 inches + ¾ inch = 4¾ inches).

Step 2. Rather than fold the strip lengthwise to find its center, stitch the two different fabric strips together with *wrong* sides together, using a ¼-inch seam. Press the seam to one side.

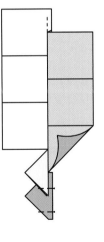

Step 3. Lay the strip on the table with the seam allowance down and the wrong side up. Mark, cut, fold, and press as described in Steps 3 through 6 in "One-Color Prairie Points" on the opposite page.

PERFECT PIPING ACCENT

Piping is another edge treatment that can add a spark of color and interest to your quilt. A thin band of flat or filled piping will set the border apart from the quilt top or the binding off from the border.

Step 1. Cut strips for your piping in the same manner as you would cut binding strips. They can be either straight-of-grain or bias strips. For flat piping, strips should be ¾ to 1 inch wide. For filled piping, cut your strips about 1½ inches wide. Piece together enough strips to fit around your quilt, measuring as you would for binding.

Step 2. Fold the long piping strip in half lengthwise, with *wrong* sides together. Press for flat piping. For filled piping, insert a thin cording, as shown, and use a zipper foot on your sewing machine to stitch the piping closed to contain the cording.

Step 3. Hand baste the piping to your quilt edges, whether before the border is added or at the edge of the border before the binding is added. Then, add the border or binding. The machine stitching will hold both the piping and border or binding in place. If your piping is filled, use the zipper foot to sew the border or binding in place, too.

Hanging Sleeve Savvy

While you can add a hanging sleeve to a quilt at any point in its life, adding it during the binding process can save you a step. Simply hem the short ends of your sleeve fabric, then fold the fabric in half lengthwise. Align both raw edges of the sleeve with the raw edges at the top of the quilt and pin them in place. Attach your binding, and the raw edges of the sleeve will be stitched in place at the same time. Now you only have to sew the lower edge of the sleeve in place by hand.

successful
QUILTING

Successful Quilting

Have you ever heard someone say, "It's not a quilt until it's quilted," or "It's the quilting that makes the quilt"? Even though you may have spent many hours piecing or appliquéing your quilt top, technically it's not a quilt until the top has been stitched together with a layer of batting and a backing. The stitching that holds these three layers together can be done by hand or machine. There are also quicker alternatives, such as tying (again by hand or machine) or machine tacking the layers together. No matter which method you prefer, this section is packed with tips, techniques, and creative ideas to help you finish your project.

GETTING READY TO QUILT

Whether you plan to quilt by hand or machine, the first step is getting your quilt top ready for quilting. Even if you prefer *tying* (using strong thread, yarn, or ribbon to tie knots through the layers to hold them together) or *tacking* (taking several stitches over top one another at intervals over the quilt top to hold the layers together) over quilting, you'll still need to mark your designs on the quilt top and baste the layers together before you begin the process.

CHOOSING A QUILTING DESIGN

This may well be one of the toughest decisions you'll make regarding your quilt. After all, if quilting makes the quilt, you want the quilting design to be right!

If you've ever been faced with project directions that simply say, "quilt as desired," you've undoubtedly been frustrated, too. How do you know or decide what to quilt? If you're making a traditional quilt and want to follow in the footsteps (or stitches) of quiltmakers who came before you, you may want to try one of these traditional patterns:

Outline quilting: Outline quilting is traditionally done ¼ inch away from the seam lines. This lets you avoid quilting over layers of seams plus helps to emphasize your quilt patches.

Baptist Fan: This allover fan motif is quilted right over the whole quilt top, regardless of the pattern of the quilt. A look at some antique quilts will reveal that this style of quilting was used just as commonly on appliqué quilts as it was on patch-work types.

Baptist Fan

Teacups: Another popular design of yore, teacups, or pumpkin seeds, were often used to fill in large areas, such as setting squares, setting triangles, and borders. You can make your own

teacup quilting design simply by tracing a teacup or saucer from your kitchen cupboard.

Teacups or pumpkin seeds

Cross-hatching or grids: Like the teacup motif, cross-hatching is a great design for filling in a large open area on your quilt top. You can make a simple ½-, ¾-, or 1-inch grid with a ruler or masking tape (see page 101). Or you can enhance your grid by using double or triple lines, as shown. Cross-hatching doesn't have to form little squares, either. A diamond-shape grid is just as nice.

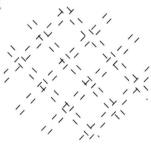
Cross-hatching

Echo quilting: Here's a traditional type of quilting that doesn't really require advance marking. You simply quilt around your motifs and then quilt around them again, ⅛ to ¼ inch outside the first row of quilting, as shown. Continue adding rows until the quilting around one motif meets the quilted rings around an adjacent motif. If you really want to echo the quilting of spectacular antique quilts, try making your echo rows even closer together—a mere ¹⁄₁₆ inch apart!

Echo quilting

MARKING A QUILT TOP

There are many ways to mark a quilt top for quilting, and no one method is the best for every situation. Ask yourself two questions before selecting a marking method. First, how will you be quilting—in a hoop, on a quilt frame, with your machine? And second, what type of fabrics are you quilting—primarily light, primarily dark, or a scrap mixture?

For instance, the marking method for hand quilting in a frame, where the quilt is handled very little, would be very different from the marking method for a machine-quilted project that will get handled, turned, bunched, and rolled frequently. Likewise, the method you choose for a multifabric scrap quilt might not be at all suitable for a delicate appliqué project.

A variety of marking methods are explained here, along with pros and cons of each, to give you better insight into the appropriate uses of each method.

Try as many marking devices as possible to see which ones work best for you on different fabrics or in different situations. Label your samples and keep them on hand for future reference.

QUILT MARKING TOOLS

Pencils

There are times when you'll find the best marking device is a pencil, either the traditional, fine-tip lead pencil or one of today's newer versions.

Pros: Extra-sharp, hard lead pencils are excellent for marking intricate designs, since the thin line will hardly be visible after quilting, even if you don't wash the quilt. Long-lasting markings are helpful for hand quilting in a hoop where the quilt is handled more than in frame quilting.

Cons: Pencil markings don't always wash out, so be sure to test on a scrap of your fabric first. Lead pencil markings can smudge if your lines are too thick or too heavy.

What to Look For:
• Use a *#3 or #4 pencil*. Both contain harder lead than the typical #2 lead, which can smudge. Keep

Better Safe Than Sorry

Traditional marking techniques usually involve a traditional lead pencil or other sort of marking pencil. Although it's not always practical to test a marking pencil on each piece of fabric in your quilt, do test it on scraps containing the same fabric content. Test markers on darks and lights, and see if they are easy to remove. You may even want to leave the marks on the fabric for a few weeks, and then try the removal process. If a marker smudges or leaves stubborn stains that will show after quilting, it's best to make another choice for marking your quilt.

the pencil sharpened for a very fine line that won't show when your quilting is completed.

• *Mechanical pencils* are available in many lead widths, and you can change the hardness of lead to suit your needs by purchasing a variety of refills.

• *Karisma water-soluble pencils,* available at quilt shops, leave a black line that washes out of fabric.

• *Berol Verithin pencils* are another favorite of many quilters. The colored lead is hard, so the pencil holds a point longer than some other drawing pencils. White, yellow, and silver are all useful colors to have on hand for marking different shades of fabric.

• *Dixon Textile pencils* are another type of removable marker you might want to try.

Chalk Products

Chalk markers are available in a variety of products from pencils to stompers.

Pros: Most chalk products are easy to use, and chalk lines can be easily brushed away after quilting. There's no need to wash the quilt to remove the markings.

Cons: Chalk lines sometimes disappear before you've finished quilting. For best results, mark only a small portion of the quilt at one time, especially if you are using a hoop, which must be repositioned during the quilting process.

What to Look For:

• *Chalk pencils* are available in many colors. Most contain thicker lead than a standard pencil, so they leave a wider line and may not be appropriate for marking intricate patterns. General's Multi-Pastel Chalks are a good choice.

• *Tailor's chalk* is a triangular or rectangular piece of compressed chalk that leaves a very fine line on the fabric because its edges are honed to a sharp edge. It's commonly available in white, but other colors are available for marking light fabrics. Again, test on a scrap of your fabric first.

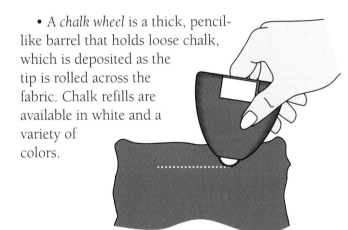

• A *chalk wheel* is a thick, pencil-like barrel that holds loose chalk, which is deposited as the tip is rolled across the fabric. Chalk refills are available in white and a variety of colors.

• *Stompers* are chalk-filled bags that are pounced up and down on a quilting stencil placed on top of fabric. When the stencil is removed, the chalk lines remain to guide your stitching.

Chalk stomper

BLUE RIBBON TECHNIQUE

Masking Tape

Masking tape can be used to mark accurately spaced lines on your quilt top. Just position the tape, quilt alongside it, and remove it. For parallel lines, reposition the tape on the opposite side of the quilted line and repeat.

Pros: The straight lines of the tape make it an excellent choice for marking straight lines, whether they be parallel lines or grids. Masking tape is a great time-saver, since you don't have to spend time marking lines before you baste your quilt layers together. You can simply mark as you go.

Masking tape is fairly economical, too, since the same length of tape can be reused many times before it loses its ability to stick in place. Narrow, ¼-inch tape is helpful for outline quilting, since it eliminates the need for eyeballing a ¼-inch distance from seam lines.

Cons: If left in place for too long, masking tape can leave a residue on the quilt top, so always remove tape when you're through quilting for the day. Also, it's not particularly helpful for curved lines, although narrow tape can be bent to mark slight curves.

What to Look For:

• Narrow masking tape is readily available at quilt shops.

• Visit your local hardware store for painter's tape, available in a variety of widths.

• Drafting tape can be found at art-supply stores.

Don't Get Stuck

Avoid using tape that's fresh off the roll because that's when it is at its stickiest and is more likely to leave a residue. Peel a length of tape off the roll, press it onto a scrap fabric two or three times to remove excess glue, then use it on your quilt top. It will still be plenty sticky, but you won't be stuck having to remove bits of tape residue.

While it pays to take some of the stickiness off a fresh piece of tape before using it to mark your quilt top, it also pays to buy a fresh roll of tape before beginning a project. Don't try to make do with old tape because it tends to get stickier with age.

Hera Marker

This Japanese tool scores a crisp crease in fabric when pulled across it. Just position the quilt top or basted layers on a hard surface and pull the hera toward you to mark a design.

Pros: The creases remain visible for a fairly long period of time, but in general, the less handling the quilt receives during quilting, the longer the lines will remain. Creases barely show when quilting is completed, since the quilting stitch itself makes an indentation in the fabric where the crease is. However, to remove an unwanted mark, spray it with a fine mist of water. Designs marked with a hera are equally well suited to hand or machine quilting.

Cons: Some quilters find it difficult to see the creases on darker fabrics, so experiment with your fabric before marking your entire quilt. While a hera works great for drawing straight lines along a

ruler edge or for freehand design marking, it is not as easy to use with a purchased quilting stencil.

What to Look For: Hera markers are packaged specifically for quilt marking, so look for one at your local quilt shop or from a quilt mail-order source.

You may find that hera creases are easier to see when you crease your fabric after the layers have been basted together. The added loft of the batting lets the hera sink in more, which emphasizes the creases.

Tear-Away Quilting Designs

Preprinted quilting designs are available on opaque paper in assorted styles and sizes to fit a variety of quilt blocks. Pin in place on the basted quilt for machine quilting. After quilting on the lines, tear the paper away, as shown.

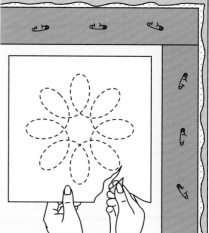

Pros: Tear-away designs are handy for machine quilting, and they come in a variety of patterns and sizes, including designs for 8-, 10-, and 12-inch setting squares and borders.

Cons: Designs are not suitable for hand quilting. Since paper is opaque, accurate placement is not as easy as with transparent designs or quilting stencils.

What to Look For:
• Blank tear-away papers are available for making your own designs.
• You can make your own tear-away sheets by tracing designs onto transparent tracing paper.

For large tear-away quilting designs, purchase large sheets or rolls of tracing paper from an office-supply store.

Freezer Paper

Grocery-store variety freezer paper can be used for drawing or tracing quilting designs. Draw on the dull, or nonplastic, side of freezer paper and cut out your designs using craft scissors or an X-Acto knife. Press the plastic-coated side to the quilt top, quilt around the shapes, then peel off the paper and use it again. If you prefer, you can trace lightly around the freezer paper and remove it before quilting.

Pros: Shapes are not only easy to use but they are also reusable. This type of quilting pattern works well for filling in designs in setting squares and triangles, and the design won't rub off or smudge as traditional pencil or chalk markings can.

Freezer paper is relatively inexpensive, too, and is a great product to keep on hand for other quilt-making uses. This method can be used in conjunction with purchased quilting stencils. Simply trace

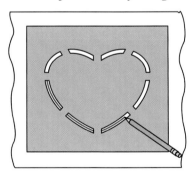

the stencil onto the freezer paper, as shown, then use the freezer paper so you don't have pencil or chalk markings on your quilt top.

Cons: If you have a large quilt in which the same motif will be repeated over and over again, you may have to make more than one of a design since the coating will eventually wear off. Freezer paper is not especially suitable for machine quilting, since rolling and unrolling a quilt can make the paper crease and peel off.

What to Look For:
• Freezer paper is usually found in either the frozen food aisle or the plastic wrap section in grocery stores.
• Gridded freezer paper is sold at many quilt shops and mail-order sources, and this type can be helpful for enlarging or reducing designs.

TRANSFERRING QUILTING DESIGNS

Unless you are using masking tape or a tear-away quilting design that is pinned to the quilt top, you'll have to transfer your quilting design onto your quilt. Here are a few pointers:

Light Fabrics

A light box will help you when transferring quilting designs from a pattern onto your fabric or template material. However, the light source method works best when the fabric you're transferring to is fairly light in color. Economical, lap-size light boxes are sold at quilt shops, but you can improvise by setting a light underneath a glass table. Place the pattern on the glass, followed by your fabric or template material, and trace. If the light is too bright in one area, diffuse it by placing a sheet of paper underneath your pattern.

You can improvise by using a window to trace patterns onto template material, provided your original pattern isn't located in the middle of a thick book!

Dark Fabrics

Stencils are another popular tool for transferring quilting motifs onto fabric. Stencils work well for any type of fabric, but they are definitely the best way to trace a design onto dark fabrics. An endless selection of prepunched designs are available at quilt shops. To make your own, you can purchase a fine-tip burner that resembles a soldering iron, made especially to melt away template plastic. Or try a double-blade X-Acto knife for cutting tracing spaces in template plastic. Stencils can then be used with a marking pencil, chalk pouncer, or tailor's chalk.

THERE'S MORE THAN ONE WAY TO BASTE A QUILT

There's no single way to baste the quilt layers together, and your decision on which method to use will likely depend upon what quilting method you'll be using. A variety of methods are explained here, along with situations when it's best to use them—or *not* use them.

Before you get ready to baste, however, you need to get your quilt backing ready. Often that means stitching together two or more lengths of fabric to make a piece wide enough for the quilt. So let's start with making the backing.

If you're making a large quilt but don't want a pieced backing, a 100 percent cotton sheet could be the answer, but only if you're machine quilting. Sheets are too tightly woven for hand quilting.

MAKING THE QUILT BACKING

Unless you are making a wallhanging or crib quilt that measures less than 42 inches wide, you will probably have to piece your quilt backing.

Step 1. To determine how much backing fabric you'll need, measure your quilt top (length and width), and add 4 inches to each measurement. Assuming you will get 42 usable inches of fabric across one fabric width, divide the width of your quilt by 42. The result is the number of fabric widths you'll need.

For instance, if your quilt top is 88 inches wide, you'll need three fabric widths (88 + 4 = 92; 92 ÷ 42 = 2.18, which is more than two widths). Although two widths in this example would *almost* be wide enough for a quilt backing, you need to take into consideration that you will have seam allowances, plus you will need extra fabric around all sides of the quilt. This extra fabric is a safeguard so that you don't run short on backing fabric as the fabric is taken up in the quilting process.

Step 2. Multiply the number of fabric widths you need (three in this example) by the adjusted length of your quilt. So, if your quilt is 96 inches long, you will need 8⅓ yards of backing fabric (96 + 4 = 100; 100 × 3 lengths = 300 inches; 300 ÷ 36 inches per yard = 8.33 yards).

Step 3. Cut the backing into three equal pieces; each piece in this example should be about 100 inches, or just less than 3 yards. Cut the selvages from each piece. Then sew the three pieces together, side by side, as shown. Use a ¼-inch seam allowance. Press the seams open or to one side, as desired.

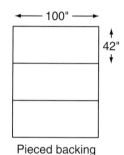

Pieced backing

CHOOSING BATTING

There are so many batting choices available to quilters today that deciding on the right one for your project can be tricky. Polyester, cotton, and wool batts are all readily available, and most come in a variety of *lofts* (the thickness of the batt, which can range from about ⅛ to ¾ inch).

Choose your batting based on the answer to these two questions: Will you be quilting by hand or machine? What type of look do you want your finished project to have? For instance, do you want it very flat, so all of your stitches show; slightly fluffy, for that rumpled antique look; or very full, as in a tied comforter?

Many cotton battings can be dried in a clothes dryer, but don't agitate them in the washing machine, or you'll have nothing left but shreds.

Antique Look with Batting

If you want an antique heirloom look in your next project but don't want to wait 50 years or so to get it, use a cotton batting and machine quilting. Don't prewash the batting. After quilting and binding, wash your quilt and dry it in the dryer. The cotton batting will shrink, giving your quilt that lovingly used look.

Fiber Content

For quite a while, polyester batts have been the choice of many quilters simply because they are available at quilt shops and craft stores everywhere, they don't have to be closely quilted to hold their shape, and they are easy to launder.

Now, new and improved cotton batts, as well as wool batts, are more readily available, and lots of quilters love them because they can produce a finished look much like quilts of yore. If you choose cotton or wool, carefully read prewashing instructions before using (some don't have to be prewashed) and check to see if the batt you chose needs to be quilted as closely as every 2 inches or if you can quilt your designs farther apart.

Loft

The choices for loft are many, ranging from low loft to high loft to extra loft. Choose a loft based not only on the finished look you want to achieve but also on the quilting technique you'll be using.

For example, if you want a big puffy quilt and choose extra loft, be aware that the batting will be harder to hand quilt than a lower-loft type. For extra loft, tying or knotting may be a better finishing technique to use.

A lightweight batting is easiest to machine quilt. Some quilters prefer cotton battings for machine quilting because the cotton fibers tend to hug the quilt top and backing, helping to prevent the layers from shifting as you move the quilt about.

Experiment with different types of batting so you can make your choice based on the look and feel you want for a particular project. If you are using cotton batting, however, it's important to follow the package instructions for preshrinking it and for how closely it needs to be quilted.

Some quilt shops sell batting sample squares that are large enough to make a pillow top. Buy different varieties for sample machine-quilting sandwiches.

No Creases, Please

If you are using packaged batting, chances are there will be creases in it when you open it. Unfold or unroll the backing at least 24 hours before you plan to use it to let it "breathe" and uncrease. Or toss it in your dryer on the no-heat setting for a few minutes to fluff out the creases.

CLASSIC HAND BASTING

Traditional hand basting with a needle and thread works well for hand quilting. The thread holds the layers together snugly, and it's not difficult to remove even if quilted over. If you plan to quilt on a floor frame, however, you may not need to baste. Check your frame's directions for basting instructions.

Step 1. Cut or piece together a backing that is approximately 3 to 4 inches larger on all sides than your quilt top. (See "Making the Quilt Backing" on page 104) Press the backing to remove wrinkles, and press the seams as desired. Cut a piece of batting the same size as or just slightly smaller than the backing.

Step 2. Place the backing wrong side up on the floor or another large, flat surface, such as a table, and center the batting on top of it. Smooth out any wrinkles in the batting. Position the quilt top right side up on top of the batting, checking all sides of the quilt to make sure it is centered on the first two layers. Pin to secure the layers.

You may find it helpful to tape your backing fabric to the floor or table (or pin it to the carpet with T-pins) to keep everything stable and in place as you baste.

Step 3. Thread a needle with a long strand of white thread and tie a knot at the end of it. Beginning at the center and working out toward each edge, or starting at one edge and working toward the opposite edge, baste the layers of the quilt with a simple running stitch of about 2 inches on top of the quilt and ½ inch underneath. Create a grid of vertical and horizontal basting lines on the quilt, approximately 6 inches apart, as shown.

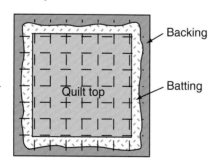

Backing

Batting

Quilt top

Be flexible when basting your grid. If possible, avoid basting through seams or across areas that you plan to quilt. Your basting lines do not have to be perfectly straight.

Relief for Sore Fingers

If basting a large quilt gets to your fingertips, try basting with a long, thin needle, such as a size 7 darning or sharp, or use a curved needle made especially for tying and basting quilts.

TAILOR BASTING

This hand-basting technique borrows a trick from another type of sewing. The stitches are a little more secure than those in regular running stitch basting, yet they are quick to make.

Step 1. Prepare the quilt for basting, as explained in Steps 1 and 2 of "Classic Hand Basting."

Step 2. Thread a needle with a long strand of white thread and tie a knot at the end of it. Insert your needle down through the layers from the top of the quilt. Take a horizontal stitch across the back, bringing the needle up through the layers approximately ½ inch from where it was inserted.

Step 3. Take a diagonal stitch on the top side of the quilt, reinserting the needle through the layers approximately 1½ inches below the spot where the first stitch was made (under the knot). Take another horizontal stitch in the back of the quilt, bring the needle to the front, and repeat the diagonal stitch. Keep stitching in the same manner until you have basted a grid of diagonal stitches across the top of the quilt, as shown.

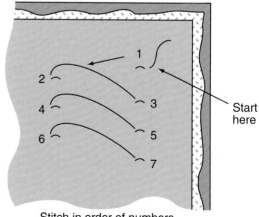

Start here

Stitch in order of numbers

PIN BASTING

Although pin basting can be used for hand quilting, it is the method of choice for machine quilting. Pins can be removed or simply moved aside as you near them while machine quilting. Thread basting, on the other hand, tends to be difficult to remove after it has been stitched over by machine, and it can get caught in the toe of your presser foot.

you know will be quilted. If your quilt will be handled a lot, be sure to close the pins. For smaller projects, you can leave the pins open to save time.

As a general rule, a fist placed knuckles down on any part of the quilt should be touching at least one pin. If your fist doesn't touch a pin, add more pins to securely hold the layers together.

Keep Those Dry Cleaner Pins

Ask your friends to save the safety pins they receive with their dry cleaning. These rustproof pins will help you build your basting pin collection quickly—and economically.

Step 1. To minimize the folding and puckering that sometimes occurs on the back of a quilt as it moves through the machine, the backing should be stretched smooth and taut before the other layers are placed on top of it. If you are working on a smooth floor, stretching can be accomplished by securing the backing to the floor with strips of masking or electrical tape.

When working on a table, large binder clips purchased at an office-supply store can be used to clip the backing to the edges of the table. If the table is not as large as the quilt, position the center of the backing at the center of the table and use the clips to hold it securely in place. Next, center the batting and quilt on top of the backing. Baste the section of the quilt that is on the table, then shift the layers around to finish basting, securing the backing to the table edges on the unbasted sides after each shift. The weight of the pins will help stretch the other sides.

Step 2. Use #0 or #1 nickel-plated (rust-resistant) safety pins to pin the layers together. Beginning at the center and working toward the quilt's corners, insert pins approximately 3 inches apart. Position the pins a little to either side of areas

Save Your Fingers

A typical double-bed quilt may require 300 or more safety pins for basting. To help eliminate the sore fingers that result from opening and closing so many pins, use the serrated tip of a grapefruit spoon to press the shaft closed, or purchase one of the quilting aids made especially for that purpose. If you plan to do quite a lot of pin basting, you might consider investing in special safety pin grip covers, which make the pins easier and more comfortable to handle.

Another trick is to simply leave the pins open after you remove them. You'll save the steps of closing them for storage and reopening them again to use them.

BLUE RIBBON TECHNIQUE

BASTING GUNS

Basting guns are similar to the tool used in department stores to attach price tags to clothing with nylon "threads." Instead of attaching tags, quilters can use a specially designed basting gun to insert short plastic tacks through all layers of a quilt to hold them together securely. This "basting" method is suitable for both hand and machine quilting.

QuiltTak was the first basting gun model on the market, but other brands are available now, too. These guns resemble glue guns, but a built-in needle replaces the heating element. When the needle is inserted through all quilt layers and the trigger is pulled, one end of a plastic tack travels through an opening in the needle and emerges on the back side of the quilt. The other end of the tack remains on the front to hold the layers together, as shown.

you pull the trigger, the layers will be held together as before, but both ends of the tack will be on the front of the quilt, as shown.

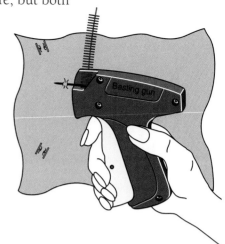

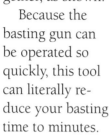

Because the basting gun can be operated so quickly, this tool can literally reduce your basting time to minutes.

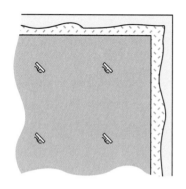

The plastic tacks can remain in your quilt until it is completely quilted. However, if one is in the way of your quilting, merely snip the end and remove it. Just be careful not to snip your quilt!

Some quilters prefer to have both ends of the plastic tack on the top side of the quilt, as this holds the quilt layers together even more snugly. Insert the needle through all layers, then insert it back through all layers to the quilt front. When

Look, No Holes!

If you fear that pins or a basting gun will leave unwanted holes in your quilt, make sure your pins are #0 or #1 weight. Or, choose a basting gun with a fine tip. Even so, the point where the pin of the gun tip enters the quilt will spread the fibers apart to let the metal enter the quilt. When a pin or the gun tip is removed, simply brush over the area with your fingernail to return all fabric threads to their original locations.

CLASSIC HAND QUILTING

At its simplest, the stitch used for hand quilting is nothing more than a running stitch that travels through all layers of the quilt to hold them together. At its best, the patterns formed by these simple stitches enhance the quilt top, adding dimension and design that make the quilt truly spectacular.

HAND-QUILTING SUPPLIES

Using the right supplies will set you on your way to perfecting your quilting stitch.

Needles

Short needles, called *betweens,* are used for hand quilting. Betweens are numbered according to size; the larger the number, the smaller the needle. It's true that smaller needles will help you produce smaller stitches, but if you're just starting out, it's easier to get the feel of the quilting stitch by using a larger needle that is easier to handle. Be aware that needles vary from manufacturer to manufacturer, so try a few brands to find out which ones work best for you.

Purchase a package of betweens that contains an assortment of sizes to see which size is easiest for you to handle. As you gain experience, you can shorten the length of your stitches simply by switching to a smaller needle.

Threads

Quilting thread is an absolute must for hand quilting. This thread is stronger than regular hand-sewing thread, which is important since your stitches have to withstand a lot of wear and tear over the years. Quilting thread is available in cotton or cotton-covered polyester. Pure, 100 percent cotton thread is preferred by many quilters, especially if they've used 100 percent cotton fabrics and batting in their quilt. The cotton won't wear away at your quilt fibers as polyester tends to do over time, but it does tend to tangle more easily than polyester. Quilting thread comes in an array of colors, so you can use matching or contrasting thread, depending on your desired look.

If your quilting thread tangles, try running it over a block of beeswax. The slight coating helps prevent knots.

Thimbles

A good thimble is a must for hand quilting. It protects your finger from the top of the very fine quilting needles, and it gives you the leverage needed to push a tiny needle through the three quilt layers. There are so many types of thimbles available that it may take several tries before you find the one you like best. Ask your quilting friends what they prefer, or ask for recommendations at your local quilt shop. In general, here's what to look for:

Fit: Choose a thimble that fits on the middle finger of whichever hand you quilt with. It should fit comfortably—not so loose that it can twirl around, but not so tight that it's uncomfortable.

Band-Aid to the Rescue

If your thimble fits fine in the warmer months but tends to spin on your fingertip when the temperatures drop, try this trick. Instead of buying two different size thimbles, simply wrap an adhesive bandage around your quilting finger before slipping your thimble on in cold weather. The bandage will fill up the gap and grip the thimble to your finger.

Style: Quilting thimbles come in metal or leather and with an open or closed top. If you are not used to wearing or using a thimble, a leather one can break you in gently to the idea. Look for one with a metal tip inside, though, or the continual pricking of the leather will wear it down, and you'll soon be feeling the needle right through your thimble.

If you choose an open-top thimble (which gives you room for your fingernail), be sure to look for one with a lipped edge so the needle can't slip up under your nail.

Cost: Thimbles come in all price ranges, too. That's not to say that inexpensive ones can't do the job. Usually, the more expensive thimbles last longer, but if you find a less expensive one that fits good and works for you, use it and replace it as needed.

Try Hand Quilting

To practice hand quilting, whether you are new to it or you simply want to improve your stitch, baste together a *quilt sandwich* (two layers of muslin with a layer of batting in the middle) for practice. Make sure your quilt sandwich is large enough to fit in your quilt hoop. If you want, trace one of the quilting patterns on pages 119 to 120 onto the top of your sandwich, or simply quilt in a free-form style.

Step 1. Place your basted quilt top in a quilting hoop to hold it securely but not too taut. You will need a little bit of ease so you can rock your needle back and forth. If your quilt is pulled too tightly in its hoop, you will have a hard time making small, evenly spaced stitches.

After your quilt is in the hoop, but before you tighten the screw, thump your fist in the center of the quilt to give it just enough slack for easy quilting. Then tighten the hoop screw.

Step 2. Thread a between with approximately 24 inches of quilting thread, and tie a knot at one end. Bury the knot by inserting the needle into the quilt top and layer of batting about 1 inch away from the starting point, as shown in **A.** Tug gently

on the thread to pop the knot through the quilt top, burying it inside the layer of batting, as shown in **B.**

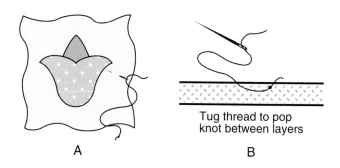

Tug thread to pop
knot between layers

A   B

Step 3. Hold your stitching hand on top of the quilt and your other hand beneath the quilt so you will be able to feel the needle. Use the thimble to hold the needle perpendicular to the top of the quilt, and insert it completely through all three layers, stopping just as you feel the tip of the needle hit your finger underneath. Use the underneath finger to guide the tip of the needle back up through the quilt, just until the tip of your thumb (or your thumbnail) feels the needle reemerging. Use the thimble finger to direct the needle where you want it to reenter the quilt, and push down on the top of the needle. As you do this, use the thumb of the hand on top of the quilt to push down the area that lies just in front of where the needle will emerge. Repeat, making one stitch at a time.

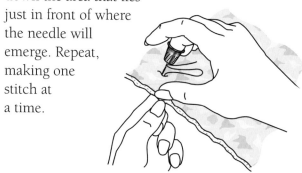

Step 4. When you are comfortable with the rocking motion of the needle, try loading the needle with two or three evenly spaced stitches before pulling the thread

through the layers, as shown. Gradually increase the number of stitches on the needle. Check periodically to be sure your stitches are even on the front and back of the quilt.

A few layers of masking tape on the under-neath finger that will do the guiding will be thin enough to allow you to sense the emerging needle but thick enough to protect your finger from repeated punctures.

Step 5. To end a line of quilting, bring the needle to the top of the quilt, just past the last stitch. Make a knot at the surface of the fabric by bringing the needle under the thread where it comes out of the fabric and up through the loop of the thread it creates, as shown.

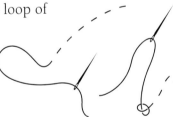

Consistency Is Key

Almost every beginning quilter worries that her stitches are too big and yearns for the secret to making them smaller. The answer is to strive for *even,* consistently spaced stitches; don't worry too much about their length. Your stitches will become smaller as you gain more experience.

Step 6. Repeat the knot and insert the needle into the hole where the thread came out of the surface. Run the needle inside the batting layer for about 1 inch and bring it back to the surface. Tug gently on the thread, and the knot will pop through to the layer of batting. Carefully clip the thread close to the top surface of the quilt.

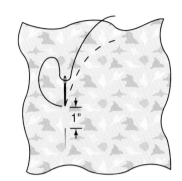

Look for a Demo

It's often easiest to improve your stitch by watching someone who is more experienced than yourself and see what techniques they use to make small, even stitches. Most quilt guild shows include demonstrations, and at many shows, a quilting frame is set up and continuously staffed by guild members. So call your local quilt guild and plan to visit the next quilt show—to see the wonderful quilts *and* to improve your quilting stitch.

QUICKER HAND QUILTING

For speedier hand quilting, you can use pearl cotton (#3 weight) or another sturdy thread in a crewel needle size (5 to 7) to quilt simple, allover designs on your quilt. Make running stitches of approximately five stitches per inch. As an alternative, do freehand quilting around the shapes in your quilt.

While this technique isn't suitable for all types of quilts, it's a fast and fun way to add a folk art look to some of your projects. And your quilting will be finished in half the time.

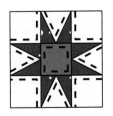

Quick Knot

Tie a quick quilter's knot at one end of your length of thread by holding the threaded needle and one end of the thread against the forefinger of your right hand. Wind the thread around the needle twice, then pull it down the length of the needle, keeping it between your thumb and forefinger. Work the wound portion down the entire length of the thread, so that when you reach the end, you'll have a tiny knot at the very end. Trim away the excess tail.

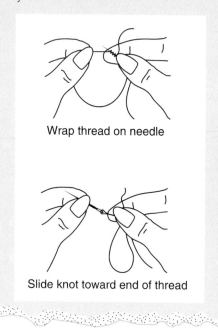

Wrap thread on needle

Slide knot toward end of thread

TYING A QUILT

Tying, or knotting, results in a puffy, cloudlike comforter. The look can be exaggerated by using a very thick, extra loft batting. If you can't find a batting as thick as you'd like, layer two medium-loft batts together. Tying is easy to do, so it's a great way for a youngster to finish her first patchwork project. And it's a quick alternative to hand quilting.

Ties can be plain or decorative to suit the look of your quilt. Be sure to read batting labels before you start to tie. Polyester batting is probably your best bet for tying, since some cotton battings need to be closely quilted to prevent them from shifting.

Tying How-To

Step 1. Select a durable tying thread that complements your quilt. Pearl cotton (#5 weight), embroidery floss (as many strands as you like), yarn, and ⅛-inch-wide ribbon are a few options. The thread should be strong enough to withstand tugging, flexible enough to knot easily, and thin enough to pass through the three layers of the quilt. If the quilt will be washed, make sure the tie material you choose is washable, too. In fact, prewashing pearl cotton and floss in vinegar water to set the color is a good idea.

Step 2. Layer the quilt as instructed in Steps 1 and 2 of "Classic Hand Basting" on page 106. Use straight pins to mark and hold the layers together at each place that will be tied.

Step 3. Thread a crewel needle, or curved needle made especially for tying, with approximately 30 inches of thread. Do *not* knot the end. Take a ⅛- to ¼-inch stitch at the first pin, pulling the thread through the layers of the quilt, as shown in **A**, until you have about a 3-inch tail. Leave the needle threaded and tie the ends securely in a square knot, right over left, then left over right, as shown in **B**. Trim the tails evenly. Repeat until all ties are completed.

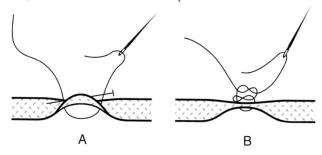

A   B

More Tying Options

• Instead of using knots, tie bows on the front of the quilt.

• For less visible ties, tie the knots on the back of the quilt.

• Use ties to enhance only specific portions of a quilt. For example, ties make great cat whiskers and butterfly antennae.

• Thread the ties through plain or decorative buttons.

• For more visible ties, tie the knot over additional strands of decorative threads or ribbons.

QUILTING AND EMBELLISHING BY MACHINE

Quilting by machine has opened up a whole new arena for quiltmakers. Machine quilting can be faster than hand quilting, thus many quiltmakers have turned to their machines because it lets them complete projects instead of having a growing pile of unquilted tops.

But machine quilting can be much more than a quick way to finish a quilt. Wonderful decorative threads—from sparkling metallics to vibrant rayons to variegated couching threads—let you add designs and embellishments beyond your wildest dreams. This section will provide you with the basic tools and supplies you need for machine quilting, how-to directions for machine-guided and free-motion quilting, and some ideas for incorporating machine quilting and embellishing into your projects.

MACHINE QUILTING SUPPLIES

Threads for Machine Quilting

When choosing thread, keep in mind that the designs will be outlined with a continuous line of stitches, rather than with the separated stitches that result from hand quilting, so a heavy or contrasting thread will be very visible on the front of the quilt. Your thread choice will be dependent on the look you want to achieve and can be plain cotton, transparent nylon, or a decorative metallic. For areas that will be heavily quilted, choose a lightweight thread. For quilting that is farther apart or for children's quilts, a heavier, more durable thread would be suitable.

Consider the longevity of the project and how it will be used when you choose thread. If you are working on a 100 percent cotton quilt that you consider to be an heirloom, choose a 100 percent cotton quilting thread. Because it is more rigid, thread containing polyester may, with time and use, cut through the fibers of your cotton quilt.

Many thread companies label the thread size on the spool. The first number is the weight, and the second number is the number of strands that make up the thread. For example, 50/3 indicates the thread weight (50) and the number of strands (3). As the weight designations increase, threads actually become lighter.

If you prefer not to see the quilting thread at all, choose size 0.004 monofilament, available in clear or smoke. Use clear for quilting on light fabrics and smoke for quilting on dark fabrics.

Cotton thread should be used in the bobbin, even if you use monofilament or metallic thread in the needle. Choose a lightweight thread for the bobbin, such as those sold for use in the bobbin when making lingerie. Experiment to see which thread combinations work best for you and your machine, but in general, the bobbin thread should not be heavier than the needle thread.

For details on specific types and brands of threads, see "Quilting and Decorative Threads" on page 114.

Needles

Refer to your sewing machine owner's manual to see if a specific needle is recommended for machine quilting. In general, a size 80/12 is a good all-purpose choice. Refer to "Quilting and Decorative Threads" on page 114 for information on needle size as related to specific thread choices.

For smooth quilting, always insert a new sewing machine needle at the beginning of a new machine-quilting project.

Specialty Feet

While you can do straight stitch machine quilting with a regular presser foot, a walking foot makes the process much easier, and the results you achieve will be more professional looking. For free-motion quilting, an embroidery, or darning, foot is needed.

Walking foot: Also called an even-feed foot, this specialty foot helps the top layer of your quilt feed through the machine evenly with the bottom

Quilting and Decorative Threads

Thread Type	Used For	Appearance	Suggested Needle Size
Bobbinfil #70 (Madeira; strong, lightweight polyester)	Use in bobbin for machine embroidery or when quilting with lightweight thread	White, so it is visible on back side of project	As required for top thread
Clear or smoke monofilament	Machine quilting and invisible machine appliqué (size 0.004)	Invisible on the finished piece	Machine, 70/10 or 80/12; machine quilting, 75/11
DMC 50 (lightweight [100/2] cotton)	Machine embroidery and quilting	Provides a delicate appearance when heavy quilting is done	Machine, 70/10 or 80/12; machine quilting, 75/11
Embroidery floss	Outline stitching, hand appliqué, and hand decorative stitching	Delicate or bold, depending on the number of strands used	Crewel, sizes 5–7
Madeira Super Twist	Machine embroidery and appliqué	A blend of two threads gives a textured, sparkle effect	Large-eyed machine, 90/14
Metallics (Sulky)	Machine embroidery, appliqué, quilting, and couching	Adds a metallic sparkle to machine stitching	Machine, 80/12 or 90/14 topstitch
Mettler Machine Embroidery (lightweight [60/2] cotton)	Primarily machine embroidery, but also used for quilting	Soft look for machine embroidery; even more delicate appearance in machine quilting	Machine, 70/10 or 80/12; machine quilting, 75/11
100% rayon machine embroidery (Sulky, Madeira)	Machine appliqué and embroidery	Adds luster to machine stitching	Machine, 80/12 or 90/14 topstitch
Pearl cotton #30	Hand quilting and tying; works well for big, folk art style stitches	Country, folk art look	Crewel, sizes 5–7
Stream Lamé or Sulky Sliver (flat, shiny, ribbonlike thread)	Use for machine embroidery and couching	Adds sparkle to your machine embroidery or machine quilting; more delicate appearance when used to quilt	Machine, 80/12 or 90/14 topstitch
YLI Lingerie & Bobbin Thread (nylon)	Use in bobbin for machine embroidery or when quilting with lightweight thread	White or black, so it is visible on back side of project	As required for top thread

layer. The machine has feed dogs that normally pull the fabric along through the machine. But since a quilt has several layers, the top ones don't benefit from the feed dog action, and your quilt layers can shift. The walking foot works in much the same way as the feed dogs, pulling

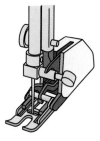

Walking foot

the top layer through your machine. This foot works best for straight-line or slightly curved quilting.

Embroidery foot: Also called a darning foot, this type of presser foot is usually a standard piece of equipment that comes with the sewing machine. It can be metal or plastic, and the bottom of the foot is an open circle that lets you view the sewing area, as shown on the opposite page. An embroidery foot has a spring action, so it can bounce along the top of your quilt, allowing you to move your quilt around. This foot, combined with lowered feed dogs, enables you to do free-motion quilting, such as stipple or meander quilting. (See pages 116 to 117 for how-to directions for these types of quilting.)

Embroidery foot

(See pages 116 to 117 for how-to directions for these types of quilting.)

End the Size Confusion

The size and weight designations for sewing notions can undoubtedly be confusing. Here's a list of typical notions and how they are sized:

• Hand needles: Size of needle decreases as the numerical designation increases.
• Machine needles: Size of needle increases as the numerical designation increases.
• Safety pins: Size of pin increases as the numerical designation increases.
• Thread: Weight decreases as the numerical designation increases.

MACHINE-GUIDED QUILTING

This method of quilting is used for in-the-ditch and other straight-line quilting, such as outline quilting and quilting traced patterns that are straight or only slightly curved. Best results are achieved by using a walking, or even-feed, foot. The action of the walking foot combined with the feed dogs helps eliminate tucking that could take place on the underside of the quilt. The walking foot allows you to pivot and turn wide curves, but it is not meant to stitch around sharply curved designs.

Many sewing machine manufacturers offer a walking foot made especially for their machines. Generic versions are also available from sewing machine dealers and some quilt shops. Generic models come in high-, low-, and slant-shank models, so refer to your sewing machine owner's manual before purchasing one.

Practice Pays

Before you begin machine quilting your actual project, practice machine quilting with your desired thread on small quilt sandwiches assembled with the same materials used in your quilt.

Try Machine-Guided Quilting

Step 1. Mark straight quilting lines on a muslin sandwich or piece a simple block, such as a Nine Patch, to practice in-the-ditch stitching. Prepare the practice quilt for machine quilting using the pin-basting method on page 107. Install a new needle in your sewing machine, and insert the correct top and bobbin threads.

Step 2. Attach the walking foot to your machine as instructed by the manufacturer.

Step 3. Take one stitch through all layers, and pull the bobbin thread up onto the top of the quilt, as shown. Insert the needle back into the hole where the bobbin thread comes up. Instead of making a knot, adjust your stitch length and take six to eight very small stitches—use the smallest stitches you can take with the machine still advancing the quilt. Hold the loose threads out of the way as you sew. Gradually return to a longer stitch length of approximately 10 stitches per inch.

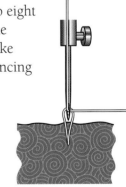
Tug top thread to pull up bobbin loop

If you are using a fairly thick batting, try a little bit longer stitch to account for the loft of the batt.

Step 4. Machine quilt on the marked lines. For a pieced block, stitch as close as possible on the low side of the seam line. Avoid stitching into the high side (the side where the seam allowances are pressed).

Step 5. Continue sewing, stopping and pivoting as necessary to finish a seam. If stitching must pass over a pin, remove it as you come to it. When you near the end of a seam, take six to eight tiny stitches as you did in the beginning to lock the stitching in place. Clip the threads and begin a new line of quilting.

Anchor Your Blocks

Anchor the quilt layers by first stitching a grid, which can consist of a vertical and horizontal seam or an allover set of lines, such as those shown in the diagram. Then go back and complete the quilting lines within the grid. This method will prevent your layers from shifting before you get to the more intricate quilting designs.

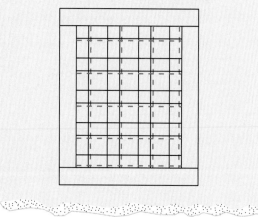

FREE-MOTION QUILTING

Free-motion quilting is done with the feed dogs lowered, which means that your sewing machine cannot advance the quilt—you have to do the work. You control the stitch length and direction by where and how quickly you move the quilt as the needle moves up and down. Although it takes some practice to coordinate your hand and foot speeds, in time you'll master this skill. Because you can move your quilt in any direction, you have lots of freedom in creating quilting designs.

Continuous quilting designs are perfect for free-motion quilting, as shown, because they allow you to quilt longer before you have to stop, tie off threads, and begin a new line of stitching at another point in the design.

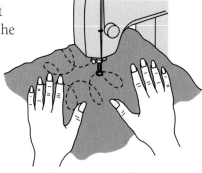

Free-motion quilting

Free-motion quilting is also great for *stipple* quilting and *meander* quilting, as described on the opposite page.

For any type of free-motion quilting, use your sewing machine's darning foot. If you don't have a darning foot, Big Foot, a large, clear plastic darning foot, is available at many quilt shops, with models that fit most types of machines.

Free-motion quilting requires more practice than straight-line machine quilting, but the speed at which you are able to produce intricate designs and complete your quilting projects makes it well worth the practice time and effort.

Prepare several small sample quilts and experiment with "drawing" a variety of shapes with the needle. If you keep your samples small enough (6 × 6 inches), you don't even have to baste them together.

Roll Up the Sides

When machine quilting a larger project, roll the quilt from both sides to minimize bulk, leaving an opening at the area you intend to quilt first. Reposition the quilt as necessary.

Stipple Quilting

Stipple quilting is a tightly formed pattern that resembles the shape of jigsaw puzzles, as shown. You form the design randomly, not following a traced design, by moving your quilt forward, backward, and sideways while maintaining an even speed on your machine's foot pedal.

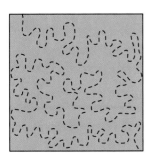

Stipple quilting

The Right Speed

While your first inclination may be to start out slowly, you will end up with very big stitches if you don't give your machine enough speed. The trick is to coordinate the speed of the machine with the speed at which you move your quilt about.

If you have a half-speed button on your sewing machine, select that option, then put your foot all the way to the floor as you stipple quilt. You'll be prevented from going too fast, yet as long as you keep the pedal to the metal, you won't be going too slow.

Try Stipple Quilting

Step 1. Prepare the quilt for machine quilting using the pin-basting method on page 107. Install a new needle in your sewing machine, and insert the correct top and bobbin threads.

Step 2. Attach a darning or freehand quilting foot to your machine. Lower the feed dogs. (Refer to your sewing machine owner's manual for instructions if necessary.)

If your feed dogs can't be lowered, cover them with two or three layers of masking tape for smooth sailing when you quilt.

Step 3. Take a stitch and pull the bobbin thread up onto the top of the quilt. Insert the needle back in the hole where the bobbin thread comes up. To lock the threads, begin sewing, but move the fabric very slowly to make several tiny stitches. Remember, you control the stitch length by your own movements, not by adjusting your machine. The faster and farther you move your quilt at a time, the bigger your stitches will be.

Step 4. Continue sewing, placing a hand on each side of the quilt, as shown on the opposite page. Move the quilt under the needle to fill in an area of quilting, such as a setting triangle. Try to look just ahead of the needle at all times to see where your stitching is headed. Find a machine speed that is comfortable for you and keep it consistent, since stops and starts can be noticeable on the finished piece. When you reach the end of a design, take several small stitches again to lock off the seam. Clip the threads close to the quilt top, or leave them long enough to thread on a needle so they can be woven between the layers.

Meander Quilting

Meander quilting is stitched freehand just as stipple quilting is done, but with one big difference. And big is the key word. Meander quilting rambles over a bigger area of the quilt top instead of forming a tightly quilted area. Meander quilting can be done over an entire quilt top without regard to the design of the pieced blocks, as shown in the diagram.

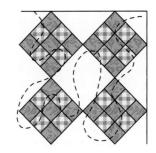

Meander quilting

Just like stipple quilting, however, you need to coordinate your machine's speed with the speed in which you move your quilt top. With a little practice, you'll find just the right mix of power and speed, just as you discovered when putting your foot on a car's gas pedal when you learned to drive.

It Pays to Plan Ahead

Whether you are stipple or meander quilting, it does pay to plan ahead. You don't want to work your stitching into an area that traps you and prevents you from continuing without having to cut your thread, as shown. Plan a starting point and an exiting point before you start to stitch. Then work around the area in the direction you have planned, and you can quilt large areas without stopping.

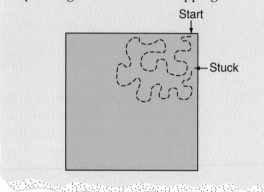

Start

Stuck

EMBELLISHING WITH SPECIALTY THREADS

Once you feel confident with the basics of machine quilting, you will open up a whole new world of possibilities for enhancing your quilts. Metallic threads, rayon threads, and invisible threads can all give your quilts unique looks, so you may want to experiment. "Quilting and Decorative Threads" on page 114 can help you get started.

Couching

Couching is one technique that adds a lot of impact, is fun to do, and is easy, too. You can add texture, color, and quilting all at the same time. Couching is simply laying down a decorative thread or yarn and attaching it to

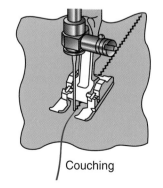

Couching

your quilt top with a zigzag stitch. Couching can be done in a straight line, as shown, or in a meandering fashion. Use your imagination and make couched cross-hatching, waves, or shapes that repeat the design in your fabric.

You can couch a single thread or yarn, twist two or more together, or even couch a strand of beads, ribbon, or other decorative trim. Depending on your desired look, you can use monofilament thread to zigzag so it doesn't show, or try one of the metallic, variegated, or rayon threads to couch for a festive finish. Before you make your final selections, remember that some trims are not machine washable, so take that into consideration if you will need to wash the finished product.

Coffee Mugs Mean No Tangles

When couching, keep the threads or yarns that you are applying in coffee mugs on your sewing table or on a TV tray at your side. The mugs are big enough to let the spools bounce around as they unwind, yet they keep the spools separate and untangled. Best of all, the mugs help to keep your hands free so you can guide your quilt.

Couch threads in the same manner you would machine quilt, starting by pulling up the bobbin thread and taking a few tiny stitches to start. When you've completed your couching pattern, leave a 3-inch tail on all threads. Use a crewel needle to weave the ends between the layers of your quilt.

Decorative Bobbin Threads

Some decorative threads are too heavy to use in the needle of your machine for quilting, but that doesn't mean you can't use them at all. If you don't want to couch them onto the surface of your quilt, wind them onto bobbins and quilt from the back.

If you use a large print fabric for the backing, you can simply quilt along the design of the backing fabric. Or try random meandering quilting, and you won't have to mark your designs.

Step 1. Since you'll want the decorative bobbin thread to show on the top side of your quilt, mark your quilting design on the wrong side of the quilt (the quilt backing). If your design needs to fit in a particular area on the quilt top, you may find it necessary to stitch the design from the top first to give you a guideline for quilting from the back.

Use either a monofilament thread that won't show under the decorative thread, or hand baste the design area. Hand basting will be removed when the machine quilting is completed.

Step 2. With your decorative thread in the bobbin and cotton thread in your needle, machine quilt following the directions for free-motion quilting on page 116 or machine-guided quilting on page 115.

Step 3. Turn your quilt over, remove any hand-basted guidelines, and admire the beautiful thread designs!

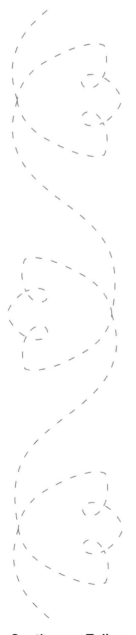

Continuous Tulips

Continuous Diamonds

Teacups or Pumpkin Seeds

Baptist Fan

part two

A QUILTER'S GUIDE TO COLOR AND FABRIC

THE
color wheel

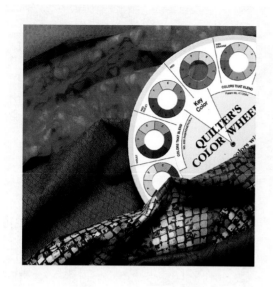

The Color Wheel

You don't have to be an artist to use basic color principles in your quiltmaking. The color wheel is a wonderful tool—it provides a colorful, visual way to learn and share a common color vocabulary. Some of the terminology that follows may be familiar to you, some may be new. But learning the lingo is the best way to be sure we are all talking about the same thing when we discuss and study color.

In this book we will study a 12-color wheel, with each color on the wheel distinct from all others. It is by varying these colors—making them darker, lighter, or combining two of them—that all other colors are formed. Once you learn a few basic principles of color, you will become more confident in selecting colors and mixing fabrics in your quilting projects.

COLOR WHEEL VOCABULARY

PURE COLORS

The 12 colors on the **The Color Wheel** are rich, vivid colors, as shown below. They are, for example, the reddest red and the greenest green possible. Quite simply, they are all the most intense versions of themselves. Therefore, they are called *pure* or *intense* colors.

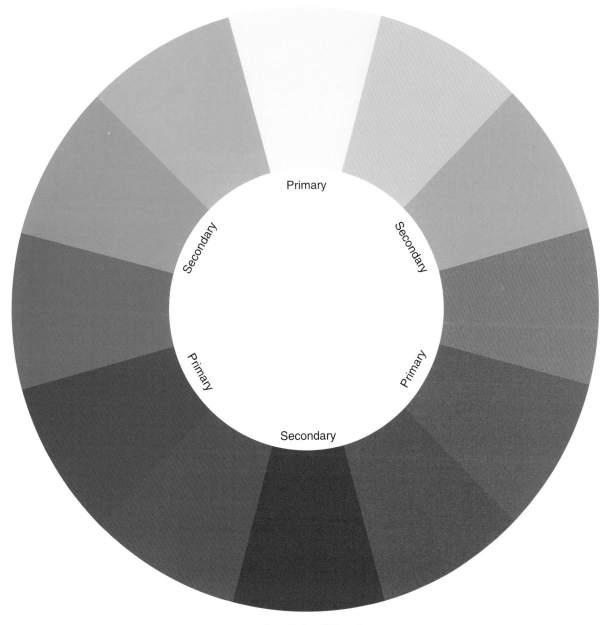

The Color Wheel

PRIMARY AND SECONDARY COLORS

The primary colors—which you probably remember from elementary school art classes—are red, blue, and yellow. They are set on the color wheel at points that are equal distances from each other, thus forming an equilateral triangle, as shown in red at right. All pure colors are derived from them.

If we were painters, we could mix the three primary colors together to make all of the other colors on the wheel, including the secondary colors, which are green (equal parts of blue and yellow),

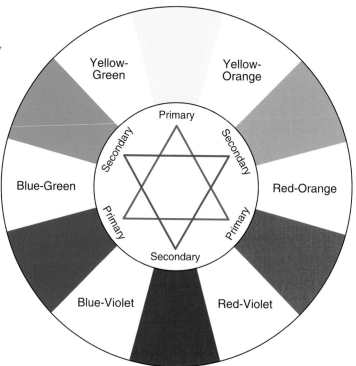

Primary and Secondary Colors

Blue and yellow make green

Red and yellow make orange

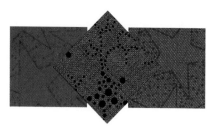

Red and blue make violet

orange (equal parts of red and yellow), and violet (equal parts of red and blue), as shown at left. Notice that the secondary colors are halfway between the primary colors and also form an equilateral triangle, shown in blue on the color wheel above. These pure colors—red, blue, yellow, orange, purple, and green—are the most powerful colors because they cause the greatest visual impact. The other six colors are formed by mixing the primary and secondary colors.

VALUE

Any color on the color wheel can be made lighter or darker, and that process is called varying the color's *value*. Values of a color that are darker than the pure color on the color wheel are called *shades*, while values that are lighter than the pure color are called *tints*.

Continuing with our painting analogy, an artist simply needs to add black paint to a pure color to make a shade of that pure color. The greater the percentage of black added, the darker the shade of the original color. For instance, if black is added to pure blue, you'll end up with a shade such as navy blue, as shown at the top of the **Blue Color Values** chart below. On the other hand, by adding white to pure blue, you'll achieve a tint such as baby blue or powder blue, as shown at the bottom of the chart.

If you hear quilters talking about how many shades of a color they used in their quilts, they're probably using the word shade to refer to how many different color *values* they used. Quilters rarely use the terms shade and tint, so to be clear we'll simply refer to light, medium, and dark values.

Make a Value Sample

Referring to the **Blue Color Values** chart for guidance and following the directions on page 128, use your own fabrics to make a sample set of values in one color. While mixing paints to create different color values is an easy process, selecting fabrics of different color values can be a bit trickier. After all, unless you are dyeing your own fabrics, your color palette is limited to the fabrics in your sewing room. Don't be discouraged if this exercise seems a bit tricky at first; the benefit of trying this technique is that you'll soon be looking at color in a whole new way! And you can always fill in the gaps in your value sample during your next visit to a quilt shop.

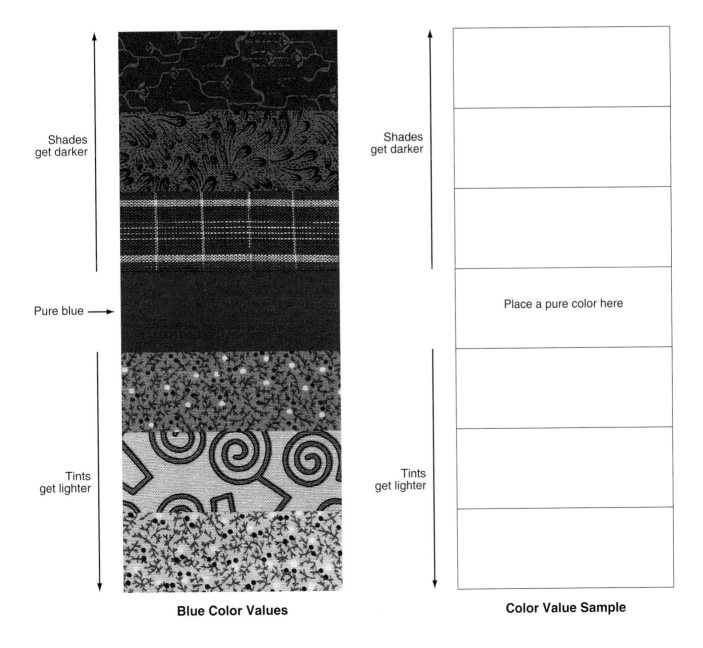

Shades get darker

Pure blue →

Tints get lighter

Blue Color Values

Shades get darker

Place a pure color here

Tints get lighter

Color Value Sample

Step 1. Pull out all the fabrics you have in the color you've chosen and spread them out in front of you. Organize them from dark to light.

If you find it difficult to tell which of two fabrics is lighter or darker, view them from across the room. This will make subtle distinctions between values easier to detect.

Step 2. Using the **Color Value Sample** chart on page 127, paste the *purest* color in the center

rectangle of the chart. Then lay out the other fabrics by value. Paste up tints below the pure color and shades above the pure color, just as in the **Blue Color Values** example.

INTENSITY

The 12 colors on the wheel can be varied in a second way, by changing their *intensity*. Remember, the colors on the wheel are described as being the most intense or purest versions of themselves. When gray is added to colors they become toned down, or duller and weaker in intensity. Therefore, a *tone* is simply a grayed version of a pure color.

Clear, bright versions of colors in several values

Grayed versions (tones) of same colors

Color Intensity

The grayness of colors is one of the hardest concepts to see, although we use it all the time. When faced with a large stack of fabrics, it is sometimes hard to see the slight differences in color intensity. Study the fabric examples in the **Color Intensity** chart on the opposite page to see how different a grayed version of a color can look from the pure color.

Make an Intensity Sample

Step 1. From your fabric stash, pull out colors for which you have many different intensities. Find as many examples of different intensities as you can. You might be surprised to find that your collection probably contains many low-intensity fabrics.

Step 2. As with the color value example, lay your fabrics on the table in front of you and separate them into groups by color.

Step 3. Within each color group, locate the purest color. Paste a swatch of each to the left column of the **Color Intensity Sample** chart below. Then find grayed or toned-down swatches of each color and paste them in the right column.

When making your samples, avoid crinkles in your paper by using a glue stick or brush-on rubber cement to paste your fabric samples. These work well even on photocopy paper, so don't be afraid to use either type of glue if you're pasting samples on copies of your book pages.

Paste clear colors here   Paste grayed versions here

Color Intensity Sample

MORE COLOR TERMS
AND COLOR SCHEMES

Once you are familiar with the basic terms used to refer to the color wheel, you can use them to plan and discuss quilts and color schemes. But first, there are a few more color terms and concepts that are important to know.

NEUTRALS

A *neutral* is actually a noncolor. Black, white, and gray are *true neutrals,* shown below, as they contain no color. Neutrals are useful in any quilt, since they act as resting places for the eyes. They also soften colors that are placed next to them, and they make good backgrounds. As you'll see,

neutrals contribute to many of the color schemes discussed later.

Quilters regularly use muslin and light beiges as neutrals, so they can be considered *quilters' neutrals,* shown below. Technically, of course, they are not neutral since they do contain some color. But because these light beiges are so close to being colorless, quilters use them all the time for backgrounds, where they act as neutrals.

The secret to keeping beiges neutral is to use light or medium values. Dark beige becomes brown, which is a very strong, dark color, not a neutral.

True Neutrals

Quilters' Neutrals

Make a Neutrals Sample

Go through your fabrics and pick out some prints, not solids, that are neutral. You're bound to have many, as most quilters incorporate neutrals into every quilt. Choose some true neutrals (black, gray, and white), as well as some quilters' neutrals (light beiges and off-whites).

Paste your fabric neutrals on the **Neutrals Sample** chart below to keep a record of all types of neutrals quilters use.

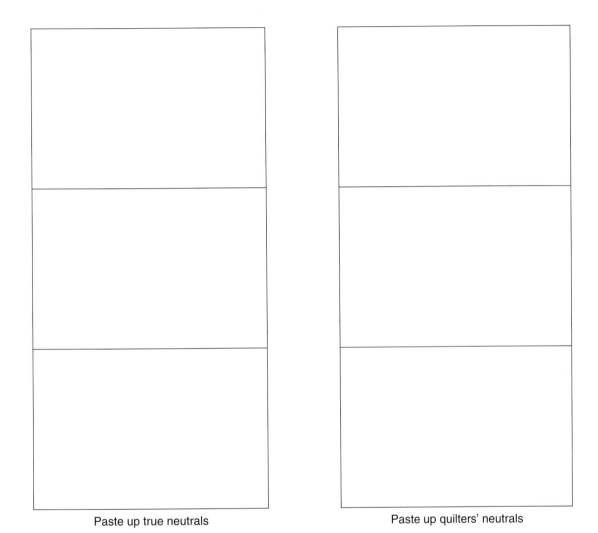

Paste up true neutrals   Paste up quilters' neutrals

Neutrals Sample

MONOCHROMATIC OR ONE-COLOR SCHEMES

Mono means one, and *chromo* means color. Together, monochromatic simply means a one-color scheme, and it's the easiest color scheme to work with. To plan a quilt with a one-color scheme, first choose only one of the 12 colors from the color wheel. If you wish, you may add any neutral background fabric, or you may simply stick to assorted values of your one color.

Monochromatic color schemes are easy to work with because there are not a lot of choices to be made. At the same time, because there isn't much variety, a monochromatic quilt can become boring if you're not careful.

If you decide to limit yourself to one color, include fabrics in many values, intensities, or tones to add variety and interest to your overall quilt design.

Monochromatic Example

The section of the **Courthouse Steps** quilt shown below is an excellent example of a monochromatic quilt. This quilt primarily uses shades of browns and quilters' neutrals, which are themselves very light shades of brown. The quiltmaker added lots of variety in the value of the brown fabrics and even more variety in the prints she selected, but it remains a one-color quilt.

As you can see, although the color scheme was limited to just one color (except for a stray purple, green, or blue print) and the quilt block itself is quite simple, the graphic impact is very dramatic in this antique quilt.

Courthouse Steps
by Ann Fryer, owned by Randolph County Historical Society, Moberly, Missouri

ANALOGOUS COLOR SCHEMES

Colors that are right next to each other on the color wheel are called *analogous* colors. The beauty of analogous colors is that they *always* coordinate or go together. Knowing about analogous colors provides every quiltmaker with a variety of useful color schemes, each guaranteed to be successful.

The reason analogous colors go together so well is that they are very similar. Choose two, three, or even four analogous colors to create your color scheme, and you will automatically have a pleasing color combination. Just take a look at the **Analogous Colors** fabric swatches on the opposite page. See how easily the colors blend together?

You can begin an analogous color scheme at any point on the color wheel. Whether you choose red, yellow, or purple as your starting point, the color you begin with plus its surrounding colors will match beautifully.

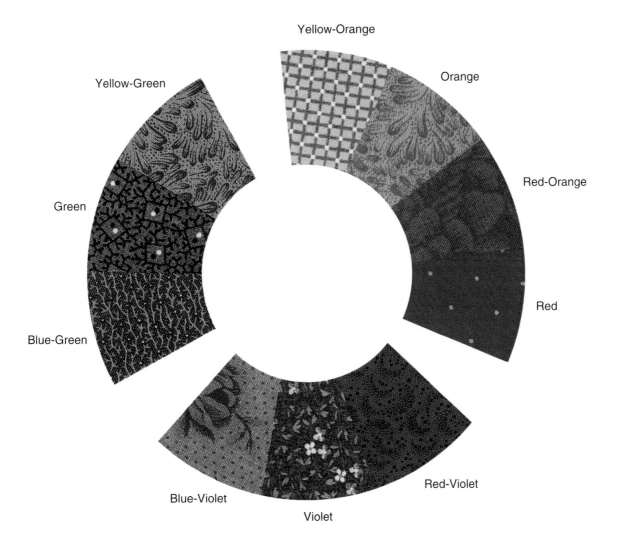

Yellow-Orange

Orange

Red-Orange

Red

Red-Violet

Violet

Blue-Violet

Blue-Green

Green

Yellow-Green

Analogous Colors

Make Analogous Color Schemes

Using the color wheel as your guide, select several sets of analogous colors and paste up your examples in the **Analogous Colors Sample** chart, shown below. You can expand the variety of fabrics by choosing fabrics of any value or intensity.

Paste up two sets of analogous colors

Analogous Colors Sample

Analogous Example

Examine the **Amish-Style Scrap Baskets** quilt shown below for a moment. Notice that it contains three analogous colors—blue, purple, and magenta—which are right next to each other at the bottom of the color wheel. Also notice that limiting colors does not necessarily mean that you have to limit the number of fabrics you use. This quilt contains many different fabrics in a variety of values. The colors are mostly grayed in intensity, and the background fabrics are grays and beiges, making a soft, peaceful quilt. The burgundy inner border and the almost royal blue background fabric found in the basket blocks stand out, as these colors are much more intense than many of the others in the quilt.

Amish-Style Scrap Baskets
pieced by Naoko Anne Ito and quilted by Betty Schoenhals

COMPLEMENTARY COLOR SCHEMES

One of the most exciting color concepts is complementary colors, because complementary colors *always* work well together. Every color on the color wheel has one and only one complement, and the two are directly opposite one another on the color wheel. Lay a ruler from the center of any color on the **Color Wheel** (shown at right) across the wheel to the color opposite it to visually study the combinations. The complementary pairs of pure colors are (beginning with yellow and moving clockwise):

yellow and purple
yellow-orange and blue-violet
orange and blue
red-orange and blue-green
red and green
red-violet and yellow-green

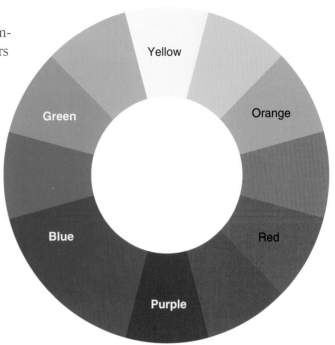

Color Wheel

Not only does every color on the color wheel have a complement, but the complementary colors physically finish each other. This means that in our eye the two complements provide opposite images that complete the color wheel. For example, red and green are complements; red is a primary color and green is made of equal parts of the other two primary colors, blue and yellow. So together, our eye sees the complete circle of the color wheel, and this provides a comfortable harmony for our eyes. Therefore, complementary colors, if used in good proportions, always make a successful color scheme for a quilt.

 If a quilt you're working on is starting to look a little less spectacular than you'd hoped, decide what the quilt's main color is, then add a dose of its complement. It can add the spark of color you need to liven up your quilt.

Treat Complements Unequally

Although complementary colors look good together, the secret to combining them is to use them in unequal amounts—a lot of one and a little of the other. Used equally, complementary contrast is too strong. Looking at a quilt in which complements are used equally is like looking at vibrant polka dots or checks. The quilt will seem to

move and vibrate since there won't be a resting place for the viewer's eyes. The **Complementary Colors** illustration below gives an idea of how complements work well together when used in different proportions and how the same color combination is stronger when the complementary colors are used in equal amounts.

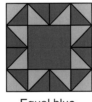 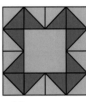 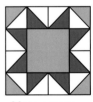

Equal blue and orange   More orange than blue   More orange than blue, plus neutral white

Complementary Colors

To get an idea of how much of each complement to use, look at the proportions of complementary colors used in some printed fabrics. You'll see that a fabric with yellow flowers on a purple background, for instance, contains a lot of purple and little touches of yellow.

Background for Complements

Complements used together are so strong that they often benefit from a neutral background. Consider the lovely red and green on white quilts we frequently see and appreciate. The white softens the two strong colors. So when you put two complements together, consider adding a neutral fabric to soften the combination and increase the impact that each color can make on the quilt. The **Red-and-Green Appliquéd Baskets Quilt** diagram below shows how striking this complementary color scheme can be, but notice how much white is used to offset the power of the solid red and green fabrics.

Illustration is based on an antique quilt owned by Cindy Rennels

Red-and-Green Appliquéd Baskets Quilt

A Perfect Accent

When one of the complementary colors is used less frequently, it becomes an accent color. So, knowing what a color's complement is provides you with an instant idea for an accent color in your quilt.

Remember, all values and intensities of two complements are complementary and may be included in your color scheme. Don't limit your thinking and color combinations to pure colors. For example, pink, a light value of red, is a complement of green. So pink and dark forest green can be used to complement one another in a quilt.

The **Pickled Watermelon** quilt shown below is a wonderful example of a quilt that combines two complements, red and green. In this quilt, the red predominates while the green is used in much smaller proportions. The red border increases the amount of red used, and the neutral off-white background softens and breaks up the strong complementary contrast.

Use two complements, a lot of one and a little of the other, on any neutral background, and you will have a stunning quilt. Add some neutral space to soften the contrast.

Pickled Watermelon
made by Julee Prose

Working with Complements

The **Complements** chart below shows three pairs of complementary fabrics. Notice that their intensities and values are varied. In the yellow and purple pair, both fabrics are low in intensity. In the red and green pair, the red is pure while the green is grayed. In the yellow-green and red-violet pair, the red-violet is pure while the yellow-green is a dark value. Even though the values and intensities change from pair to pair, each fabric pair will still work well together because the colors are complementary. From just the three examples shown here, you can begin to imagine the limitless combinations you can create simply by using complementary colors.

Make Complementary Color Schemes

Look through your fabrics and find several pairs of complementary fabrics. While it may be easier to start by pairing pure colors, try to include a wide variety of prints, choosing different values and intensities.

Use the **Complementary Colors Sample** chart below for pasting up your combinations.

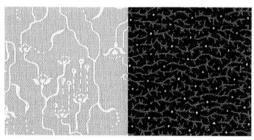

Yellow and purple—both low intensity

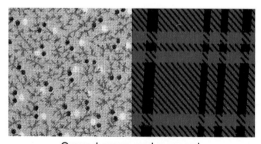

Grayed green and pure red

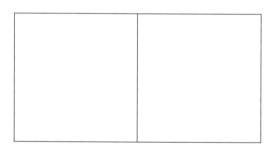

Dark yellow-green and pure red-violet

Complements

Paste up pairs of complementary fabrics

Complementary Colors Sample

WARM AND COOL COLOR SCHEMES

Different colors affect us in ways that relate to our emotional responses. For example, colors are considered to have either a warm or a cool effect. The idea that colors have warmth is the number one concept in your understanding of color because it will affect the design and mood of your quilts.

Look at the **Warm vs. Cool Colors** diagram at right and notice that a straight line drawn across the 12-color wheel will evenly divide the warm colors from the cool ones. The cool colors on the left are the blues and greens of the sky, the sea, and the grass. The warm colors on the right are the yellows, reds, and oranges of fire and the sun.

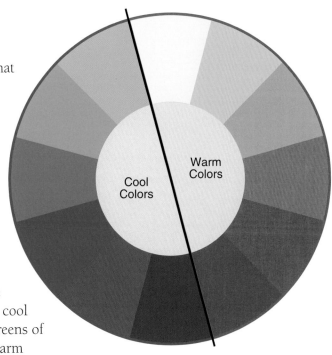

Warm vs. Cool Colors

Color Warmth Is Relative

When a color is considered warm or cool, this characterization is made in relation to the other colors used with it. For example, notice that on the color wheel, violet is in the middle between warms and cools. However, violet may appear to be either warm or cool depending on the other colors you combine with it. If you use violet next to red-violet, it will appear to be cooler than the red-violet. On the other hand, when violet is used next to blue-violet, it will appear to be the warmer of the two colors.

Yellow is always a warm color. In fact, it is the strongest color on the color wheel, so it is wise to remember the adage, "A little yellow goes a long way."

Look at the two sets of colors that demonstrate **Relative Color Warmth,** below. The first set—green/blue/violet—is a cool combination, and violet is the warmest color in the set. The second set—violet/red-violet/red—is a warm combination, and the same violet fabric is now the coolest color.

Violet fabric is the warmest of the group

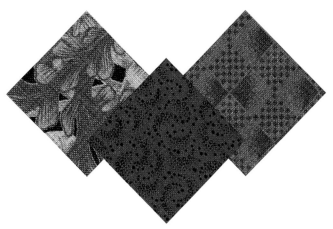

Violet fabric is the coolest of the group

Relative Color Warmth

Warmth Is Stimulating

A warm color scheme makes a stimulating quilt. The **Red-and-Orange Baskets** quilt shown below is a good example of a warm color scheme. It is a dynamic quilt because it combines two pure, warm colors (gold and red) on a dark background. The red stands out because it is pure and warm and is used much more in the quilt. The gold triangles stand out even though they are much smaller, because yellow is such a powerful color.

Red-and-Orange Baskets
made by Katie Young and owned by Irene Metz

Cool Is Restful

While warm colors stimulate our senses, cool color schemes are soothing. The simple green and white **Antique Double Nine Patch** quilt shown below is striking because of the clear contrast of one medium soft color on white, yet the mood is cool and calm. Any cool color on a white background would provide the same feeling.

Antique Double Nine Patch
from the collection of Cindy Rennels, maker unknown

Warm and Cool Colors Together

Warm and cool colors used together make a vibrant quilt. When you combine colors that are so different in mood, you can't help but create excitement and movement.

A good example of this theory is shown in the quilt **Summer's End,** shown below. The quiltmaker successfully mixed many warm and cool colors, not to mention a large variety of fabrics.

This quilt is soft in feeling because of its low-intensity grayed plaids and hand-dyed fabrics, yet full of life because it combines warm and cool colors.

Remember that when you use complementary colors you are combining warm and cool, too, which is another reason complementary color schemes are so compelling and exciting.

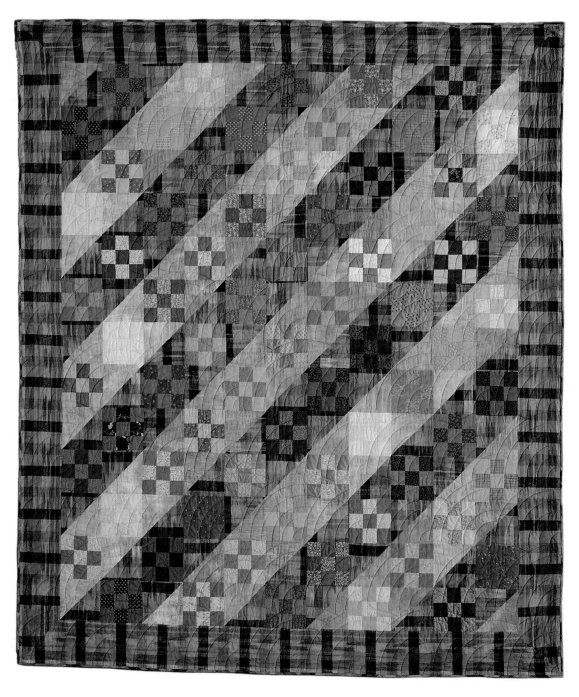

Summer's End
made by Judy Miller

Make a Warm and Cool Fabrics Sample

Pick a variety of warm and cool fabrics from your collection or scrap basket. Be sure to include different values and intensities. Don't worry about whether the fabrics "go together." They're not a future quilt; they're only samples to remind you of warm and cool colors.

Paste the warm colors together on the left and the cool colors together on the right in the **Warm and Cool Colors Sample** chart, shown below.

Paste up warm colors

Paste up cool colors

Warm and Cool Colors Sample

EARTHTONE COLOR SCHEMES

Earthtones are browns, rusts, and beiges—colors associated with the earth. The rusts are the dark shades of the orange and yellow-orange colors on the right side of the color wheel, which means they are usually warm in feeling.

You've probably noticed that browns do not appear on the color wheel. That's because they are mixtures of many colors on the wheel. They are usually not neutral because they not only contain colors, they are also dark in value, which, added to their color, makes them strong.

The earthtones have been the most popular colors for quiltmakers of all generations. Natural dyes have made beautiful browns and rusts available for many centuries. The invention of commercial dyes in the mid-nineteenth century made earthtone fabrics widely available to quilters, which is one reason we see wonderful antique brown quilts from that period. But earthtones remained a popular color scheme throughout the

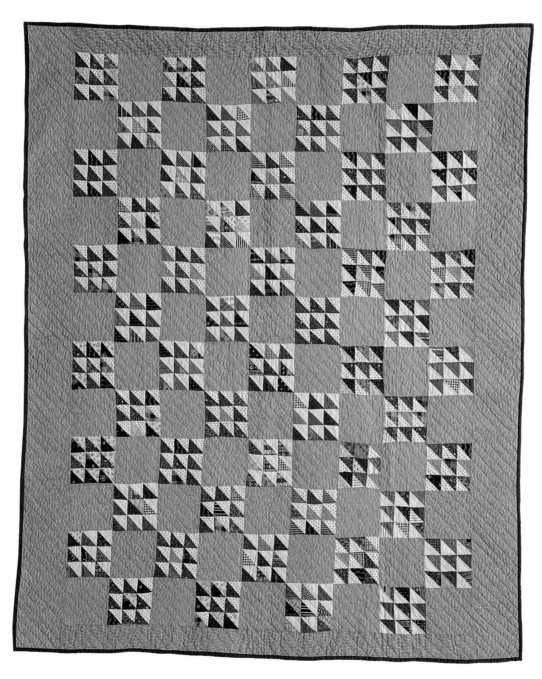

Wild Geese
pieced by an unknown maker, quilted by Shirley McElderry

history of quiltmaking, and today they have become a staple in quilters' color palettes.

One reason for the popularity of earthtones is that they are easy to work with because they are restful and quiet in mood. Even beginners feel comfortable working and experimenting with earthtones. The **Courthouse Steps** quilt shown on page 132 is a glorious study in mid-nineteenth century earthtone fabrics, as is the **Wild Geese** nine-patch variation shown on the opposite page. Both quilts feature simple block patterns that allow the quiltmaker to use many fabrics. Each quilt exudes a calm and restful feeling, despite the combination of dozens of fabrics, because the colors are earthtones.

The **Snowball and Nine Patch** quilt shown below is a contemporary version of an earthtone scrap quilt. Most of the fabrics are browns, and the dark fabrics stand out, creating the design against the light beige background. The touches of color in the green and yellow add spark to the quilt but don't disrupt the overall quiet, earthy feeling.

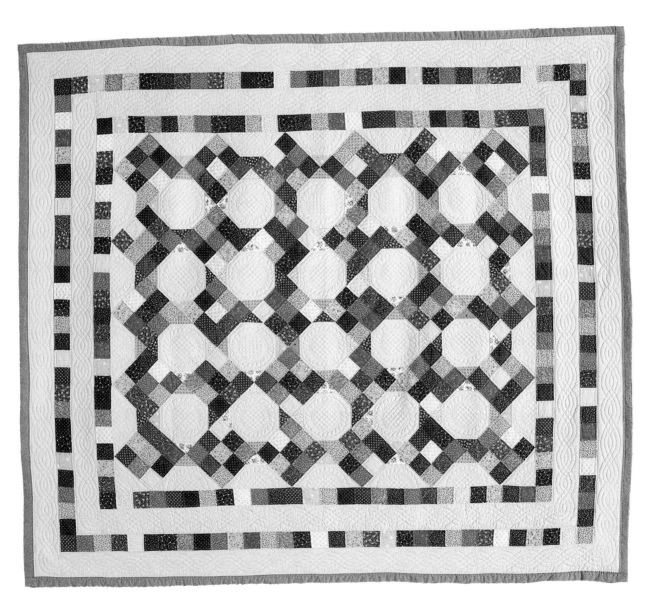

Snowball and Nine Patch
made by Carolyn Miller

Make an Earthtones Sample

Collect as many samples of earthtone fabrics as you can, including different values and intensities. Remember, the beige quilters' neutrals fit in here, too. Be sure to include a variety of prints, not just solids.

Paste your examples on the **Earthtones Sample** chart, shown below.

Paste up browns, rusts, tans, and quilters' neutrals

Earthtones Sample

SPLIT COMPLEMENTARY COLOR SCHEMES

The split complementary color scheme is a fun one to play and design with. It contains four colors that go together beautifully, including a guaranteed perfect accent. And, while the name may sound a little intimidating, you already know all of the color terms you need to design a quilt using split complements.

First, choose three analogous colors you like, such as blue, blue-violet, and violet. Remember, analogous colors are colors placed next to one another on the color wheel. For the fourth color, look directly across the color wheel from the middle of your three colors. In the blue-to-violet example, you'd find yellow, as shown in the **Split Complementary Colors** swatches on the opposite page. The fourth color may be used in small amounts as an accent color, or it may be used as a major color in the quilt. The split complementary color scheme is easy to plan because it is guided by a formula, but the results won't give away your secret. No matter which color you start with, your split complementary color scheme will be full of wonderful color play because it will include both analogous and complementary colors.

 *Remember, every value of the four colors you choose will work in the color scheme. You don't need to limit your choices to just the pure color values.*

Make a Split Complementary Sample

Step 1. From among your fabrics find three analogous colors such as red, red-violet, and violet. The fabrics you used earlier as examples of analogous colors will do if you can't find different ones.

Step 2. Use the color wheel on page 135 to find the complement. Remember, it's the color directly opposite the *middle* of your three analogous colors. Paste swatches of each fabric in the **Split Complementary Sample** chart on the opposite page.

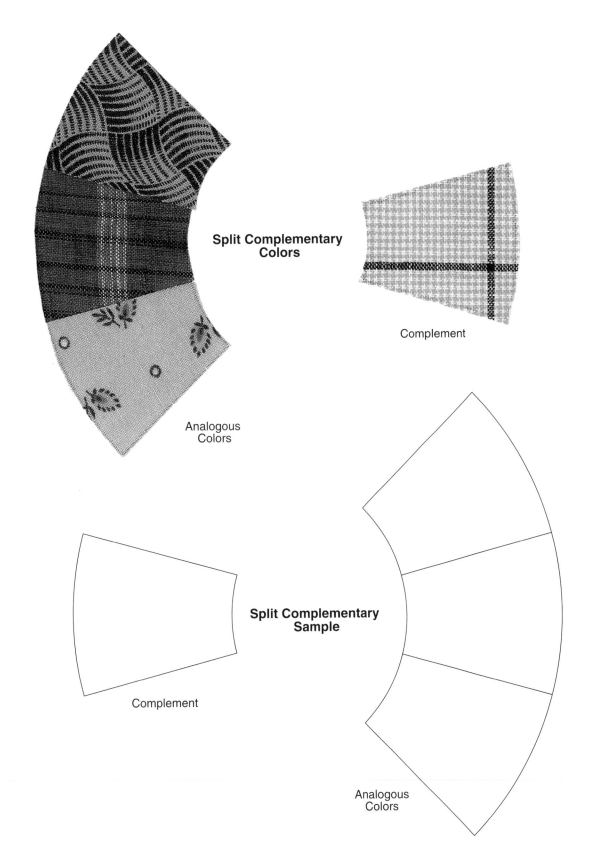

**Split Complementary
Colors**

Complement

Analogous
Colors

**Split Complementary
Sample**

Complement

Analogous
Colors

COLOR WHEEL MASTERY

Now that you've mastered the basic concepts and terms associated with the color wheel itself, you're ready to learn more about how colors behave when they interact with each other. Color contrast and behavior will help you understand why some quilt blocks seem muddled while others work well, and why some quilts seem ordinary while others are truly spectacular.

color
CONTRAST

Color Contrast

Once you know how to use the color wheel and understand the terms used to describe it, you are ready to advance your knowledge by learning how the different colors work and behave when used together. Some colors will dominate others, and how you use them together will affect your quilt's visual impact.

Whether the next quilt you plan to make is a reproduction of a charming antique or your own bright and vivid patchwork interpretation, you'll find that learning to use the principles of color dominance and color contrast effectively will add excitement to your design.

HOW COLORS BEHAVE TOGETHER

No, we're not talking about whether they behave or misbehave! The way colors behave has to do with how they interact with each other. Now that you know the basic color terms and you have sought out samples of each from your fabric collection, let's look at fabrics and colors in relation to actual quilts.

Every quilt that contains color is an example of how colors behave together. When you examine quilts in books, magazines, and at quilt shows, try to keep in mind the color terms you have learned, and you'll better understand how colors work together. You'll also have a much easier time creating dynamic color combinations in your own quilts and wallhangings.

COLOR DOMINANCE

Quite simply, different colors behave and affect us differently. When you look at a quilt or anything else with a combination of colors in it, you see some colors first and some later. Why? Because some colors dominate while others fall away or recede.

To describe a color as *dominant* means that it stands out, comes forward, or advances. It catches the viewer's eye first.

Warm Colors Dominate

Generally, warm colors will dominate a quilt. Cool colors do not catch the eye; they recede and act as the background. This means that no matter where on your design you put a cool color, it will tend to fade toward the background, and no matter where you put a warm color, it will catch the viewer's eye first and become the focus or the main design.

To remember this warm vs. cool guideline, think of looking at the sky on a bright summer day. When you look toward the sun, what do you see? The cool blue of the sky, or the hot glow of the bright sun? Although this is a strong example, the theory works for all colors.

Summer Night, shown on page 152, illustrates the dominance of warm colors beautifully. Every block in the quilt is constructed the same way— they're all simple log cabin blocks, as shown below. Therefore, in this kind of quilt we can easily see how color and its position controls what we see.

Log Cabin Blocks

In this quilt, the quiltmaker used only two colors: cool blue and warm yellow. Although she used many fabrics in graduated values of each color, most of the fabrics are close to pure in intensity and the overall effect is one of a bright blue and a bright yellow. You can't help but notice how powerful the warm yellow star is. Even though it is a pure color, the powerful yellow advances to the front of the design, leaving the cool blue to automatically recede and become the background of the quilt.

This quilt illustrates perfectly that the quiltmaker controls what we see by where she puts the warm and cool fabrics. Just imagine what the quilt would look like if she had reversed the color placement and the star were blue! There would simply be a big, blue hole in the center of a very yellow quilt.

Summer Night
made by Karen Stone

Pure Colors Dominate

Pure colors are stronger than grayed or toned-down colors, so the intense colors of the color wheel will dominate any grayed colors.

The striking **Grandmother's Flower Garden** quilt, shown on the opposite page, is another example of how color—rather than pieced lines—controls design. In this quilt, the yellow background takes over because it is warm and pure, right off the color wheel—and there's a lot of it.

Remember that yellow is the strongest color on the color wheel. The flowers are usually the dominant design feature in this traditional quilt pattern, but they don't stand a chance here against the powerful yellow background. Most of the flower hexagons are toned-down blue shirtings and feed sacks, and these cool, grayed blues become background to the strong, warm yellow. Notice, however, how the few red hexagons in the quilt do stand out because they, too, are warm and pure.

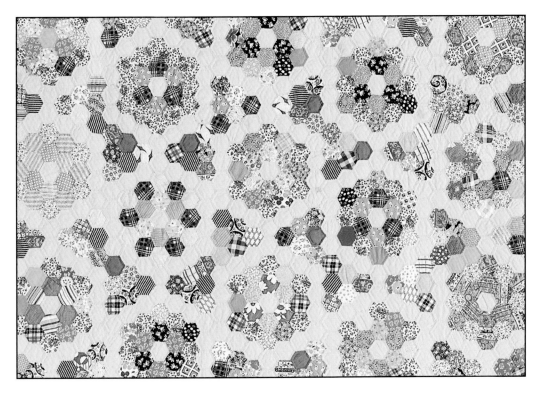

Grandmother's Flower Garden
pieced by Leila Poindexter and hand quilted by Kathryn Jones

Now take a look at how different this quilt would look if the color placements were changed (as in the diagram below). When the flowers are primarily yellow and other warm colors and the background is a cooler color, the quilt leaves the viewer with a completely different impression.

Grandmother's Flower Garden
with cool background

Dark Colors Dominate

The third principle of color domination is that dark colors generally dominate light ones. However, this concept is more flexible than the

others. Sometimes light colors stand out against dark backgrounds as a sparkle, especially if there is just a little of the light fabric in the quilt. Most often, though, the dark colors determine the shapes we see in a design.

Again, a Log Cabin quilt is a good example of how this principle works, because the blocks are all the same. This leaves only color to dictate the design. **Paths to the Diamonds,** shown on page 154, is made of a combination of prints that are mostly neutral (black, gray, and white) and red (with a little green in the print). The red fabric stands out because it is pure, dark, and warm, and the black prints also advance because they are very dark, so these are the fabrics you see first. The many grays and light fabrics blend together to form the background.

To test the dark dominance concept, close your eyes for a few seconds and then open them; when you look again you'll see the dark parts of the quilt first. It's not that you don't see the light fabrics, but that the dark colors dominate and control the design.

Paths to the Diamonds
made by Doris Heitman

All Colors Dominate Neutrals

Almost any color is stronger than black, white, gray, or light beige. The definition of a neutral is that it is so weak that it can be dominated, which is why we traditionally use neutrals as background colors. Even black—which is very dark and can dominate light values—can be a background for colors, especially when they are pure and bright.

Take a look at the **Schoolhouse Blocks** illustration at the top of the opposite page, and notice that while all the blocks are the same design, the placement of both light and dark neutrals and colors changes from block to block. You can easily see what a powerful tool color dominance is for creating a whole range of quilt blocks from just one simple block design!

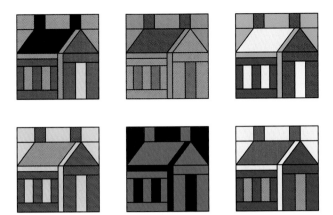

Colors dominate neutrals

Schoolhouse Blocks

DOMINANCE CHANGES

When you combine several colors in a quilt top, you are usually combining a variety of color characteristics, too, such as pure, grayed, dark, light, warm, and cool. In the **Color Dominance** fabric examples below, there are three sets of four fabrics. While some of the fabrics remain constant from one group to another, notice that by changing one of the fabrics in a group we change which fabric is dominant. As the dominant fabric is removed and another fabric is added to the set of swatches, a different fabric becomes the dominant one in the group.

 Row 1

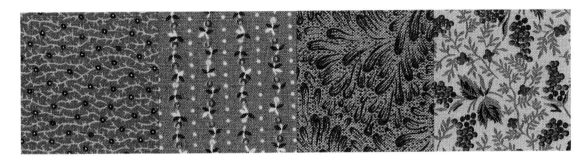

Row 2

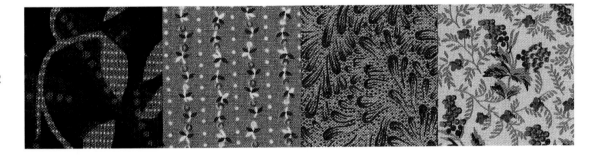

Row 3

Row 1: Blue and purple fabrics are both dark, but purple dominates because it is warmer than the blue fabric.

Row 2: Black and blue fabrics are both dark, but blue dominates because colors dominate neutrals.

Row 3: Gold fabric dominates because it is warm and is closer to a pure color than all other fabrics.

Color Dominance

Experiment with Color Dominance

The best way to learn about how dominance can change is to play with bolts of fabric at the fabric store or with stacks of fabric in your collection.

Step 1. Choose several fabrics you like together, and lay them on the table. Study them to see which fabric or fabrics dominate. Also, decide *why* they dominate.

Step 2. Make some changes to the set, one or two fabrics at a time. Be sure to change the dominant fabrics several times. For example, if the dominant fabric is a pure, warm color, try substituting a pure, cool color to see whether it, too, dominates. Try different values of the dominant colors (such as pink instead of red or rust instead of orange) to see whether they still dominate. By experimenting in this way, you will begin to see how color relationships change as you combine them differently.

If it seems hard to pick out the dominant fabric when they're right in front of you, try standing back about five feet and looking at them again. From that distance, your eye eliminates line and shape and you see only color.

A Lot of One Color Can Dominate

It stands to reason that a lot of any color will make it stand out more within a group of fabrics. Even though the color may not dominate the overall design of the quilt, it will become important in the quilt simply because of its volume.

For example, a large amount of a pale blue used with small bits of a warm red will make what we call a blue quilt. However, the warm color will still be the first element we see and will thus dictate the design of the quilt. A lot of a strong, pure color, even a cool color, will definitely increase its strength and dominance in the quilt.

MAKE SAMPLES OF HOW COLORS BEHAVE

On the following pages are two pairs of quilt block drawings that you can use with your own fabrics to illustrate how colors work and behave to-gether. Trace the blocks to make templates and cut fabric patches to the exact size of the printed blocks. Don't include seam allowances, since these blocks will be pasted together, not sewn. Trace or photocopy the blocks so you can paste several samples onto separate sheets, rather than in your book.

Warm and Cool Colors Sample

Step 1. Select three fabrics that go together—two cool colors and one warm color—to use with the **Bachelor's Puzzle Blocks,** shown on the opposite page. If you want a neutral background fabric, use it as a fourth fabric.

Step 2. Cut pieces for your sample block using templates of the shapes in the block, then lay out a pleasing color design in Block A. When you're satisfied, rub the glue stick over the entire block drawing and paste the fabric to the paper.

Step 3. In Block B, reverse the position of the warm and cool colors. For example, if you used a warm color in the four "X" sections, now use a cool fabric for those pieces. Stand back and notice how different your two blocks look, even though they are made using the same design and fabrics.

If you have fusible web on hand, you may find it easier and neater to work with than glue. Fuse webbing to the wrong side of the fabrics before you cut out the shapes. Then cut your shapes, finalize your block design, and press your pieces onto a photocopy of the blocks.

Complementary Colors Sample

Step 1. Choose two complementary colors and one neutral fabric to use with **Aunt Sukey's Choice Blocks** on page 158. For Block A, cut fabric pieces to make a block using the two complementary fabrics equally. Arrange your pieces and glue them to the paper. Study this design to see how busy it looks.

Step 2. Use the same two complements in Block B, but use more of one than the other as you lay out your pieces. When you are pleased with the effect, paste the pieces to the paper. Compare the blocks and note how little you used of one complementary color to achieve a pleasing quilt block.

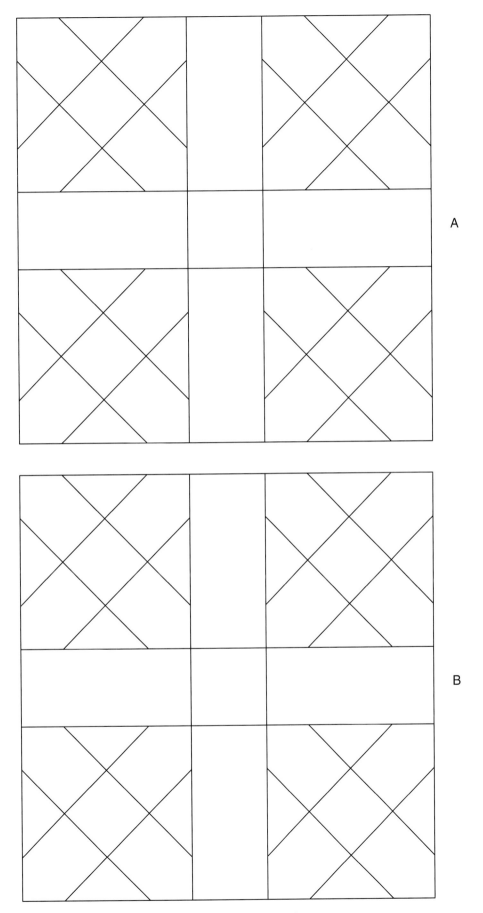

A

B

Bachelor's Puzzle Blocks

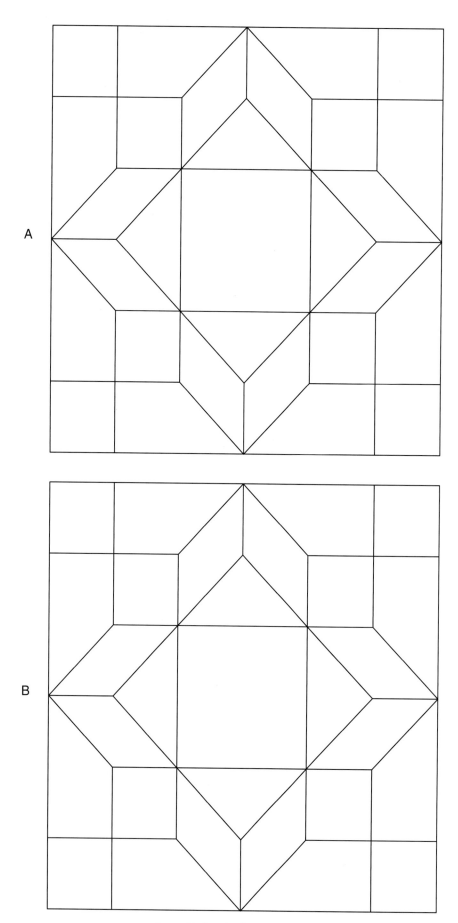

A

B

Aunt Sukey's Choice Blocks

Color Contrast

ANALYZING QUILT BLOCKS

Take a moment to look at the blocks below. Do you know the answer to the questions, "Why does one flower stand out more than the other?" and "Why do the two Joseph's Coat blocks look so different even though they are pieced from the same fabrics?"

One flower block stands out more because one is made of pure red and bright green while the other flower is pale pink and washed-out green. Look at what stands out—the warm and the pure. So in the case of the paler flower, only the warm yellow-orange basket gets noticed.

The Joseph's Coat block has many pieces and the potential for many different designs. Where

you put the colors determines which parts of the design will stand out. We used the same fabrics in both blocks: a pure, warm red solid; a black print; a medium, cool blue plaid; and lighter, cool and neutral prints.

In this set of fabrics, it is a safe bet that the pure, warm red and the black will dominate, the medium blue will be next in strength, and the paler fabrics will recede into the background.

This is exactly what happens. We control what design advances in the complicated block by placing the red and black first, then playing with the subordinate colors.

One block is not better than the other, they are just different. Which block design you like best is up to you.

Flower Basket Blocks

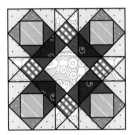 

Joseph's Coat Blocks

UNDERSTANDING AND USING CONTRAST

One of the easiest ways to enliven a quilt is to include some kind of color contrast. Contrast as a concept is not hard to understand—it is using opposite or different things together. You want contrast in your quilt to make it both interesting and exciting. The quilt pattern itself usually offers a way to play with contrast of line and shape. However, you'll want something interesting happening in color as well as in pattern, since color is the first and most noticeable aspect of any quilt design.

Once you've decided on a quilt pattern or design, the next step is to decide on the colors. As soon as you put two colors together, you are using color contrast—some combinations just provide more contrast than others. In this section, we'll examine the different types of contrast you can use

and degrees of contrast you can achieve when planning your quilt color schemes.

ONE COLOR ON WHITE

The simplest color scheme is one color on white. It can be delicate or dramatic in effect and has been used by quilters for generations. Since white is neutral, it will become the background for any colors set against it. If you choose a one-color-on-white scheme and use only a single colored fabric, there is obviously no contrast between colors. The only contrast possible in this color scheme is value contrast. Since the white is light, putting any color against it will provide some degree of contrast. The darker the value, the higher the degree of contrast.

The **Blue-and-White Cherry Baskets** quilt shown below is a lovely example of low contrast in a one-color-on-white quilt. There is no *color contrast* because pale blue is the only color in the quilt. And the blue is so light in value that it is almost as light as the white background and does not offer much *contrast of value*. Thus, the overall effect is delicate and soothing in feel. Pale colors on a white background create the quietest, softest color contrast.

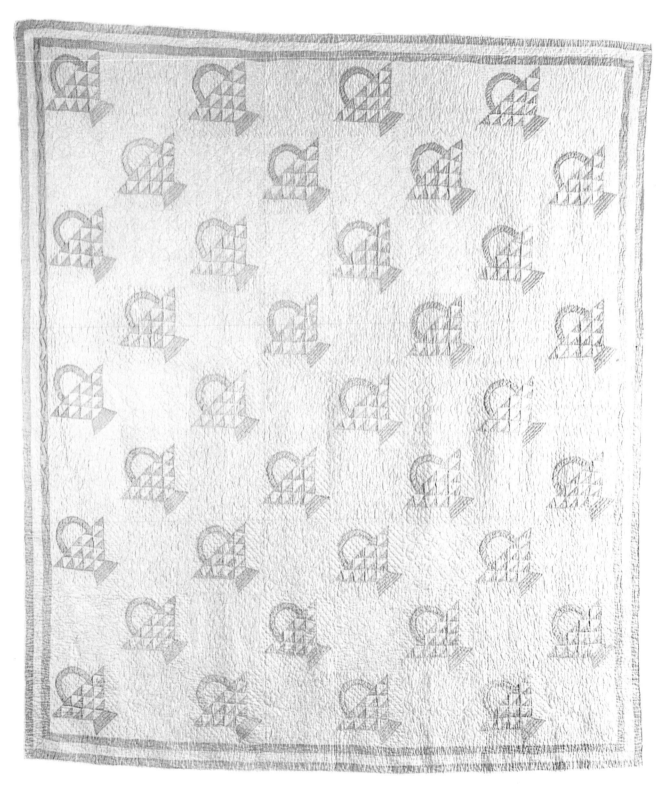

Blue-and-White Cherry Baskets
made by Susan Boyd and owned by her granddaughter, Martha Bastian

Now compare the **Blue-and-White Cherry Baskets** quilt to the red-and-white **Pineapple Log Cabin** quilt, shown below. It, too, is a one-color-on-white quilt, yet it is quite vibrant despite its simplicity of design, fabric, and color scheme. The reason for this is that the quiltmaker used a pure, strong color on white, which creates a very strong contrast of value.

Pineapple Log Cabin
made by an unknown quiltmaker and owned by Edith Leeper

CONTRAST OF VALUE
IN ONE-COLOR QUILTS

The red-and-white Pineapple quilt is dramatic because it uses high contrast of value: the solid red is dark set against the white and therefore stands out. The pale blue Baskets quilt is quiet because it uses low contrast of value: the solid blue is almost as light in value as the white.

While each of these quilts contains only one solid fabric in the single-color scheme, you can also make a one color quilt using many fabrics. For instance, the red-and-white quilt could just as easily have been pieced using a wide variety of red calicoes on a white background, rather than a single solid red.

As mentioned in the chapter "The Color Wheel," the one-color scheme is an easy one to use if you don't want to worry about combining colors. To avoid the risk of making a dull quilt, a one-color quilt may benefit from some color contrast. So try using as many different fabrics as you can, including fabrics of different scale and type (see page 179) to add textural interest.

When you are mixing lots of prints from the same color family, you'll achieve the strongest contrast of value by placing the lightest and darkest fabrics right next to each other. When you separate dark and light values with medium values, the contrast is softened or diluted.

The **Wild Geese** quilt, shown at left, is a good example of this dilution. It is essentially an all-brown quilt. However, many values of brown are used, from dark browns and deep rusts to light prints, and all are set on the medium value, beige background. Even though this is a peaceful quilt made primarily of quilters' neutrals and earthtones, the varied prints and contrast of value among them provide visual interest.

Examine the blocks closely to see how in some the contrast is very strong, while in others it is lessened because a medium-value brown was used in place of either a dark or a light triangle.

Wild Geese
pieced by an unknown maker, hand quilted and owned by Shirley McElderry

COMPLEMENTARY CONTRAST

When you use two complements together, you are using *complementary contrast.* As mentioned on page 135, complements always look wonderful together and make a strong quilt, but when used equally they seem to vibrate, which makes the quilt hard to look at. Instead, choose one as the predominant color and the other as the accent.

Since *all* values of two complements are complementary, include several values of either or both complements for a more exciting color plan.

 *A neutral background such as white, black, or beige helps calm down what can be an overpowering color combination. So try controlling the color contrast of two complements you want to use by placing them on a neutral background.*

Complementary contrast controls **Honeymoon Cottage**, shown below. This quilt shows successful use of two complements, red and green, with some soft yellow and gray added. The red dominates because it's warm, because it appears in two values, and because it's used in large spaces (such as the roof and chimney). The cool green appears only in the grass, which by comparison is a small space. The house blocks stand out clearly on the neutral white background.

Honeymoon Cottage
made by an unknown quiltmaker and owned by Cindy Rennels

WARM-COOL CONTRAST

There are times when you may not want to include contrast of value; for example, if you are designing an all-pastel quilt. To add interest to such a quilt, try to include both warm and cool colors. When they're mixed, they're always dynamic. It doesn't matter what values you include—they can be all dark or all light. Just the fact that the colors themselves are so different enlivens your quilt.

Warm-cool contrast is one of the most fun types of contrast to play with because it allows you to use any colors you want as long as you include some from each side of the color wheel.

Mountain Mirage, shown below, is a study of warm/cool contrast. A wide variety of colors and values move from warm to cool in this restful quilt. The great variety of color doesn't overwhelm the quilt because the changes in value are gradual and give the viewer's eyes a direction in which to travel.

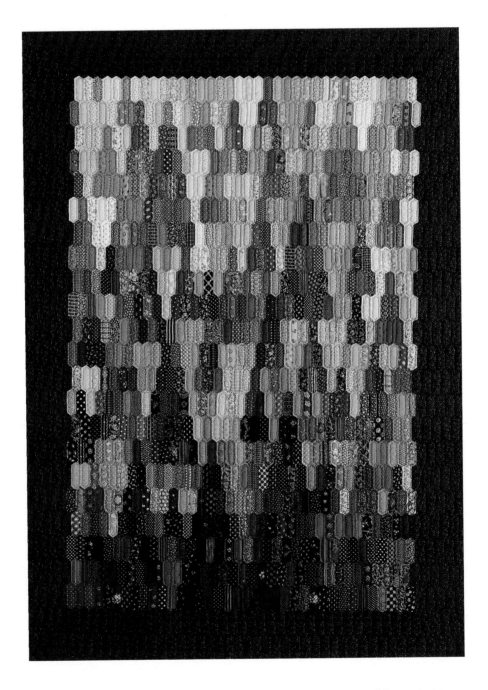

Mountain Mirage
made by Kathryn Kuhn

PURE COLORS TOGETHER

The strongest color contrast is between the strongest colors—the 12 pure colors on the color wheel. Using any number of these pure colors together will assure a vibrant quilt.

Red, White, and Blue, shown below, is just such a vibrant quilt, with three pure colors from the color wheel set on a white background. Not only are these three colors pure, but they are the primary colors out of which all other colors are mixed. Using the three primary colors alone could be quite overpowering, so the neutral white was needed to define the quilt's design. Notice how the yellow squares jump out even though they are small, because yellow is the strongest color.

Red, White, and Blue
probably made by Lillie Miller Rohrbach and owned by Lucille Powell

Amish Easter Baskets, a bright, cheerful quilt, Crayola-like in feeling, is another example in which pure colors are combined for a striking effect (shown below). Red, blue, and green right off the color wheel control the traditional design. Again, notice that the high color contrast is softened by a neutral white background.

Amish Easter Baskets
made by Elsie Vredenberg and owned by the Museum of the American Quilter's Society in Paducah, Kentucky

CONTRAST OF INTENSITY

When pure colors are mixed with grayed colors, the result is a *contrast of intensity*. The pure colors stand out, while the grayed colors recede. This combination happens naturally when you combine a great number of colors and fabrics in a scrap or charm quilt, such as in **Simply Charming**, shown below. It's full of variety in fabric and color. Notice how the pure yellows, reds, purples, and yellow-greens advance while the other fabrics recede.

Not only do some colors advance and others recede, but in this quilt the intensity of the colors changes the design we see. For example, in some sections of the quilt, the patches combine to form six-pointed stars. Yet in other areas, the less intense color fabrics are arranged so that we see a more traditional Tumbling Blocks arrangement. All the patches are exactly the same size and shape; it's the color play that dictates the design. What do you see when you look at **Simply Charming?**

Simply Charming
made by Edith Zimmer

COMBINING DIFFERENT KINDS OF CONTRAST

Usually a quilt contains more than one kind of contrast. For example, when you use pure colors on white, you are automatically using contrast of value, too. And remember the color wheel on page 139, where the wheel is divided in half, separating the warm colors from the cool ones? That means complementary contrast always includes warm-cool contrast because any two complements are across the color wheel from one another.

The exuberant **6 ÷ 3 = 5** hexagonal quilt, shown on page 168, incorporates all kinds of color contrast. It uses all the colors of the color wheel in many values, including the pure version and grayed versions of each. It includes warm colors and cool ones, and emphasizes the warm-cool contrast by the placement of the hexagons. The quilt relies on color contrast to make it bright.

The many kinds of color contrast mix with the other elements of quilt design—blocks, sashing, borders, and binding—to create lively quilts. You don't always have to think in terms of color contrast first. But color contrast will be there; it will affect the quilt. It is an idea to which you can turn when you want a way to add a bit of life to your quilt. Color contrast in quilts, as in life, is invigorating.

6 ÷ 3 = 5
made by Edith Zimmer

BACKGROUNDS AFFECT COLOR CONTRAST

When you consider which colors to use in a quilt, you need to consider background color, too. In order to stay in the background and not draw attention to itself, the fabric you choose must be neutral or a receding color.

BLACK AS BACKGROUND

Black is a wonderful background for the powerful, pure colors. It brings out their vibrance. In the Amish **Robbing Peter to Pay Paul** quilt, shown below, you can see how the black background enlivens the pure colors.

Now take a look at a few more sample block diagrams below to see how the pure colors, and even some darker or grayed ones, stand out against the black background. The black fabric makes the pure, vibrant colors sing.

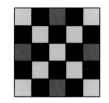

Oklahoma Nine Patch   **Roman Stripe**   **Irish Chain**

Robbing Peter to Pay Paul
made by Becky Herdle

WHITE AS BACKGROUND

White has the complete opposite effect on colors when it's used as a background. It softens colors and makes a more delicate background. Sometimes it even dulls colors. When you decide to place colors on a white background, think about contrast of value, too. Light colors, even warm ones like yellow, will blend into a white background, as you can see in the **Scrap Baskets with Nine-Patch Sashing** quilt, shown below. The dark baskets show up well, but the light fabrics and the prints with white backgrounds have less contrast of value. Although you can see them up close because they have some color, from a distance they are very close in value to the white quilt background, which makes for a quiet, soothing quilt.

Scrap Baskets with Nine-Patch Sashing
made by Wilma Sestric

BLACK AND WHITE TOGETHER

Black and white placed right next to each other are always dynamic because they create the ultimate contrast of value, the darkest dark against the lightest light. They may also be used together as background. **Barn Raising Pinwheels**, shown below, and **Oklahoma Nine Patch**, shown on page 172, both use both black and white as background. The high contrast between the black and white rows enhances the action of the many prints, most of which are bright and pure in color. Black, white, and pure colors always make for a dynamite color combination.

Barn Raising Pinwheels
pieced by Barbara Berliner and machine quilted by Cathy Sexton

Oklahoma Nine Patch
made by Carolyn Miller

GRAY AS BACKGROUND

Gray is quieting and softening wherever you put it. It is by definition medium in value, so its effects are medium, too. It recedes, it calls no attention to itself, and it is, therefore, the ultimate neutral. Look at the **Amish-Style Scrap Baskets** quilt on page 134. In this quilt, the gray background allows the blocks to stand out even though they are made of soft grayed colors themselves. They would have been lost on a black background (traditional for an Amish-style quilt) because, although neutral, the black is powerful in value and could easily overpower and deaden the low-intensity colors of the baskets.

MUSLIN AND LIGHT BEIGE AS BACKGROUND

This **Postage Stamp Baskets** below quilt contains mostly low intensity fabrics on a muslin background. Choosing a sashing for these blocks could easily have presented a problem to the quilt-maker. Too strong a sashing would have taken over and dominated the delicately colored blocks. Too light a sashing would have been too dull and faded into the muslin background. The grayed-green sashing is a perfect choice. It provides a soft contrast to the muslin background yet recedes enough to allow the colors in the baskets to stand out.

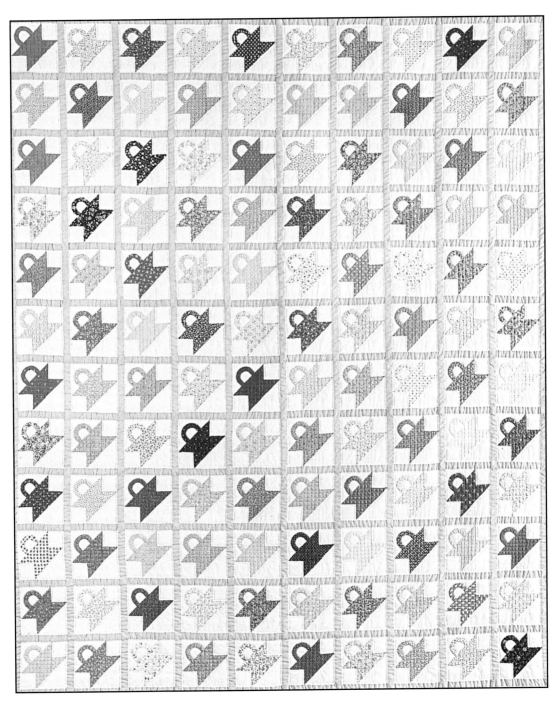

Postage Stamp Baskets
made by Martha Bastian

My Cabin Made of Logs, shown below, is essentially a red, white, and blue quilt, a warm and cool color combination that is always strong.

By replacing the traditional white background with beige, however, the quiltmaker has softened the high contrast of the usual red-and-navy-on-white color scheme and produced a more mellow quilt. Notice that although the background contains many fabrics, they are the same color and

are close in value, so overall the background remains beige.

You can add interest to your quilt's background by using a variety of prints or plaids, as shown in My Cabin Made of Logs. As long as the fabrics are basically the same color, you'll have the color effect you want, but the different prints will add a bit of spice to the design.

My Cabin Made of Logs
made by Jane Graff

BLUE AS BACKGROUND

Blue is the background color of our lives. It is always above us in the sky, varying day to day and season to season from clear, bright blues, to grayed blues, to midnight blues. It is also a cool color that recedes when mixed with other colors. Thus, it is a perfect background for quilts of all kinds. In its pure version, it was used successfully in **Summer Night,** shown on page 152.

In **Silver Anniversary,** shown below, blue is used in a grayed form. There are two background fabrics in the quilt: beige and silvery blue. The pieced rings in bright, warm pinks and roses stand out against both background fabrics. But by mixing the gray-blue and muslin backgrounds, the quiltmaker creates a secondary design for the blocks within the background, giving the quilt drama and presence.

Silver Anniversary
designed by Annie Segal, pieced by Penny Wolf, and machine quilted by Jonna Castle

COMBINING COLORS AND PRINTS

Up until now, we've been discovering how colors work together to provide impact. From complementary colors, to color dominance, to choosing background colors, we've been focusing strictly on color itself. However, unless you are making an Amish-style quilt or a traditional red-and-green appliqué quilt, you probably aren't limiting your fabric choices to just solid colors. Wonderful prints, plaids, and paisleys are all available to quiltmakers, and understanding how the printed designs affect the impact of color in quilts is important. In the next section, "Using Prints of Yesterday and Today," we will introduce a variety of printed fabric styles and show you how to use fabrics and colors effectively to plan your own quilt color schemes.

using prints
OF YESTERDAY and TODAY

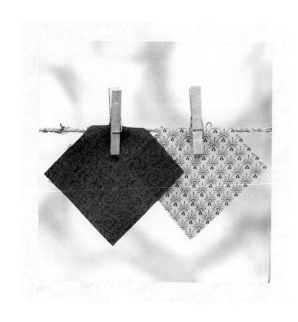

Using Prints of Yesterday and Today

An affinity for fabric is the reason many quilters make quilts. And unlike our grand-mothers and great grandmothers, we don't have to rely on leftover bits of fabric from the clothing we make to piece our quilt tops. Instead, we have almost unlimited fabric choices, ranging from traditional calicoes and homespun plaids to glittery metallics and mottled hand-dyed cottons.

To keep our interest piqued, fabric designers change the colors and patterns from season to season and year to year. Even though available colors and designs may change, fabrics continue to be made in standard, definable prints.

As a quiltmaker, it is important to recognize the different types of prints and to be sure to include all kinds in your collection. It's not just the color that makes a quilt exciting; the creative blending of lots of different types of fabrics also contributes to the visual impact.

WORKING WITH PRINTED FABRICS

Quite often, beginning quiltmakers look at a quilt top they've completed and wonder why it isn't as exciting as they imagined it would be when they first planned the colors and selected the fabrics. In many cases, the reason is not the colors used but the lack of variety in the printed fabrics. Too many medium-size floral prints or an over-abundance of pin dots and other miniature-scale prints can lead to a lackluster quilt.

It's easy to see why we as quiltmakers could fall into this trap. After all, we wouldn't dream of wearing a polka-dot blouse with a plaid skirt. However, fabrics are used differently in a quilt, so we need to learn how to combine a variety of prints for an effective quilt design, not based on fashion concerns! If you've ever hesitated to use paisleys, plaids, and polka dots in the same quilt, keep reading. By the end of the chapter, you'll see why more fabric variety leads to livelier quilts.

RECOGNIZING TYPES OF PRINTS

Prints come in different sizes and styles. Some are monochromatic, and some contain a variety of colors. Some patterned fabrics aren't even printed, they have their designs woven right into them. Woven plaids and stripes are easy to spot, since they look the same on both sides. Regardless of what type of printed or woven pattern you prefer, what's important in quiltmaking is how you combine different prints together.

 *By mixing different styles and sizes of prints, you'll be adding dimension, interest, and excitement to the overall look of your finished quilt.*

In this section we'll discuss the characteristics of print types and show you examples of each. We've left space next to our examples for you to paste up samples from your own collection of fabrics. If you don't want to glue directly into your book, photocopy these pages or just keep a notebook with a page for samples of each type of print.

 This exercise will give you a chance to review your fabric collection and will call to your attention what kinds of prints you like best. It may also suggest areas where you need to add variety to your collection, so keep a notebook handy to jot down your fabric shopping list.

Kinds of Prints

Floral: A floral print, as the name implies, contains flowers. This is the largest and most varied category of quilt fabric. Flowers may be tossed randomly over a fabric or appear in a definite direction; they may be widely spaced or close together. Notice, too, that floral prints can contain lots of color contrast or just a little, and they can also provide a great deal of or very little contrast in value, as shown below.

Floral Prints

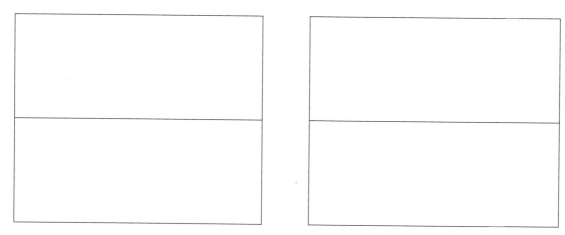

Floral Print Samples

Geometric: Geometric prints are designs based on geometric shapes such as circles, squares, and triangles, as well as checks, stripes, and plaids, as shown below. Patterns may be all over, directional, widely spaced, or packed, just as in florals. And again, the degree of contrast within the design, both in color and value, can vary greatly.

Geometric is the one category where you can have a design woven into the fabric, such as a stripe, check, or plaid, rather than printed on top of the fabric. The benefit of a woven fabric is that the design appears on both sides, so you can use either side without worrying about sewing right sides together.

Evenly spaced geometric

Check

Plaid

Random geometric

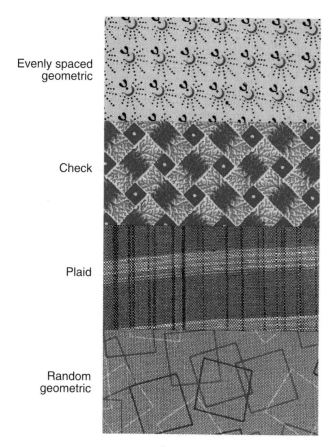

Geometric Prints

Geometric Print Samples

Conversational: A conversational or novelty print depicts a real thing. Celestial prints were popular in the nineteenth century, as were prints showing horses and riding accessories such as saddles, horseshoes, bits, and reins. Prints of games and toys were popular for children's clothing in the early twentieth century and eventually worked their way into patchwork.

Today, you can find examples of all these conversational prints, as many fabric manufacturers are producing fabrics to simulate novelty fabrics of earlier times, as shown below.

Conversational Prints

Conversational Print Samples

Abstract: Abstract prints are prints that do not portray a specific recognizable shape, unlike the floral, geometric, and conversational prints already shown. Abstract prints include (but certainly aren't limited to) designs that swirl, are irregularly shaped, or look sponge painted or hand painted, as shown in the fabric swatches below. Paste your sample abstract prints on page 182.

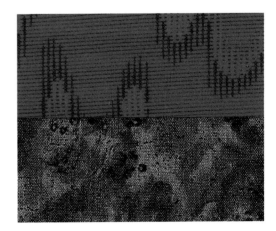

Abstract Prints

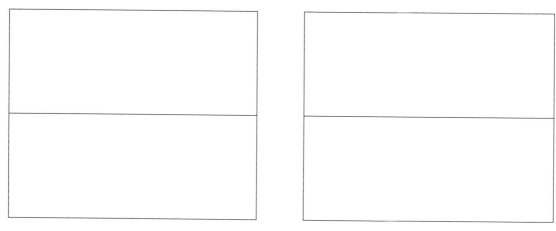

Abstract Print Samples

Ethnic: Prints with a foreign or exotic feeling, as shown below, are referred to as ethnic prints. These are Western interpretations of the fabrics of different regions of the world, such as African and Native American prints, Dutch wax prints, Indonesian batiks, Egyptian designs, and others.

 If you like ethnic prints, be sure to buy the styles you like when they are popular, as they tend to have a short life span. If you wait until the moment you actually want to use one, you may not be able to find the style print you're looking for.

African print

Dutch wax print

Indonesian batik

Japanese print

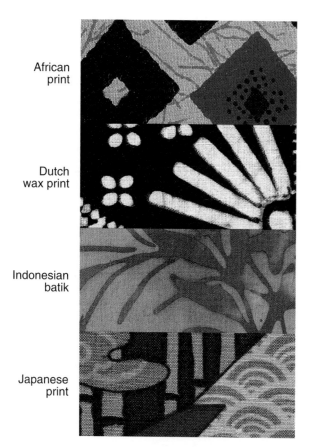

Ethnic Prints

Ethnic Print Samples

SCALES OF PRINTS

The size of the design printed on the fabric is referred to as the print *scale*. It is important that quilters understand the concept of scale, because the use of different scale prints gives impact to quilt design. Too often, quiltmakers limit themselves to small-scale calicoes, especially when first starting out. Instead of thinking small, think about variety. Our quilting forebears used a great variety of print sizes, and that partly accounts for the depth and richness of their quilts.

Many quilters don't choose a variety of prints for a quilt simply because they only want to include fabrics that they truly love. And, quite simply, they tend to like the same style of print, whether it be small-scale geometrics or medium-scale florals. When quilters shop for fabrics, they are drawn to the same types of fabrics repeatedly. To avoid the trap of using the same scale of prints, select fabrics based on what they will do for your quilt, not on how well they would fit in your wardrobe. Remember, you'll be cutting each fabric into small pieces so it won't end up looking like the huge print you see on the bolt anyway!

To see how different scales of prints work together, cut a square- or triangle-shaped window in the center of a piece of white paper. Take it with you to the fabric store and lay it over the fabrics you select to see how they will look when cut into those shapes. Don't be afraid to add variety to your quilt. If you have the right colors but your selection of fabrics still seems less than exciting, spice up your project by changing the print scales.

Print Scale

Print Scale Samples

COLOR CONTRAST WITHIN FABRICS

Printed fabrics exemplify the same color principles that were discussed in the chapter "Color Contrast." For instance, once you add a pink rosebud with green leaves to a yellow background, you've changed the appearance of solid yellow because other colors have been introduced.

The most important thing to remember about color and fabric, however, is that color is a long-distance illusion. Even a fabric with many colors in it will appear to be predominantly one color; in this example, the rosebuds and leaves won't matter. In order to tell a fabric's true color, stand back to view the fabric. From a few feet away the blend of colors will probably look different from how it does up close. Remember, you will be using tiny pieces mixed with other colors, and that, too, will affect how the fabric looks. The tiny specks of buds and leaves will not be visible from a distance, and the colors will blend into one.

In this section, we will explore the variety of contrasts available in different types of prints—from high-contrast complements to very subtle shading nuances.

Don't be overly concerned about matching every color in every print you select. It really doesn't matter whether a tiny sprig of green in a floral print matches the greens in the other prints you are considering. All greens will blend into the other colors when you view them from a distance.

SOLID PRINTS

Solids, of course, are easily classified by color. *Solid prints* are low-contrast prints on a color, usually two values of a color or black on a color. They provide interest upon close-up viewing but look like solids from a distance.

Today, even the traditional muslin (bleached or unbleached) is being supplemented by white-on-white prints, and manufacturers are providing quilters with more and more choices of neutral tone-on-tone prints. They're easy to work with because they definitely recede into the background as muslin does, but they offer a bit of variety upon close-up viewing, as shown in **Solid Prints**, below. Paste your samples of solid prints in the spaces provided at the top of the opposite page.

If you are used to using some solids in your patchwork because you find it difficult to mix prints, try replacing the solids with solid prints. While a solid print won't offer a lot of contrast, it will add more close-up interest to your quilt.

Solid Prints

Solid Print Samples

COMPLEMENTARY COLORS IN FABRICS

When prints have several colors in them, you can see that the fabric designers used the standard theories of color contrast within the printed fabrics. Complementary contrast and warm-cool contrast, both shown below, are popular in fabrics.

Because such fabrics contain high contrast and often a variety of colors, they're sometimes considered busy and hard to use. But their busyness is what makes them interesting. Try using them for larger quilt patches where the print can fill the space with detail, or use them as the basic fabric from which you pull other colors for the quilt.

**Complementary Contrast
and Warm-Cool Contrast in Prints**

**Complementary Contrast
and Warm-Cool Contrast Print Samples**

ANALOGOUS COLORS IN FABRICS

Analogous colors are also frequently used together in prints. They make beautiful color combinations in fabric just as they do in quilts. Notice how pleasing and soothing the analogous color fabrics shown below are to the eye.

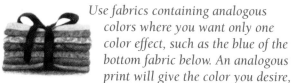

Use fabrics containing analogous colors where you want only one color effect, such as the blue of the bottom fabric below. An analogous print will give the color you desire, but make your quilt appear richer from a distance because of the subtle additions of closely related colors.

Analogous Contrast in Prints

Analogous Colors Print Samples

VARY YOUR FABRICS

Include a variety of prints in any quilt you make—variety is the spice of quilts as well as the spice of life! If you include fabrics of different color contrasts, kinds, and scales of print, you will have an interesting quilt, as exemplified in the portion of the **Scrap Half Log Cabin** quilt shown at right. The quilt contains stripes, geometrics, high contrast fabrics, and beige-on-white tiny florals, all in scraps.

Scrap Half Log Cabin
made by Sharyn Craig

IDENTIFYING AND USING PRINTS OF THE PAST

Many prints and fabric types are identified with particular periods in quiltmaking history. Even though they were not designed particularly for quilters, they were used extensively in quilts and can actually help us date antique quilts.

Today, reproduction fabrics are being made that enable us to re-create the looks of time-honored antique quilts. It is useful to know some of the kinds of fabrics found in quilts of different historical periods and how to identify them in both antique quilts and reproduction fabrics. With this knowledge you can replicate the look of an heirloom quilt if you want to. Here are some of the most important styles of prints and the periods in which they were most popular. Using any of the fabrics from these periods or combining them is what will give your quilt an historic look.

CALICOES

The calicoes quilters are so fond of have been available since the mid-nineteenth century. The word *calico* originally referred to tightly woven cotton cloth imported from Calicut, India, but it soon became the name for the brightly colored, small-scale florals, shown below, that we think of as traditional in quilts. Calicoes were widely avail-

able and found their way into quilts as well as clothing. Even today, with literally thousands of bolts of new and vibrant fabrics lining the shelves of quilt shops, calicoes remain a staple to quiltmakers.

Use calicoes sparingly. These safe, predictable fabrics often look solid from a distance, so they don't give your quilt as much texture and pattern as other types of prints would.

DOUBLE PINKS OR CINNAMON PINKS

Many variations of these small-scale pink-on-pink or floral prints, shown below, were printed from the 1860s through the 1920s. Inexpensive and widely available in stores throughout the United States, they were often used in quilts and are enjoying a new wave of popularity since reproductions are available today.

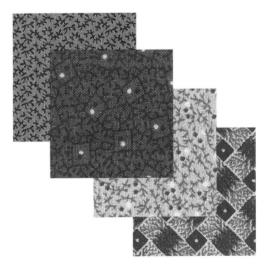

Double Pinks

Double pinks are always bright in color, so use them sparingly, too. They are very powerful, so a small amount can make quite a statement.

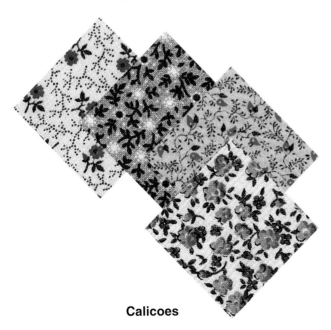

Calicoes

FEEDSACK CLOTH

During the Great Depression, feedsacks were printed with brightly colored, cheerful florals and conversational prints, as shown below. Clever homemakers didn't let the precious fabric go to waste. They used the sacks to make clothing for their families and to patch into quilt tops. When manufacturers realized that their printed sacks were being used for home sewing, they had them printed with feed company labels that would wash out so every bit of the precious fabric could be used.

Feedsack Prints

Feedsack fabrics were loosely woven and coarse compared to today's quilting cottons, so they are not good fabrics for a quilt that will get a lot of use. Reserve authentic feedsack fabrics for a special project or choose reproductions, which are printed on high-quality cotton.

GREENS

Green fabrics were popular in the early nineteenth century, but they had one disappointing feature—they faded more than any other color. At that time, green was printed by over-dyeing, combining yellow and blue. Both colors faded, often at different rates, which accounts for antique quilts with appliquéd leaves that have turned tan, yellow, or blue, or sometimes blotchy combinations of these three. These leaves were probably originally green. According to Barbara Brackman in her book, *Clues in the Calico,* late nineteenth century and early twentieth century greens "could also fade away completely, leaving ghostly white leaves and stems among the still-bright flowers."

Acid or apple green was a yellow-green calico that frequently included black and yellow in the print. Sometimes this color is also referred to as poison green, since it was the color of arsenic. Acid green is found in quilts from the mid-nineteenth century, but when these quilts were sewn the greens were probably not as yellow as they appear today. Prints of this color are also available in reproductions today, as shown below.

Acid green is very strong because it's so close to yellow, so some quilt-makers find it hard to use. Try small bits of it where you want a very bright color, or incorporate it into a project that you want to replicate the look of a nineteenth-century quilt.

Acid Green Prints

Depression green is a pale, bluish green that was quite popular from the Great Depression years up until the 1950s. Unlike acid green or other shades of green, it was usually used as a solid rather than in prints, as shown below.

Depression Green

For an authentic 1920s look, use depression green in sashing and borders around appliqué or a patchwork design full of color.

SHAKER GRAYS AND HALF-MOURNING PURPLES

These dark-hued calicoes (shown below and at right) were available throughout the nineteenth century and were widely used in quilts of the time. They were originally designed to be "worn by widows who had passed out of the stage of mourning proper, when they were expected to wear black… [and they] were favored by practical rural working

Shaker Grays

women, not necessarily bereaved, because their speckled textures and dark colors required less frequent laundering," according to Susan Meller and Joost Elffers in *Textile Designs*. Reproduction Shaker grays and half-mourning purples such as the swatches shown below are popular with quilt-makers today.

Shaker grays and half-mourning purples make great neutrals. Even though purple is a strong color, the dull purples are surprisingly good neutrals, and the prints provide visual texture to the background.

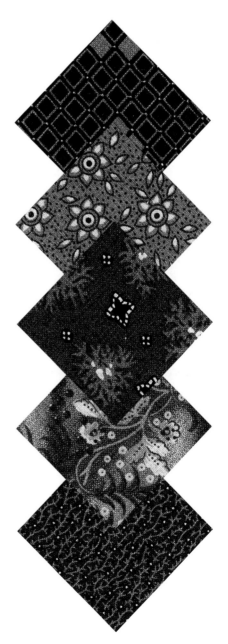

Half-Mourning Purples

INDIGOS

The word *indigo* refers to the vivid, deep blue fabric dyed from the indigo plant. In the nineteenth century, indigo prints in blue and white, several values of blue, or blue, yellow, and white were widely available and frequently used in quilts. Indigos are one of the few types of antique fabrics that maintain their color. This is because the indigo dyes were so stable. Today, quiltmakers can find reproductions of typical indigo prints, as shown below, but actual indigo dyes cannot be used to make these fabrics in the United States because when they are released during the manufacturing process they cause water pollution.

Because indigos are very close to being pure in color, they're very strong colors. They will dominate a quilt, so use them in the parts of your design that you want to emphasize.

Indigos

MADDERS

Madder is a vegetable dye derived from the root of the madder plant. It produces many different browns, rusts, oranges, purples, and reds, as shown below. Madder-dyed fabrics are seen in most quilts from the eighteenth and nineteenth centuries, because madder was the most common dye of the era.

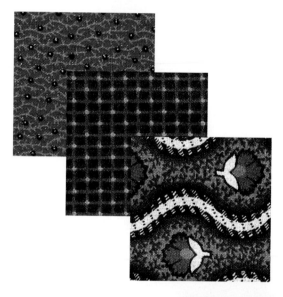

Madder Prints

NEATS

Commonplace in the second half of the nineteenth century, *neats* were small scale, simple designs printed in only one or two colors, as shown below. They could be either floral or geometric, and they were a staple fabric of the time. Neats were usually brown, red, blue, or black figures on a white background, or the reverse. Many of this style print were manufactured because they were inexpensive to print. They were used primarily in clothing such as blouses, shirts, and pajamas, but many of them made their way into quilts.

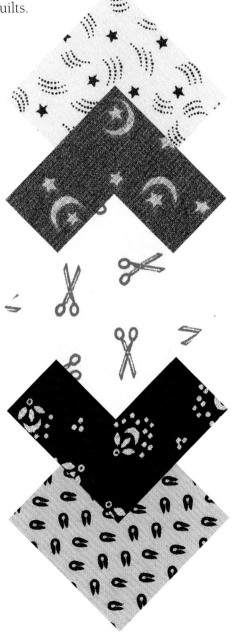

Neats

SHIRTINGS: PLAIDS, STRIPES, AND CHECKS

Popular throughout the nineteenth and twentieth centuries as clothing, the pale blue and brown shirting stripes, plaids, and checks, shown below, became widely available in the late nineteenth and early twentieth centuries. Shirtings were commonly used in turn-of-the-century scrap quilts, and are popular again today.

One way to add a bit of extra texture in your next scrap quilt is to use one or several light-color shirting fabrics for the backgrounds of your quilt blocks.

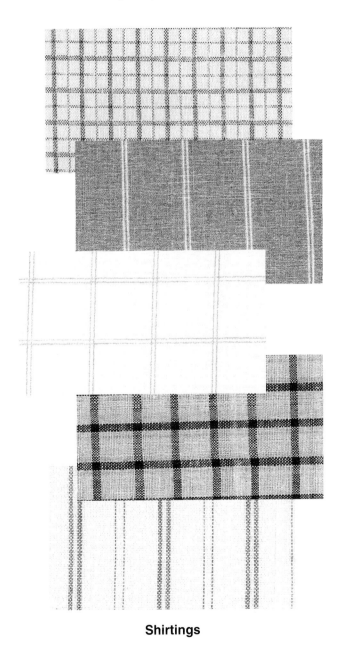

Shirtings

OMBRÉS

Also called *rainbow* or *fondu prints,* the *ombrés* contain a print over a background that shades and blends gradually from one value to another or from one color to another. These fabrics were popular from the 1840s through the 1850s and are seen frequently in quilts of that period. Reproductions, such as those shown below, are especially popular with the many quiltmakers interested in quilt history.

TURKEY REDS

Turkey red refers to a deep, rich, scarlet red. These wonderful and complicated prints became commercially available in the early 1800s. French Provincial in style, Turkey red prints contain wild, large florals and floral stripes. They are primarily red and feature black, blue, yellow, and white. Solid cloth in the same rich red was used in many quilts of the nineteenth century, and to quilters the term "Turkey red" has come to mean any print or solid in this deep, rich, slightly rusty red. Turkey red is a favorite of quiltmakers because no matter how you use it, it's always dramatic.

Ombré Prints

Turkey Red Prints

RE-CREATING THE LOOK OF BYGONE ERAS

In addition to recognizing the specific types of fabric associated with quilts of particular historical eras, there are other key characteristics that tie in with specific time periods. In this section we will discuss how to replicate the quilts of different eras by including significant colors, prints, and patterns. For each era listed below, I've also provided information regarding typical fabrics, colors, backgrounds, block designs, and styles of quilting used in quilts of bygone eras.

Mid-nineteenth century red and green quilts
Mid-nineteenth century scrap quilts
Late nineteenth century red and white quilts
Turn of the century scrap quilts
1920s pastel quilts
1920s Lancaster County Amish quilts
1930s depression quilts

Although we are concentrating on making quilts look old through color and fabric, you can more closely replicate a particular style of quilt by using the same types of quilt blocks, quilting motifs, and fabrics popular at a particular time.

Some of the quilt examples that follow are authentic antiques, while others are contemporary quilts that really do capture the flavor of earlier quiltmaking eras.

The Mid-Nineteenth Century Red-and-Green Quilts

Fabrics: Both solids and calicoes

Colors: Turkey red, green, acid green, tan, gray-blue, or yellow (Green often faded to tan or blue, thus they are frequently seen in antique red-and-green quilts from this period. Yellow is frequently seen if the design required a third color.)

Background: Bright white or muslin

Quilting: Close, tiny, and elaborate in design

Blocks: Many red-and-green quilts of this period were florals, either appliqué or a combination of appliqué and patchwork. Album and Baltimore album quilts were essentially red-and-green quilts with many colors added in much smaller doses.

*This **Red-and-Green Appliquéd Baskets** quilt, owned by Cindy Rennels, is believed to have been made between 1860 and 1870 and is typical of mid-nineteenth century red and green florals. It contains Turkey red, green, and yellow (possibly discolored green from which the blue dye faded) fabrics on a white background. The green has faded to a tan that is visible and attractive. It is filled with close background grid quilting typical of the mid-nineteenth century. The flowers in the baskets or urns are cockscombs, a motif popular during that era.*

Making Quilts That Look Antique

With all of the reproduction fabrics on the market today, it's easy to make a brand new quilt that looks like a quilt from your favorite bygone era. But the one thing that may be missing is the faded, soft, well-used look of a real antique. Part of the charm of the antique originals is the yellowed look of age or the faded softness of their colors. Sometimes it's nice to make quilts that capture the look of well-used and much-washed utilitarian quilts. Here are some pointers on making a new quilt with a built-in old look.

Yellow-Beiges and Faded Fabrics

Begin to search for and collect yellow-beiges and faded-looking fabrics. The swatches shown at right will give you an idea of the type of print and color to look for. There are many on the market, often scorned for their dullness and lack of brilliance. Collect them to use in antique-looking quilts. They can easily look as if they were once whites that have yellowed, and they would look perfect in an "old" quilt.

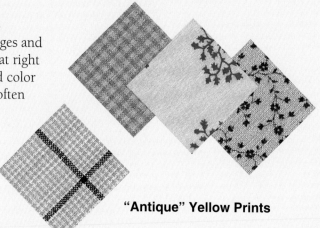

"Antique" Yellow Prints

Shirting Fabrics

Shirting fabrics in pale stripes and plaids have a faded look, and many grayed fabrics look as if they could be faded versions of vivid originals. Also, examine the backs of current fabrics. Many of them are softened echoes of the print on the front, so using the wrong side can simulate the effects that time has on fabric, as shown below.

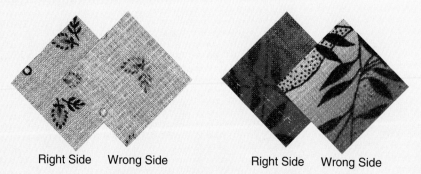

Right Side Wrong Side   Right Side Wrong Side
Wrong sides of fabrics look faded

Make Old-Looking Fabric

You can make your own old-looking fabric. Over-dyeing fabric softens the brilliance of a color and makes it look yellowed with age. Jane Nehring, who wrote the article "Aging Gracefully" for *Miniature Quilts*, recommends using a tan commercial dye available for "antiquing" fabric to give brilliant whites the desired dingy look. Or you can

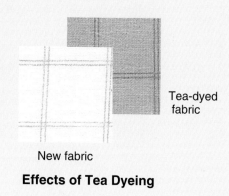

Tea-dyed fabric

New fabric

Effects of Tea Dyeing

tea dye your fabrics. To do this, use 100 percent cotton fabric, and prewash and dry it to remove the sizing. Use a small pot so the fabric bunches up and produces a time-worn, mottled look. Boil six or more tea bags in the pot; don't break the bags. Remove the pot from the stove. Dip the fabric into the pot. Don't worry about the tea bags touching the fabric, and don't stir the mixture. Let the fabric soak for 20 minutes. The resulting blotchiness will look like the authentic discoloration of time, as shown in the fabric pairs below.

Buy generic brand tea bags for tea dyeing. The cheaper brands contain more black tea, so they provide a good color. (Not to mention that they'll save you some money!)

 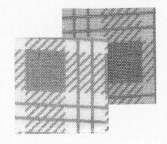 

Mid-Nineteenth Century Scrap Quilts

Fabrics: Every kind of clothing fabric, especially calicoes, plaids, stripes, and large florals for borders

Colors: Madder browns, from rust to tan, mourning purples, Shaker grays, indigos, acid green, double pinks, tan (Green faded to tan and is frequently seen in antique quilts from this period.)

Quilting: Outline of the pattern; could be close or not

Blocks: Any block; usually pieced. Overall, repeating pieced patterns such as the Log Cabin were preferred.

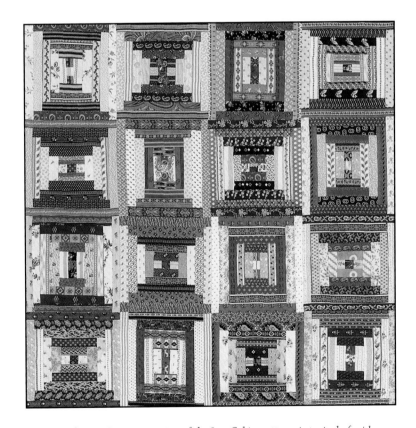

Courthouse Steps, a version of the Log Cabin pattern, is typical of mid-nineteenth century scrap quilts. In color, it contains many madder fabrics, as well as several acid greens and mourning purples. Notice the variety of prints in scale and type, including calicoes, florals, and a wonderful selection of stripes.

Late Nineteenth Century Red-and-White or Blue-and-White Quilts

Fabrics: Usually solids

Colors: Only one color, usually pure red or blue

Background: Bright white

Quilting: Any kind; could be close or not

Blocks: Any block; often repeating pieced patterns such as the Schoolhouse; sometimes alternated with white connecting blocks

*This **Red-and-White Wedding Ring** quilt, owned by Cindy Rennels, is typical of quilts made in the late nineteenth century in color and design. The fabric is a solid Turkey red, the background is a bleached white, and the quilting motifs and multiple borders are simple in design.*

Turn-of-the-Century Scrap Quilts

Fabrics: Shirtings in checks, stripes, and plaids; calicoes; and conversational prints

Colors: Being scrap quilts, they contained many colors. But because of the prevailing fabric colors available at that time, these quilts had a blue, red, and white flavor and tended to contain a lot of indigo blue, double pinks, black on white prints, black on red prints, and grays.

Quilting: Usually a simple outline of the pattern; could be close or not

Blocks: Any block; often simple, overall, or repeating pieced patterns, such as the Nine Patch block

All American Schoolhouses, made by Sharyn Craig, while not an antique quilt, captures the color and flavor of turn-of-the-century quilts, which were often mainly blue, red, and white. It uses several reproduction indigo blue prints, including a celestial print typical of the time. The red calicoes are authentic in feeling, and the quilt has a slightly faded look typical of the well-used, frequently washed utilitarian quilts of that era.

1920s Pastel Quilts

Fabrics: Usually solids

Colors: One or many pastels

Background: Usually bright white and prominent

Quilting: Varied; could be close, such as small grid quilting, or not

Blocks: Many were florals, either appliquéd or pieced; baskets were a popular motif, as is evident in these two examples

*This **Carolina Lily Medallion** quilt, owned by Cindy Rennels, exemplifies 1920s quilts in color and theme. The pieced baskets float on a large, open, white space covered with grid quilting. The fabrics are all solids, and the goldish beige baskets were probably originally a soft green. Note, too, that the flower stems and sepals are a very light bluish green, a slightly faded version of depression green.*

*Many pieced quilts of the 1920s were one-color-on-white, as is this **Fruit Baskets** quilt, but pastels replaced the strong red-on-white and blue-on-white of earlier decades. The quilting is elaborate, probably to add interest to the quiet charm of the otherwise simple quilt. Quilt owned by Cindy Rennels.*

1920s Lancaster County Amish Quilts

Fabrics: All solids, sometimes wool or sateen

Colors: Purples, blues, turquoises, magentas, dark greens, and red

Background: Usually black, although other dark colors such as green, purple, or red were also used for backgrounds. This contemporary version has a dark navy background.

Quilting: Black thread; elaborate and decorative, including feathered wreaths and borders

Blocks: Pieced; simple, large, full-quilt designs, such as Center Diamond and Bars

*This contemporary **Spiderwebs and Dewdrops** wallhanging, made by Susan Stein, is Lancaster County Amish in flavor and color, though not in design. The dark background makes the cool, pure colors appear vibrant and strong. The quilting in variegated metallic thread, while not authentic, stands out against the navy and adds sparkling accent to the open space.*

1930s Depression Quilts

Fabrics and Colors: Feedsack florals in bright and pastel colors, depression green and bright pink; greens and pinks were most often solids

Background: Unbleached muslin

Quilting: Varied from utilitarian to elaborate

Blocks: Varied; often patterns that use small scraps, such as the Wedding Ring

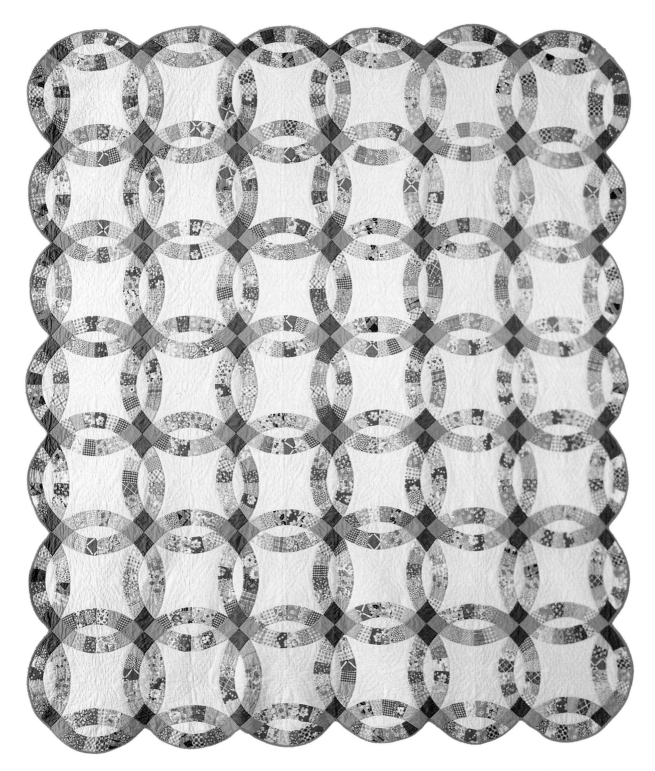

*The Double Wedding Ring was a popular design in the 1930s. This **Feed Sack Wedding Ring** quilt, owned by Bertha Rush, exhibits all of the characteristics of depression-era quilts: scraps of feedsack prints, muslin background, depression green and rosy pink solids, and lovely fill quilting.*

PLANNING EFFECTIVE
color schemes

Planning Effective Color Schemes

The planning stage of quiltmaking is often the most fun. It is at this stage that we consider the quilt's purpose, its future owners and their preferences, the wealth of tempting fabrics available, the myriad of quilt blocks possible, the layout, the size, the set, the quilting pattern, and so much more. It is the stage of excitement. Cutting, sewing, and quilting are more methodical, but they all lead toward the magical moment when the quilt is complete. The planning is full of challenges (and some might even say it's fraught with danger!), and color is one of the factors that makes it so.

Color will play an important role in how the finished quilt looks, so let's consider how you can use your new knowledge of color and fabric at the planning stage to help make the whole process exciting, fun, and rewarding.

LEARNING WHERE TO BEGIN

There are lots of things to consider when planning a quilt color scheme; perhaps that's why so many quilters feel overwhelmed when it comes to selecting fabrics. In this section, I've broken these color considerations down into useful bits of key information so planning your next quilt will be easy.

CONSIDER HOW COLOR AFFECTS MOOD

One of the most exciting things about color is that it affects us physically and emotionally. A great deal of research has been done on how color affects people. Although we are often unaware of it, we are affected every day by the colors that surround us. Our natural outdoor environment consists of cool sky blues and grass greens, which are soothing to us. Advertisers and product packagers use their knowledge of color-mood research to catch our attention and entice us to buy their products. They know that warm colors attract our attention, so they use them in their product packages. Hospitals and restaurants also use color to create appropriate atmospheres.

It only makes sense that as quilters we can use the same knowledge of how color affects mood to create the kinds of quilts we want. To see how to use this information effectively, here's a summary of the effects colors have on human beings.

How Colors Affect Us

Cool colors soothe and relax: Blue is placid and passive, but it can also be cold. Green is stable and tranquil, conveying hope and peacefulness.

Warm colors stimulate and excite: Red is exciting, stimulating, and agitating. It also conveys passion. Yellow is bright, cheerful, and buoyant.

Pastel colors suggest light: They are graceful and have a feeling of airiness.

Pure colors suggest buoyancy: Pure, primary colors project lightheartedness.

Muted colors suggest stability: Grayed tones are more serious than pure ones.

You often know what feeling or mood you want a quilt to convey. Now that you know how colors affect mood, you can plan a quilt that will fulfill its purpose. For example, if you want to make a quilt to comfort an ill friend, consider the peacefulness of cool colors. If it is a quilt to make a child happy, you may want to include bright, pure colors. If your quilt is to be a dramatic eye catcher at a quilt show, consider a warm color scheme.

Look at the quilt diagrams below and at the top of page 206. Each diagram is of the same quilt pattern, but the colors have been changed. See for yourself how tranquil the **Cool Colors** quilt seems when compared to the exuberance of the **Primary Colors** quilt. Note, too, that the quilt designed primarily with **Warm Colors** (see page 206) makes a powerful statement.

Cool Colors

Primary Colors

Warm Colors

CONSIDER COLOR AND CONTRAST

Using colors to set the mood is only the first step in quilt design, and quite often it is a subconscious decision. You can also add what you know about color and value contrast to your quilt planning. Since low contrast is relatively quiet while high contrast is stimulating, you can use the type of contrast that best suits your quilt. Using the same quilt diagram as in the above examples, you can see how different degrees of contrast can dramatically change the mood of an entire quilt. In the diagram below, we've used complementary contrast (red and green) and value contrast (pure red and a light, grayed green), and set them both on a pure white background. This is just one example of how different types of contrast can be used. Refer to the chapter "Color Contrast" to remind yourself of the choices.

Complementary Contrast

CONSIDER THE AMOUNT OF COLOR

How much of a particular color you include will affect the relative strength of that color in the quilt. A lot of any color will make it strong in the sense that it is quite visible, even though it may not jump out at the person viewing the quilt. A quilt with a light blue background decorated with red dots will remain blue in feeling, even though the red dots will tend to jump out because they are pure and warm. Because the red dots are tiny, they will simply act as accents on the blue quilt, as shown below.

Red dots advance, yet
quilt appears blue overall

ASK YOURSELF QUESTIONS

First, ask yourself what you want the quilt to do and what mood you want it to convey. All of your color decisions depend upon the answers to these questions. What colors you choose and what kind of contrast you decide upon depend upon your quiltmaking goal.

For example, if you decide to make a quiet quilt, combine a palette of cool colors with low contrast of some kind. If you want to make a stimulating quilt, choose primarily warm colors or a mixture of warm and cool colors, and make sure your fabric selection provides high contrast of some kind.

PUTTING COLOR TO THE TEST

TEST COLOR SCHEMES

"Try before you buy" is a good motto for quilters who are unsure of their color ideas. A quick way to see how color affects a quilt design is to use crayons, markers, or colored pencils to color the design before you spend money on fabric. To do this, choose a design from a book or magazine and draw it on graph paper. Then make multiple copies on a copy machine, and color the design in different ways. Or, make one copy of the design and lay a piece of tracing paper over it. Color on the tracing paper; lift the paper and color another combination on a new sheet. You can get a lot of mileage out of only one drawing and you don't need access to a copy machine.

When you're coloring, you don't have to be precise; just a few blocks will give you an idea of how your color plan will effect the look of the quilt.

Use colored pencils rather than markers to map out your color scheme. You can use them for subtle shading to give the effect of pastel fabrics, whereas markers may be a little too bright to really represent your fabrics.

PLAN A SMALL QUILT

Let's take a simple quilt block, the Basket block, and pretend you want to make a small quilt with just four Basket blocks with a strip-pieced sashing between them. The inspiration for this block is **Scrap Baskets with Nine-Patch Sashing**, shown at right. This scrap quilt uses many fabrics on an off-white background. Notice that some baskets stand out because of contrast of value, while others get lost for the same reason.

In this color exercise, you'll be trying several different color variations of the same pattern. It's the color decisions that will affect how the quilt will look. Even with this simple design, you still need to ask yourself some questions:

- Do you want your quilt to be a bright or a tranquil one?
- Do you want the baskets to stand out against the background or blend in with it?
- Which do you want to stand out more, the baskets or the sashing?

Here are several color options to consider after you have answered these questions. Suppose I want a quiet quilt in which the baskets stand out against the background and are stronger than the sashing, as shown in **Color Option 1** on page 208. I can choose several cool blues and greens for a quiet effect, but I need high contrast so the baskets will stand out against the white background. I can't achieve high contrast through color because the blues and greens are closely related, so I need to achieve it through contrast of value. To do that, I can make my background very light and my baskets either dark or pure.

Scrap Baskets with Nine-Patch Sashing
made by Wilma Sestric

If the color combination seems too dull, I can add a little of a warm color, such as a pale tint of yellow. If I put the yellow in the baskets and keep the sashing cool, the warm will help emphasize the baskets.

Take a look at the resulting basket quilt I've planned. Notice how the blue, green, and yellow in medium to dark values on a white background work together to make a calm color scheme without being too quiet or boring.

Color Option 2 shows what happens when I answer the same set of questions differently because I'd like a vibrant quilt. I choose the complementary colors red and green because complements always provide high color contrast, and add a neutral white background. Remembering that it's important to use complements in unequal amounts, I opt to use more red than green. The resulting quilt is high in value contrast as well as color contrast. Not only do the blocks provide contrast, but the bold sashing does, too. If I want to de-emphasize the sashing, I can make it predominantly green.

Take a look at the Basket quilt in **Color Option 3**, shown below at right. My answers to the basic color questions are less clear in this quilt. The cool greens and blues in the baskets at first suggest a peaceful color scheme, especially when combined with the quilters' neutrals. But for fun, I want to create a strong sashing, so I choose red. The baskets still stand out against the background because of value contrast and because the background is a neutral beige, yet the bright red sashing makes a strong secondary design in the quilt top.

Now try your hand at using color to change a quilt using the **Scrap Basket Color Plan** on the opposite page. Make a few copies of the color plan, either with a photocopier or by tracing. Play freely with colored pencils to make a color scheme. Then try another color scheme after asking yourself the three questions at the top of page 207. Pretend you want a certain effect and see if you can achieve it. In just minutes you'll be able to play with different colors and see the variety of looks that are possible.

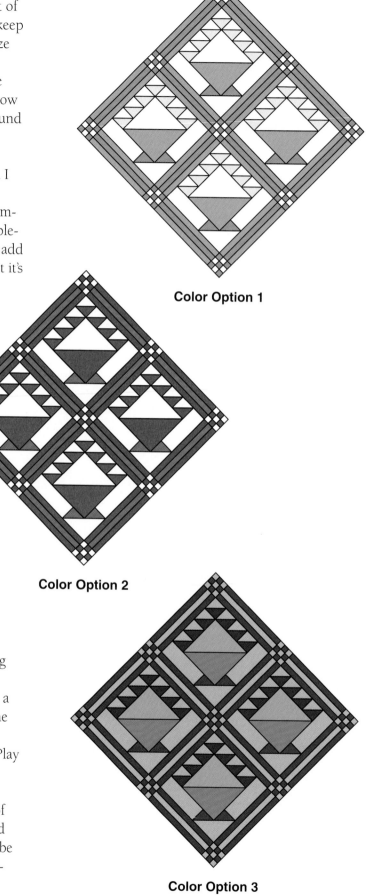

Color Option 1

Color Option 2

Color Option 3

Make your own Basket quilt color scheme

Scrap Basket Color Plan

Setting these two quilt blocks together in a quilt top is fairly common. Yet you can create a variety of different effects with this simple design just by varying the color placement. The partially colored diagram below at left shows that when different parts of a design are emphasized, the resulting quilts will be completely different! Here, too, coloring with pencils is a quick way to explore the possibilities of a block.

Emphasize a Background—or Not

Coloring is a good way to try out different background colors, too. The **Double Wedding Ring Color Plan**, shown below, illustrates how different the same quilt would look if you changed just one fabric—the background. You don't even have to color the entire drawing. Just color enough to get the feeling of the backgrounds you are considering.

USE COLOR TO EMPHASIZE PARTS OF A DESIGN

The Basket block is a simple design. Although we could emphasize the basket or the sashing depending on where we put certain colors, the design remains the same. Many blocks, however, can look completely different depending upon how you color them. One such example is the **Snowball and Nine Patch** combination, shown below.

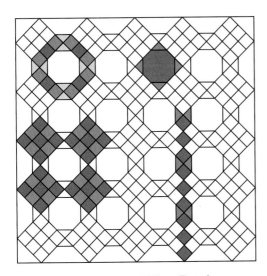

Snowball and Nine Patch

Double Wedding Ring Color Plan

Practice Makes Perfect

Since it's a lot easier (and much less expensive) to plan a quilt on paper than out of fabric, we've provided three sets of quilt blocks that you can use for your own creative exercises. Look at the original quilts from which we've taken the blocks (notice they are all variations of a simple Nine Patch block), study the sample colorings we have provided, and then try your hand at designing your own quilts. Try to emphasize different areas of the overall design with each color plan.

 Now's a great time to experiment with a color scheme that you've never worked with before. There's no fabric investment to make, and you might even surprise yourself and enjoy the result! After all, this is always a fun part of quiltmaking.

Summer's End
made by Judy Miller

Color ideas for Summer's End

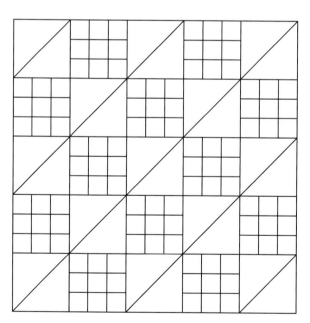

Create your own color scheme

Summer's End, shown on the opposite page, features a strong diagonal line. Notice how the line of the quilt design can be emphasized or de-emphasized, however, simply by changing the contrast of value used in the triangle squares that separate the Nine Patch blocks.

Oklahoma Nine Patch, shown at left, also incorporates diagonal lines in the quilt design, but this time the diagonals are set in a barn-raising style. By changing the original black and white triangle squares to a more placid, analogous color scheme, the quilt will take on a whole new look. Yet another approach would be to use an Amish color scheme for a third entirely different look.

Oklahoma Nine Patch
made by Carolyn Miller

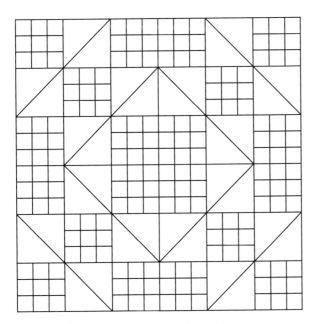

Create your own color scheme

Color ideas for Oklahoma Nine Patch

On the Road Again…Paducah Bound, is also a Nine Patch quilt, but in this quilt design, the blocks were turned on point to achieve the diagonal, medallion-type setting. Notice that by altering the color choices you can emphasize different areas of the design so either diamonds, nine patches, or pinwheels become more visible. What area of the design would you emphasize with color?

On the Road Again…Paducah Bound
made by Nancy Chizek

Color ideas for Paducah Bound

Create your own color scheme

TIPS ON CHOOSING COLORS

A TRIED-AND-TRUE COLOR PLAN

One of the easiest ways to choose a beautiful color scheme for a quilt is to use a theme fabric. A theme fabric is one that contains several colors and is often a large, busy print. Because the fabric designer knew all about color and chose harmonious colors, you are guaranteed a successful color scheme if you use this fabric as the basis for your color selections.

The first step is to find a fabric you like that contains several colors. Carry the fabric around as you search for additional fabrics in these colors. Look at the sample fabrics below. Notice that the theme fabric contains analogous warm colors, a neutral, and contrast of value. If you pull out the colors as you look for coordinating fabrics—such as beige, lavender, maroon, or rusty red—your color scheme is set!

In addition to following the colors in a theme fabric, pay attention to how much each color is used in the theme fabric. If it's used just a little, that's a good indication that you should use just a little of that color in your quilt, too.

The theme fabric system of color planning works at any time and is particularly useful for beginning quilters who may be unsure of their own color preferences.

STRIKE A BALANCE

You already know that when working with complementary colors, it's important to use more of one complement than of the other. The same sense of proportion holds true when you work with advancing and receding colors in a quilt. For the best results, use more of the receding colors (cool, light, or muted colors) than you do of the advancing colors (warm, pure, or dark colors). If you use too many strong, advancing colors, they will overpower the quilt.

The two Schoolhouse blocks shown below illustrate this point. Imagine how overpowering a whole quilt made from the red and yellow blocks with that busy sashing would look. There are so many components made of advancing, strong colors that the viewer wouldn't know where to look first. In the second block, the red house stands out nicely against the aqua sky, and the dark blue sashing and red stars make a nice frame around the house without detracting from it.

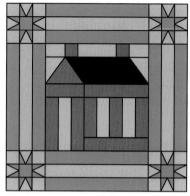

Too many advancing colors; house, sashing, stars, and background all fight for attention

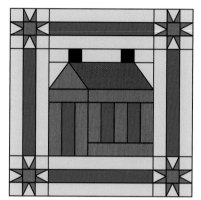

Using more receding colors lets house stand out, yet sashing and stars frame it nicely

A LITTLE YELLOW GOES A LONG WAY

As we discussed in the chapter "The Color Wheel," yellow is the strongest and most brilliant color on the color wheel. You need much less yellow in proportion to other colors.

Look at the **Mennonite Four Patch/ Nine Patch** quilt at right. The color scheme is simple: brown, green, red, and yellow. The quiet, earthy brown is used in the greatest proportion and the yellow, red, and green are used in about the same small proportions. Notice how you see the yellow grid pattern immediately and then the red patches. The yellow takes over this quilt, just as it always does. Can you imagine how this quilt would have looked if the quiltmaker had swapped the placement of the vibrant yellow and the soft brown? Don't be afraid to use yellow in your quilts, just use it sparingly, or soften its power by using a pale tint of yellow.

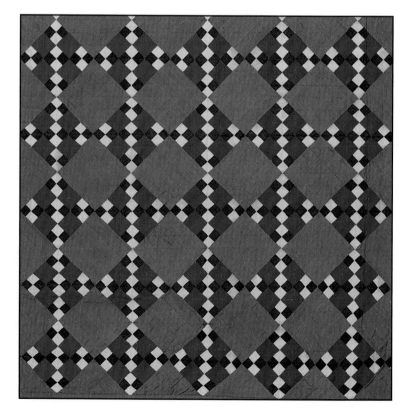

Mennonite Four Patch/Nine Patch
owned by Joan Townsend

NEVER USE A COLOR ONLY ONCE

Be sure to use every color in your quilt more than once. Echo the colors in some way, whether in small pieces or in large elements somewhere else. Repeating colors will help to balance the quilt. For example, take a look at **Simply Charming,** below. Notice how the bright green patches seem to pop off the page. If this shade of green had been used in only one spot, your eye would have been drawn to that area of the quilt, where it would have stopped. Instead, the quiltmaker used this vivid green in several places so it became a tool to move your eye over the entire quilt top. Repeated use of this green makes it seem less unexpected.

Using a color more than once doesn't mean you have to use the same exact fabric more than once. The quilt below is a charm quilt, with each patch cut from a different fabric. The fabrics aren't repeated, but the colors are.

Simply Charming
made by Edith Zimmer

CHOOSING THE RIGHT BORDER

The right border can make or break a great quilt. Here are four important tips to help you select the right fabric and make sure your quilt gets the border it deserves.

1. Watch your proportions. The amount of border fabric is usually huge in comparison to the patchwork pieces or appliqué in the center of the quilt. Therefore, whatever color you put in the border will make a very strong statement. If you don't want too bold a border, select a soothing color fabric.

2. Echo colors in the quilt top. The border is a good place to echo a color you want to emphasize from the center design. If you choose the strongest color, however, remember that you will be using a lot of it and it may be too dominant and overpower your quilt.

Conversely, if you choose too light a color, the border will appear to fall off the quilt. It will be lifeless or dull and might as well not even be there. Consider the second strongest or a moderately strong color from the center for an appropriate border color.

3. Don't start a new color in the border. A border needs to blend with the quilt somehow. If you are using a new fabric, which quilters often do, be sure it repeats a color or a value found in the center of the quilt. The border fabric should also be of the same intensity and mood as the center. It's fine to use a new fabric, just not a whole new color.

4. Use a narrow inner border of a stronger color. If you want to repeat a strong color but don't want to use too much of it, use it in a narrow inner border. Then finish off the quilt with a second, wider border made of a less powerful color. This was done successfully in the **Sunshine and Shadow** quilt, shown below. The quiltmaker brought out the red in the Log Cabin blocks nicely by repeating it in the narrow inner border. Had the red been used in the wide outer border, it would have overpowered the dramatic pattern of the quilt. Used sparingly, however, it makes a strong echo to the many red prints in the Log Cabin blocks. The outer border repeats the value and color of many of the center fabrics, and its neutral brown color frames the quilt but doesn't detract from the design.

Sunshine and Shadow
made by Bettina Havig and owned by Joyce Gross

BINDING:
YOUR FINAL COLOR CHOICE

The binding is your last chance to make or break your color scheme, and it's also a good place to echo a strong color. Because it is so narrow, it provides just a touch of the color you choose. A bit of color contrast is also fun, and it shows off the binding nicely.

Barn Raising, shown below, illustrates all of the key points on selecting borders and bindings. The electric blue inner border repeats and brings out a color that was used sparingly within the quilt. It would probably have been too strong a color for the wide outer border, so a calmer dark blue is used there. It, too, repeats a color from the center. The fuchsia binding, however, begins something new at the very outside of the quilt. Although it is purer and thus stronger than the related colors used in the center, it is an analogous color to the others in the quilt, which helps it blend in. However, the fuchsia is still distinct enough to add that final bit of whimsy and fun.

Barn Raising
made by Mark Stratton, quilted by an Amish family

your fabric
COLLECTION

Your Fabric Collection

As soon as you set aside the leftover fabrics from your first quilt, you've begun a fabric collection! For quilters, fabric is our resource. We may add to that resource frugally by simply saving the scraps from each quilt we make, or we may begin to collect ahead as we see fabric we love and feel sure we will need at some time in the future.

This chapter covers three concepts that will help you plan your quilts and build your fabric collection. First, we'll analyze quilt patterns so you can make a fabric checklist for any quilt you want to make—in any color scheme. Then we'll look at your personal fabric stash to see what you have, what you don't have, and what you can do to systematically add to your collection and expand its versatility. Finally, you'll find ideas for organizing and storing your precious yards, fat quarters, and leftover bits of fabric so they'll be protected and ready to use when you need them.

ANALYZING QUILTS FOR COLOR

Use the **Color Inspiration** chart below to help you analyze the quilts in this book and others that you see and like. It will help you determine why you like a particular quilt and what aspects of its color, contrast, and design you'd like to incorporate into a quilt of your own. Then you'll be better prepared to plan and design your own color schemes.

If the idea of analyzing quilts in this systematic way seems a little foreign or unnatural to you, don't worry. After you try it a few times the process will become easy and almost automatic when you view a quilt, whether you admire it in a book or see it hanging at a quilt show.

Make a quilt photo album to hold snapshots you take at quilt shows or classes you attend. Slip a photocopy of this chart in next to the quilts you particularly like, and use it to jot down notes or ideas about colors and fabrics for future reference.

Color Inspiration

QUILT NAME: _____

What color hits me first? Why? _____

List the colors used: _____

_____

_____

Check for the types of contrast.

Are they present? How are they used?

☐ *Contrast of Value* _____

☐ *Complementary Contrast* _____

☐ *Warm-Cool Contrast* _____

☐ *Pure Color Contrast* _____

☐ *Contrast of Intensity* _____

High contrast or low contrast? _____

What color is the background? _____

Are neutrals used? Which ones? _____

Determine the mood of the quilt.

Choose one or more adjectives to describe how this quilt makes you feel: _____

What created that mood? _____

_____

Why does this quilt appeal to me? _____

_____

PLANNING MY NEXT QUILT

Record information about your quilt in the **Quilt Planner** below, and fill in the information and fabric swatches on the opposite page. Copy the pages so you can use them again, each time including a picture or sketch of the quilt design for color planning purposes. You can paste up fabric swatches you're considering, then take the quilt planner and samples along when you shop for additional fabrics.

Quilt Planner

QUILT PATTERN: _____

QUILT SIZE: _____

Number of main design blocks needed: _____   Borders: _____

Number of alternate blocks needed: _____   Binding: _____

Insert Quilt Drawing or Color Plan here:

KEY QUESTIONS TO HELP MY PLANNING

There are many factors to consider when planning a quilt. Before you choose a block and begin picking out fabric, ask yourself the following questions:

What mood do I want the quilt to convey?

_____

_____

_____

_____

What colors will help me convey this mood?

_____

_____

_____

_____

What kind of contrast will help me convey this mood?

_____

_____

_____

_____

What part of the design do I want to emphasize?

_____

_____

_____

_____

What neutral or neutrals will I use?

_____

_____

_____

_____

How many fabrics do I need?

_____

_____

_____

_____

FABRICS SWATCHES AND YARDAGE REQUIREMENTS

Organize your fabrics in order by how much they will be used in the quilt, and jot down yardage requirements for an easy-reference shopping list.

Prior to shopping, color or paste fabrics in the blocks to remind yourself of the color fabrics you'll be looking for.

Fabrics	Yardage Needed
Fabric A	_____
Fabric B	_____
Fabric C	_____
Fabric D	_____
Fabric E	_____

Color or Paste Swatches

DEVELOPING A VERSATILE FABRIC COLLECTION

When it comes to planning or selecting the fabrics for a quilt, there are two ways to go about it. You can either take your quilt book or pattern to the fabric store with you and purchase all new fabrics for the quilt you want to make, or you can "shop" at home first. Once your fabric collection begins to grow, you'll have the option of looking through your many fabrics and selecting ones you'd like to use for a project. You can mix and match, add and delete, spread the fabrics out over the table or floor, and really begin working with the fabrics as a planning tool. Then you'll only need to shop for fabrics to fill in the gaps, rather than purchasing enough fabric for an entire quilt.

ANALYZING YOUR FABRICS

To make your fabric collection really work for you, however, it is important to know what colors and print styles you have readily available to you and which types you'll need to purchase. Rather than rummaging through an insurmountable stack of unorganized fabrics (or through boxes or storage bins), it's really helpful if you can get a good idea of your collection's strengths and weaknesses at a glance.

Later in this section you'll find handy ideas for organizing your growing collection. Here, however, we'll focus on the kinds of fabrics you've been collecting and what gaps might be developing. For instance, do you tend to have a lot of variety in red prints, but seem to be lacking purple ones? Or do you seem to favor grayed or toned-down colors over pure, intense ones?

We each have our favorite colors and styles of prints, whether they be large scale, pastel florals, or brightly colored homespun plaids. But remember, it's the variety of fabrics you use that will spice up your quilts, so it's good to have all styles of prints and an excellent variety of color available to work with in your sewing room. On the next 12 pages you'll find a **Color and Print Analysis** chart for each of the 12 colors in the basic color wheel. These charts show examples of the pure colors and light, dark, and grayed values of each color. Next to each color value there is space to record how many different fabrics you own of each color and print style. By evaluating your entire group of fabrics and determining how many pieces you have of each color, you'll quickly see where your collection is strong and where it could use some additional fabrics to round out the color wheel.

Yellow	Color and Print Analysis				
	Floral	Geometric	Abstract	Ethnic	Solid
Pure — Small scale					
Medium scale					
Large scale					
Light — Small scale					
Medium scale					
Large scale					
Dark — Small scale					
Medium scale					
Large scale					
Grayed — Small scale					
Medium scale					
Large scale					

Yellow-orange	Color and Print Analysis				
	Floral	**Geometric**	**Abstract**	**Ethnic**	**Solid**
Pure — Small scale					
Pure — Medium scale					
Pure — Large scale					
Light — Small scale					
Light — Medium scale					
Light — Large scale					
Dark — Small scale					
Dark — Medium scale					
Dark — Large scale					
Grayed — Small scale					
Grayed — Medium scale					
Grayed — Large scale					

Orange		Color and Print Analysis				
		Floral	Geometric	Abstract	Ethnic	Solid
Pure	Small scale					
	Medium scale					
	Large scale					
Light	Small scale					
	Medium scale					
	Large scale					
Dark	Small scale					
	Medium scale					
	Large scale					
Grayed	Small scale					
	Medium scale					
	Large scale					

Red-orange		Color and Print Analysis				
		Floral	Geometric	Abstract	Ethnic	Solid
Pure	Small scale					
	Medium scale					
	Large scale					
Light	Small scale					
	Medium scale					
	Large scale					
Dark	Small scale					
	Medium scale					
	Large scale					
Grayed	Small scale					
	Medium scale					
	Large scale					

Red	Color and Print Analysis				
	Floral	Geometric	Abstract	Ethnic	Solid
Pure — Small scale					
Medium scale					
Large scale					
Light — Small scale					
Medium scale					
Large scale					
Dark — Small scale					
Medium scale					
Large scale					
Grayed — Small scale					
Medium scale					
Large scale					

Red-violet	Color and Print Analysis				
	Floral	**Geometric**	**Abstract**	**Ethnic**	**Solid**
Pure Small scale					
Pure Medium scale					
Pure Large scale					
Light Small scale					
Light Medium scale					
Light Large scale					
Dark Small scale					
Dark Medium scale					
Dark Large scale					
Grayed Small scale					
Grayed Medium scale					
Grayed Large scale					

Violet		Color and Print Analysis				
		Floral	Geometric	Abstract	Ethnic	Solid
Pure	Small scale					
	Medium scale					
	Large scale					
Light	Small scale					
	Medium scale					
	Large scale					
Dark	Small scale					
	Medium scale					
	Large scale					
Grayed	Small scale					
	Medium scale					
	Large scale					

Blue-violet	Color and Print Analysis				
	Floral	Geometric	Abstract	Ethnic	Solid
Pure — Small scale					
Medium scale					
Large scale					
Light — Small scale					
Medium scale					
Large scale					
Dark — Small scale					
Medium scale					
Large scale					
Grayed — Small scale					
Medium scale					
Large scale					

Blue	Color and Print Analysis				
	Floral	Geometric	Abstract	Ethnic	Solid
Pure — Small scale					
Medium scale					
Large scale					
Light — Small scale					
Medium scale					
Large scale					
Dark — Small scale					
Medium scale					
Large scale					
Grayed — Small scale					
Medium scale					
Large scale					

Blue-green	Color and Print Analysis				
	Floral	Geometric	Abstract	Ethnic	Solid
Pure — Small scale					
Medium scale					
Large scale					
Light — Small scale					
Medium scale					
Large scale					
Dark — Small scale					
Medium scale					
Large scale					
Grayed — Small scale					
Medium scale					
Large scale					

Green	Color and Print Analysis				
	Floral	Geometric	Abstract	Ethnic	Solid
Pure — Small scale					
Medium scale					
Large scale					
Light — Small scale					
Medium scale					
Large scale					
Dark — Small scale					
Medium scale					
Large scale					
Grayed — Small scale					
Medium scale					
Large scale					

Yellow-green		Color and Print Analysis				
		Floral	Geometric	Abstract	Ethnic	Solid
Pure	Small scale					
	Medium scale					
	Large scale					
Light	Small scale					
	Medium scale					
	Large scale					
Dark	Small scale					
	Medium scale					
	Large scale					
Grayed	Small scale					
	Medium scale					
	Large scale					

FABRIC SHOPPING LIST

Once you've determined the state of your fabric collection, you can plan for future growth. If you've found that you need more yellows or greens or grays, you can set out to remedy the situation. The **Fabric Wish List,** shown below, is a handy checklist that you can take with you each time you visit your local quilt shop or fabric store, when you travel to quilt shows, or as you browse through mail-order catalogs.

Of course, you don't have to dramatically increase the number of fabrics you own right away. Filling in the shopping list can just serve as a reminder of the types of fabrics you want to look for when you have the opportunity. Try purchasing one or two of the colors from your checklist the next time you're shopping. You'll be surprised how easy it is to acquire a wonderful array of fabrics in a relatively short period of time. Soon, you won't have to make a special trip to the fabric store to begin a new quilt. Everything you need will be available right in the convenience—and comfort—of your own sewing room.

 A painless way to grow your fabric collection is to always buy a little too much for each project. An extra ⅛ or ¼ yard of each fabric will add a lot more variety to your collection—and your future quilts—without costing a bundle.

Fabric Wish List

Check each box that applies for the colors you need. For example, if you need yellow fabrics, make a check to indicate whether you need to buy pure or light yellow. Then indicate the print scale and style of prints you'd like by using the codes below. Photocopy this blank Wish List so you can reuse it as often as you like.

Key:

Print Scale
S = small
M = medium
L = large

Print Style
F = floral   E = ethnic
G = geometric   S = solid
A = abstract

	Dark	Medium	Light	Grayed	Pure	Print Scale	Print Style
Yellow							
Yellow-orange							
Orange							
Red-orange							
Red							
Red-violet							
Violet							
Blue-violet							
Blue							
Blue-green							
Green							
Yellow-green							
Black							
Gray							
White							
Quilters' neutrals (beiges to browns)							

WHAT TO DO WITH ALL THAT FABRIC

PREPARE BEFORE STORING

Wash and dry fabric as soon as you bring it into your home. Washing helps get rid of excess dye, removes the sizing, and pre-shrinks the fabric. Fabric may not need ironing if you remove it from the dryer immediately, but do iron it if it is wrinkled. Then fold it to the size that fits your storage area and put it away. If you put away fabric that has some wrinkles that haven't been pressed, it will be much harder, maybe even impossible, to get them out later without rewashing the fabric.

 *Some fabrics bleed more than others because they contain more dye or because their dye is less stable. To save time and conserve water, you can prewash a variety of fabrics together in one washer load or basin. To keep colors from running and ruining other fabrics while prewashing, add a dye fixative (such as Synthropol) to the water. This product is used by hand-dyers to set the color in fabrics.*

ORGANIZE YOUR STORAGE SPACE

At some point in your quilting life, storing fabric will probably become a challenge. Storage cabinets and shelves are available in many sizes and price ranges. Stores that specialize in storage and closet design have excellent units that we quilters can adapt to our needs. Whatever type of storage or display area you have or plan, keep in mind that fabric needs to be protected from excessive light (natural and indoor), dampness, and dust. Here are some easy storage ideas that just about any sewing area can accommodate:

• Stackable, plastic storage boxes. They keep fabric clean and tidy, and the see-through type lets you see what's inside so you know without opening every box whether fabrics are sorted by colors or by darks and lights.

• Under-the-bed, flat storage boxes. If your sewing room is small, you can use this type of container to stash fabric out of the way under the bed or the sofa.

• Closet shelves. Storing fabric in the closet keeps it out of the light. If your closet has only one shelf overhead, consider adding several more at lower heights for easy access. When the door is closed, your fabric is out of sight and the room is neat. This works well when your sewing room is also the guest room or the family room.

• Open shelves. This method keeps fabric close at hand where it can inspire you and be ready to jump off a shelf and into a quilt at a moment's notice. The drawback, however, is that depending on the lighting conditions in your sewing room, the fabric can be exposed to harsh sunlight.

 If you like the ready-access open shelves provide but are concerned about sunlight fading your fabrics, attach a roller shade to the shelf or slip fabric with a rod pocket over a curtain rod and attach it to the top shelf of your storage area. Pull down the shade or slide the curtain across the shelves to protect your fabrics when they're not in use.

ORGANIZE YOUR FABRIC

Once you have lots of fabric, it's time to organize it for your convenience. That way, you'll be able to find a particular fabric immediately when you need it. Here are a few things to consider in sorting your fabric. They may perfectly fit your needs or at least give you some ideas for organizing your fabric collection.

Sort by Color

In general, sort fabrics by color and put all values and intensities within a color group together. This gives you instant perspective on where your collection is limited, and you can set about filling in the gaps on future shopping expeditions.

Separate Piles

Separate out certain kinds of fabric so that you can find them easily. Here are the types of piles you may want to keep, but depending upon the fabrics you collect, you may have one or two others to add.

Solids. You may find it easier to keep solids separate from prints, since you use them in different types of projects. For example, when working on an Amish-style quilt where you would use only solids, you can reach for what you need without a lot of searching. Within the set of solids, sort by color.

Wide stripes. These often contain many colors and would be hard to classify by any one color.

Large pieces. Keep your eyes open for sale fabrics you would like to use on the backs of your quilts and buy many yards. Store these fabrics on a separate shelf so you know they are to be used for quilt backs. This keeps me from cutting off bits of fabric for various projects until you don't have enough left for a backing.

Hand-dyed fabrics. These are usually small pieces and they tend to get lost in large piles of fabric. Besides, you'll probably want to reserve them for special projects. Subdivide the hand-dyed stack by color.

Antique fabrics. These precious fabrics are both fragile and expensive, so store them separately, too.

Temporary Piles

You can separate fabrics temporarily by current projects or themes, such as a stack of depression fabrics for a period quilt or a pile of plaids for a folk art quilt.

Determine the yardage to buy of a particular fabric by how you think it will be used. For example, a large-scale theme print could be used for borders or setting squares, so 3 yards or so would be a wise purchase. Accent fabrics can be as small as quarter- or fat quarter-yards and still be useful. For quilt backings, consider whether the fabric is likely to be used for a wall-hanging or a bed-size quilt. Remember, a queen- or king-size quilt can require as much as 7 to 10 yards of fabric!

START PLANNING YOUR NEXT QUILT

Now that you have gained a better understanding and appreciation of how colors and print styles work together to add a wonderful visual texture to your projects, you're armed and ready to plan and stitch your best quilt ever! Knowing how colors work and behave together will give you the confidence to try new ideas and color schemes. Remember to have fun experimenting with different color and fabric options to design your own quilts, and don't be afraid to try something new.

About the Authors

Susan McKelvey is a well-known expert on color who is especially interested in making color understandable to quilters. She has written several books and articles on color, as well as on other quilting subjects, such as writing on quilts and designing quilt labels. Through her company, Wallflower Designs, she designs and distributes quilting books, patterns, and supplies. She teaches quilting throughout the United States, and her quilts have appeared in quilt shows, galleries, and museums.

Before discovering quiltmaking in 1977, Susan earned her B.A. in English at Cornell College and her M.A. at the University of Chicago. After earning her M.A., Susan then taught English in Illinois, Iowa, and Maryland, and with the Peace Corps in Ethiopia. She has also worked as a test development manager at Westinghouse Learning Corporation.

Susan and her husband, parents of two grown children, currently live in rural Anne Arundel County, Maryland, with two rescued golden retrievers and two beautiful cats, all of whom think they were born to grace quilts!

Janet Wickell has been quilting for many years, but it became a passion in 1989, when she discovered miniature quilts. She is a sponsor of Minifest, the only national show and seminar devoted to small quilts. For the past several years Janet has been a freelance writer and has contributed to many books for Rodale Press, including titles in The Classic American Quilt Collection series. She teaches quilting and hand marbling fabric, and she enjoys herb gardening, photography, and reproducing quilt patterns in stained glass. She is currently working on her first book about miniature quilts. Janet lives in the mountains of North Carolina with her husband, daughter, and a growing menagerie of animal friends.

Resources and Recommended Reading

The following resources may provide additional insight in the study of color or fabric styles.

Albers, Joseph. *Interaction of Color.* New Haven: Yale University Press, 1975.

Birren, Faber. *Creative Color.* West Chester, Pa.: Schiffer Publishing, 1987.

Brackman, Barbara. *Clues in the Calico: Identifying and Dating Quilts.* McLean, Va.: EPM Publications, 1989.

McKelvey, Susan. *Color for Quilters.* Vol. II. Millersville, Md.: Wallflower Designs, 1994.

Meller, Susan, and Elffers, Joost. *Textile Designs: Two Hundred Years of European & American Patterns for Printed Fabrics.* New York: Henry N. Abrams Publishers, 1991.

Nehring, Jane. "Aging Gracefully: Gentle Ways to Make a New Quilt Look Old." *Miniature Quilts,* no. 17 (April 1995): 21.

Quiller, Stephen. *Color Choices.* New York: Watson-Guptill Publications, 1989.

Acknowledgments

Companies That Contributed Fabric

Our thanks go to the companies that generously contributed the fabrics that so beautifully illustrate the color concepts in this book:

EZ International
Fasco
Marcus Brothers
Osage County Quilt Factory
P&B Textiles
Piney Woods
RJR
The Souder Store
South Sea Imports

A Quilter's Guide to Color and Fabric

We also gratefully thank the many exceptional quiltmakers and collectors who graciously permitted us to show their quilts in part two of this book as examples of the principles of working with color and fabric.

Martha Bastian, Mexico, Missouri
Barbara Berliner, Columbia, Missouri
Nancy Chizek, Ann Arbor, Michigan
Sharyn Craig, El Cajon, California
DSI Studios, Evansville, Indiana
Jane Graff, Delafield, Wisconsin
Joyce Gross, Petaluma, California
Doris Heitman, Williamsburg, Iowa
Becky Herdle, Rochester, New York
Naoko Anne Ito, Berkeley, California
Kathryn Jones, Marshall, Missouri
Kathryn Kuhn, Monument, Colorado
Edith Leeper, Columbia, Missouri
Shirley McElderry, Ottumwa, Iowa
Irene Metz, Harleysville, Pennsylvania
Carolyn Miller, Santa Cruz, California
Judy Miller, Columbia, Maryland

Museum of the American Quilter's Society, Paducah, Kentucky
Lucille Powell, Gilbertsville, Pennsylvania
Julee Prose, Ottumwa, Iowa
Annie Segal for Quilters' Newsletter Magazine, Golden, Colorado
Randolph County Historical Society, Moberly, Missouri
Cindy Rennels, Clinton, Oklahoma
Bertha Rush, Hatfield, Pennsylvania
Wilma Sestric, Ballwin, Missouri
Susan Stein, St. Paul, Minnesota
Karen Stone, Dallas, Texas
Carly and Mark Stratton, Pasadena, California
Joan Townsend of Oh Suzannah, Lebanon, Ohio
Elsie Vredenberg, Tustin, Michigan
Edith Zimmer, San Diego, California

A Quilter's Guide to Easy Quilting

We extend a sincere thank you to the talented quiltmakers and quilt collectors who shared their quilts for part one of this book.

Bluebirds of Happiness, owned by Marian Costello Mongelli of Norristown, Pennsylvania. This quilt appears on pages 48 to 49 and is a project in *The Classic American Quilt Collection: Baskets.*

Crazy Wedding Ring, made by Joanne Winn of Canton, Ohio. This quilt appears on pages 70 to 71 and is a project in *The Classic American Quilt Collection: Wedding Ring.*

Spiderwebs and Dewdrops, made by Susan Stein of St. Paul, Minnesota. This quilt appears on pages 70 to 71 and is a project in *The Classic American Quilt Collection: Wedding Ring.*

Grandmother's Flower Garden, made by Leila Poindexter and quilted and owned by Kathryn Jones of Marshall, Missouri. This quilt appears on pages 70 to 71 and is a project in *The Classic American Quilt Collection: One Patch.*

Plaid Houses, made by Doreen Hugill of Mount Elgin, Ontario, Canada. This quilt appears on pages 70 to 71 and is a project in *The Classic American Quilt Collection: Schoolhouse.*

Amish-Style Baskets, made by Naoko Anne Ito of Berkeley, California. This quilt appears on pages 70 to 71 and is a project in *The Classic American Quilt Collection: Baskets.*

Scrap Half Log Cabin, made by Suzanne Nelson of Neffs, Pennsylvania, and designed by Sharyn Craig of El Cajon, California. This quilt appears on pages 96 to 97 and is a project in *The Classic American Quilt Collection: Log Cabin.*

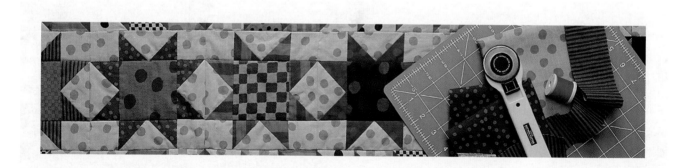

Buyer's Guide

If you can't find tools or quilting supplies mentioned in this book

at your local quilt shop, contact any one of these mail-order sources,

which carry a wide variety of quilting supplies and notions.

Clotilde, Inc.
B3000
Louisiana, MO 63353-3000
(800) 772-2891
www.clotilde.com
   Sewing notions and quilting supplies, including the Little Foot presser foot, the Big Foot free-motion quilting foot, walking feet, fusible web, thimbles, rotary-cutting equipment, pins, needles, and marking tools

Connecting Threads
P.O. Box 8940
Vancouver, WA 98668-8940
(800) 574-6454
www.connectingthreads.com
   Quilting supplies and notions, including fabrics, threads, patterns, pins, needles, iron-on labels, rotary cutting tools, value finder, markers, light tables, stencils, and battings

Hancock's of Paducah
3841 Hinkleville Road
Paducah, KY 42001
(800) 845-8723
www.hancocks-paducah.com
   Sewing notions and quilting supplies, including fabrics, batting, rotary-cutting equipment, pins, needles, threads, marking tools, template plastic, and basting guns

Keepsake Quilting
Route 25B
P.O. Box 1618
Center Harbor, NH 03226-1618
(800) 865-9458
www.keepsakequilting.com
   Quilting supplies and notions, including fabrics, patterns, quilt kits, the Little Foot presser foot, the Big Foot free-motion quilting foot, pins, thimbles, templates, quilting frames and hoops, and cotton, polyester, and wool battings

Nancy's Notions
333 Beichl Avenue
P.O. Box 683
Beaver Dam, WI 53916-0683
(800) 833-0690
www.nancysnotions.com
   Sewing notions and supplies, including fusible web, pins, needles, thimbles, the Little Foot presser foot, the Big Foot free-motion quilting foot, walking feet, specialty threads (including metallic, couching, bobbin, and monofilament), marking tools, and rotary-cutting equipment

Quilter's Catalog
House of White Birches
P.O. Box 9025
Big Sandy, TX 75755
(800) 347-9887
   Quilting patterns and supplies, including batting, basting guns, the Little Foot presser foot, and rotary-cutting equipment

Quilts and Other Comforts
B2500
Louisiana, MO 63353-7500
(800) 881-6624
www.quiltsonline.com
   Notions and supplies for quilters, including coordinated fabric packs, patterns, quilt kits, thimbles, pins, needles, marking tools, rotary-cutting equipment, the Little Foot presser foot, the Big Foot free-motion quilting foot, batting, quilting patterns, and quilting hoops and frames

Index

Underscored page references indicate tip boxes. **Boldface** references indicate tables.